"Based on Luke-Acts Scott Harrower has mounted an exegetical challenge to the strict realist reading of Rahner's rule that evangelicals would be foolish to avoid. The biblical accent does not fall on the imitation of the Trinity's inner life but on the imitation of Christ in the economy of salvation. The onus is now on those who champion the rule or something like it in its strict form to meet the challenge."

—**Dr. Graham A. Cole**
  Anglican Professor of Divinity at
  Beeson Divinity School, Samford University
  Author of *Do Historical Matters Matter to Faith?* (2012)

"The book leverages its investigation of Luke-Acts to lodge a protest against a widespread, highly influential, but seldom critically examined movement in modern Trinitarian methodology. . . . I commend this book as an excellent piece of research theology, the kind of solid work that captures the theological moment, advances the next few steps into new territory, and indicates where future progress lies."

—**Fred Sanders, from the foreword**
  Associate Professor in the Torrey Honors Institute, Biola University
  Author of *The Deep Things of God* (2010)

"'Rahner's Rule' has exercised massive influence over recent theology. To this point it has not, quite surprisingly, been subjected to adequate biblical scrutiny. In this insightful work, Scott Harrower takes important steps to provide such scrutiny. The result is a book that will repay careful study, and even those who are not fully persuaded by all the arguments will benefit from engagement with it."

—**Thomas H. McCall**
  Associate Professor of Biblical and Systematic Theology at
  Trinity Evangelical Divinity School
  Author of *Which Trinity? Whose Monotheism?* (2010)

Trinitarian Self and Salvation

Trinitarian Self and Salvation
An Evangelical Engagement with Rahner's Rule

Scott D. Harrower

☙PICKWICK *Publications* · Eugene, Oregon

TRINITARIAN SELF AND SALVATION
An Evangelical Engagement with Rahner's Rule

Copyright © 2012 Scott D. Harower. All rights reserved. Except for brief quotations in critical publications or reviews, no part of this book may be reproduced in any manner without prior written permission from the publisher. Write: Permissions, Wipf and Stock Publishers, 199 W. 8th Ave., Suite 3, Eugene, OR 97401.

Pickwick Publications
An Imprint of Wipf and Stock Publishers
199 W. 8th Ave., Suite 3
Eugene, OR 97401

www.wipfandstock.com

ISBN 13: 978-1-61097-674-9

Cataloging-in-Publication data:

Harrower, Scott D.

    Trinitarian self and salvation : an evangelical engagement with Rahner's rule / Scott D. Harrower.

    xviii + 172 p. ; 23 cm. Includes bibliographical references.

    ISBN 13: 978-1-61097-674-9

    1. Rahner, Karl, 1904–1984. 2. Trinity. 3. Economy of God. 4. Bible. N.T. Luke—Criticism, interpretation, etc. 5. Bible. N.T. Acts—Criticism, interpretation, etc. I. Title.

BT111.3 H35 2012

Manufactured in the U.S.A.

I would like to dedicate this work to my best friend and wife:

Kate you are a *rare, deep, star*.

I also dedicate this work to our children, Dante, Grace, and Angela:

our own twinkling trinity.

Contents

Foreword by Fred Sanders / ix
Acknowledgments / xv
Abbreviations / xvii

1. Contemporary Evangelical Rahnerism / 1
2. The Rahnerian Background / 26
3. The Messianic Office of God the Son in Luke–Acts / 73
4. God the Father and God the Son / 107
5. God the Son and God the Spirit / 126
6. Conclusion / 155

Bibliography / 159

Foreword

Modern Trinitarian theology has rejoiced in its discovery of the way God has made himself known in the economy of salvation. Operating under the broad guidance of Rahner's Rule ("The economic Trinity is the immanent Trinity, and vice versa"), Christian theologians have traced the presence of Father, Son, and Spirit in the events of salvation history, and argued with new vigor and confidence that the relationships we see among the trinitarian persons here below are revelations of eternal triune structures immanent to the very being of God. Much of the energy and excitement of modern trinitarianism, a thriving and prolific ecumenical undertaking, have come from this project of reading the character of the eternal Trinity directly from the events of the economy.

The recent rush to the economy has much to commend it. If the doctrine of the Trinity had become austere and remote from the gospel over the centuries, the modern reorientation served to correct that tendency by locating the contents of trinitarian theology in the midst of the events of biblical history. The prevailing winds of what one writer has called "neo-economic trinitarianism" also dispersed a farrago of speculative metaphysical accounts of the inner life of God, distracting constructs that cumbered the theological prospect. Trinitarianism has lately been developed in greater proximity to the gospel, largely thanks to a widespread, generalized "loose reading" of Rahner's Rule.

Such a re-centering of trinitarianism onto the economy, with its renewed attention to salvation history and its eschewing of speculation, should have resulted in a wealth of new biblical insight. If a doctrinal hypothesis is true, after all, it ought to prove itself fruitful for Bible reading. It ought to throw a more helpful light on the Bible, highlighting neglected themes and giving new prominence to terms that had heretofore been obscure. But theologians operating under the banner of Rahner's Rule did not, generally speaking, use the new emphasis to seek treasures new and old in the text of Scripture. And professional exegetes have not rushed gratefully to the side of systematicians with news of discoveries made possible by the conceptual tools of the new trinitarianism. Modern trinitarianism has often enough congratulated itself on being more biblical than previous generations ("I thank God that I am not like the men of the middle ages!"), but with few exceptions the slogan "more biblical" has signified a hermeneutical wave of the hand at the general sweep of biblical history, the broad outlines of the entire scope of the canonical narrative. Valuable as this perception of the big picture may be, what has been lacking is detailed reading, the kind of close exegesis that engages hard facts, peculiar details, thick descriptions, and unexpected phraseology; the kind of thing that could either confirm or problematize the whole paradigm established by Rahner's Rule.

Curiously, that kind of close study has not been carried out by self-conscious devotees of Rahner's Rule, but now is being undertaken by a school of interpreters who find themselves at odds with a "strict realist reading" of the rule. In other words, it is not Rahner's Rule that has finally motivated more careful exegesis, but the backlash against it. That backlash has so far been primarily doctrinally articulated (see the works of Molnar, Badcock, Sanders, Rauser, Jowers, *et al.*, cited below), but in the present work, Scott Harrower attempts a more directly exegetical critique of the strict realist reading of Rahner's Rule. Harrower's claim is that Rahner's Rule (strictly applied) fails to do justice to the theology of Luke-Acts, which constitutes about a third of the New Testament. In the philosophy of science following Thomas Kuhn's *Structure of Scientific Revolutions*, there has been a debate about how many observational exceptions are necessary to bring about a crisis in a dominant theoretical paradigm. If Harrower is right, the dominant paradigm of Rahner's Rule fails to account for a full third of the biblical data. Surely that amounts to a crisis for the reigning theory. Surely the scramble for a new paradigm should begin.

Strict adherents of Rahner's Rule assume that every relation we see among Father, Son, and Spirit in the history of salvation is an economic enactment of an eternal state of affairs. The relations of the three persons in time, that is, all have an eternal analogue immanent to God's triune being. If the incarnate Son obeys and submits to the authority of the Father who sent him (to take the example that most exercises Harrower), it is because the eternal relationship he has toward the Father is a relationship of obedience and submission. The greatest contribution that Harrower makes to the current discussion is that he tests this kind of application of Rahner's Rule by seeing if it can apply to Luke-Acts without reservation. Convinced that "if one is going to employ the [strict realist reading] of [Rahner's Rule] to the narrative of Luke-Acts, then one must apply it to the whole narrative and not selectively," he devotes several chapters to showing what would follow from interpreting all the economic-trinitarian activity of Luke-Acts as revelatory of immanent-trinitarian states of affairs. The result is *reductio ad absurdum*: The lines of authority, for example, are criss-crossed multiple times, with the Son alternately carrying out the Father's will at one moment, and then exercising dominion over the Father's self-revelation the next (much hangs on Harrower's interpretation of Luke 10:22). Similarly, Luke-Acts presents the Spirit conceiving and then impelling the Son in earlier moments, but bearing witness to and being dispensed by the Son at later moments. All of this makes perfect sense narratively and chronologically; in fact one of Harrower's strengths here is his engagement of recent Luke-Acts scholarship with its emphasis on narrative unfolding (Kavin Rowe and Andy Johnson, among others). But what if the entire sequence of reversible subordinations were to be transposed into the eternal nature of God? They would be not so much mutual submission as mutually exclusive subordination.

Harrower's overall message for trinitarian theology today is that the transcendental deduction of immanent trinitarian relations from the economy cannot be as direct as strict realists have suggested. What happens in the economy stays in the economy, and must be interpreted within the framework imposed by creation, salvation history, and the mediation of God's self-revelation through the human nature of Christ. The book leverages its investigation of Luke-Acts to lodge a protest against a widespread, highly influential, but seldom critically examined, movement in modern trinitarian methodology. While I do not agree with every line of Harrower's argument, I commend this book as an excellent piece of research theology, the kind of solid work that captures the theological moment, advances the next few steps into new territory, and indicates where future progress lies. It has prompted me to look at my own earlier work and regret that, though I correctly indicated that the future of trinitarian theology should be in the field of the theological interpretation of Scripture, I nevertheless failed to carry out any actual exegetical theology. Harrower has moved forward by undertaking a more elaborate and rigorous exegetical test of proffered theological norms. By what other standard should evangelical theology hope to make progress in understanding? It can be merely laudatory, and not very descriptive, to say that one project is "more biblical" than another, akin to saying it is more true or more correct. But Harrower's book is more biblical in the sense that is a deliberate attempt to set trinitarian theology more directly and immediately under the norm of Scripture.

Harrower's book indicates two lines of research that ought to be developed by trinitarian theologians in our time. First, the sustained attention he gives to Luke-Acts demonstrates the way a focused investigation in biblical theology can provide resources for systematic theology. In 1970, T. E. Pollard demonstrated that "it was St. John's Gospel, with its Logos-concept in the Prologue and its emphasis on the Father-Son relationship, that raised in a most acute way the problems which led the church to formulate her doctrines of the trinity and of the person of Christ."[1] The main lines of the history of the doctrine of the Trinity are indeed Johannine: logos, love, the Father-Son pairing, eternal life, life-in-himself, sending, begetting. A close reading of another canonical voice conjures the prospect of an alternative theological history, one in which the leading ideas of Luke-Acts (or more broadly of a synoptic theology) would have provided the terms and arguments for the elaboration of the doctrine. What if the leading voice had been a dogmatic theology of servanthood and messianic Lordship developed from Luke-Acts, with Johannine categories in a supporting and confirming role? The content of the doctrine would (in my opinion) have emerged recognizably the same; the same Nicene judgments would have been rendered, in different terminology. And at any rate the history of dogma is what it is. But latent within canonical Scripture are resources that are still awaiting fuller exploration and elaboration; angles from which the truth has not been described.

The second line of research suggested by the present book is in that field of historical theology, or the classic tradition just alluded to.

---

1. T. E. Pollard, *Johannine Christology and the Early Church*. London: Cambridge University Press, 1970, p. ix.

Harrower is right to prioritize direct investigation of Scripture, and to narrow his field of vision to a single canonical author. But the next step would be to take this refreshed biblical theology up into conversation with the magisterial expositors of the great Christian tradition. That conversation would bring to the surface some crucial issues that remain submerged in the present work. The most momentous of these is the venerable question of the basis of the eternal sonship of Christ. It is a question that rumbles continuously in the background of the present work. And the whole issue is most tantalizingly raised when Harrower presses the question of what Rahner's Rule might have to say about the ascension of Christ. If the economic sending of the Son from the Father has as its immanent analogue the eternal begetting of the Son from the Father (so the classic tradition of trinitarian interpretation), then what is the immanent analogue of the economic return of the Son to the Father? It is Harrower's angle of approach to the project of trinitarian interpretation of Scripture that succeeds in putting a question like this in sharper profile than I can remember seeing it before. This is theological investigation on a grand scale, and it makes me eager to enlist the advice of superiors like Augustine, Cyril of Alexandria, and Thomas Aquinas, gathered around the text of Scripture and submitting to it as the norm.

Fred Sanders
Biola University

Acknowledgments

Works like these are team-efforts within God's Church, thanks be to him above all. For their stimulating interaction with regards to the PhD thesis which provided the basis of this project, I would like to thank Dr. Graham Cole and Dr. Thomas McCall. In addition, Dr. Don Carson has been a great friend, employer, and role model for the last three years. Longstanding thanks go to Rev. Dr. Peter Adam from Ridley College in Melbourne, Australia, who has been a patient encourager and mentor, thank you Peter.

My friends at Trinity Evangelical Divinity School in Deerfield, Illinois and beyond have been great bouncing boards for thinking through the inter-connectedness of theology and not shying away from making those connections. Adam Johnson, Ben Sutton, Jonathan King, and Jules Martinez have been thoughtful friends and sparring partners at TEDS. "Vielen Dank" goes to the Marburg formation group: Roland Werner, Gernot Elsner, Thomas Dallendörfer, Tobi Wörner, Daniel Chlebek, Knafffi, Alexander Oed, Markus Lägel, Stephan Rauhut, Christoph Schmitter, Timo Schuster.

Our friends at St. Mark's Anglican Church in Camberwell, Australia, have also been faithful in all manner of encouragement and a fine example of the church body working together.

Above all, my heartfelt appreciation goes to the family with which God has truly gifted me. They have been wonderfully supportive during the entire process of embarking on a PhD and refining that work into this book. My parents have been a great encouragement and support to the extent that this project would not have been possible without them—thank you very much. Kate has been a constant source of unique light and even read and edited this work (though any mistakes are mine).

Our children have remained as excited about life as one could hope for. Thank you all.

Good Friday, 2011

Abbreviations

RR	Rahner's Rule
LRR	Loose Realist Reading of Rahner's Rule
SRR	Strict Realist Reading of Rahner's Rule
SRRT	Strict Realist Reading of the Text

1

Contemporary Evangelical Rahnerianism

THEOLOGICAL VIEWS ON THE Trinity greatly affect most aspects of Christian faith and life. For example, in terms of basic Christian belief, the current trinitarian debate about the subordination of God the Son to God the Father has great significance for Christology. In terms of Christian life, the inner life of God the Trinity has been argued to be the basis for various social, familial, and ecclesial relationships and practice. Much of this theology and its implications revolve around the methodological use of Rahner's Rule (RR). This axiom, RR, is defined as follows in Karl Rahner's classic work *The Trinity*: "*The 'economic' Trinity is the 'immanent' Trinity and the 'immanent' Trinity is the 'economic' Trinity.*"[1]

The positive aspect of this maxim is that it reconnects the human experience of God in history with the immanent Trinity, thus narrowing any perceived gap between the Trinity and faith. A second positive outcome is that if all theology is carried out with RR in view then all branches of theology will necessarily be in close relationship to trinitarian theology.[2] RR has become so significant that Vanhoozer recently

---

1. Rahner, *The Trinity*, 22 (italics are Rahner's). This work will adopt Rahner's language of "immanent" and "economic," though equivalents, such as "essential" for "immanent," will be used to avoid tedium. We will take Cole's definitions on the immanent and economic Trinity. The economic Trinity "[r]efers to the various roles of the members of the Trinity in the administration (economy) of the plan of salvation." The immanent (or essential) Trinity is the "Trinity's own eternal, internal, life as Father, Son, and Holy Spirit," Cole, *He Who Gives Life*, 286–87.

2. Rahner, *The Trinity*, 11. Erickson, *God in Three Persons*, 294–95.

stated, "One of the most important present-day litmus tests for theologians pertains to how far one accepts (or understands!) Rahner's Rule."³ Evangelicals are no exception to this need to deal with RR, and in fact many Evangelicals with a high view of Scripture do employ RR as a key theological norm. However, amongst Evangelical theologians RR is employed in different ways in order to support their various proposals. For example, despite the fact that Letham's *The Trinity*, and Erickson's *God in Three Persons*, are regarded as two of the most significant conservative Evangelical works on the Trinity,⁴ these works come to opposite conclusions on various issues based upon different interpretations of RR.⁵ This is not an isolated phenomenon.⁶ Rather, this highlights two reasons for the difficulty that RR poses. The first is that it contains an "inherent instability." As Sanders notes: "Rahner's Rule . . . lean[s] sometimes toward a more strict and total identification of economic and immanent Trinity, and sometimes toward a more carefully circumscribed account of the relationship between them."⁷ Secondly, RR is "difficult to falsify and . . . difficult to confirm."⁸ Struggles with RR and its attendant issues are not limited to the English-speaking world.⁹ In German-speaking scholarship, Stolina's 2008 work "»Ökonomische« und »immanente« Trinität?" called for a re-conception of the relationship between the economic Trinity and the immanent Trinity.¹⁰ A representative of French scholarship is Dunard, who argues that Rahner never expected his rule to be interpreted as a univocal norm.¹¹

Our current context, in which RR has been interpreted in varying ways, demonstrates the need for a decisive Evangelical methodology which a view to assessing the validity of RR, and any particular use

---

3. Vanhoozer, "Forward," in *Communion with the Triune God*, edited by Kelly M. Kapic and Justin Taylor, 11.

4. Kärkkäinen, *The Trinity: Global Perspectives*, 214.

5. Erickson, *God in Three Persons*, 331. Letham, *The Holy Trinity*, 34–36, 383–401.

6. Giles, "The Son of God Is Not Eternally Inferior, Subordinate, or Submissive"; Letham, "Reply to Kevin Giles." Sarot, "Trinity and Church."

7. Sanders, *The Image of the Immanent Trinity*, 6.

8. Jowers, "A Test of Karl Rahner's Axiom," 423.

9. Dunard, „«Trinité immanente» et «Trinité économique» selon Karl Barth. See also Bénétreau, „Appellation et Transcendence."

10. Stolina, "»Ökonomische« und »immanente« Trinität?."

11. Dunard, "Trinité immanente," 474. See also Dunard, "L'identité rahnérienne entre la Trinité économique et la Trinité immanente à l'epreuve de ses applications."

of it. Evangelicals with a high view of Scripture tend to choose either of two approaches to RR. These can be usefully described with the application of Rauser's designations. There is firstly the "strict realist reading" (SRR) of RR,[12] secondly, a "loose realist reading" (LRR) of RR.[13] Other designators for these two approaches include Sanders' designations: the "radicalizers" and the "restrictivists."[14] The approach

12. This is a literalist view that identifies the immanent Trinity and the economic Trinity without qualification. This view of RR reads the Rule as an ontological principle, not merely an epistemological principle. It asserts that God is in the economy as he is eternally within himself. Rauser, "Rahner's Rule."

13. This reading of RR affirms that the expressions "immanent Trinity" and "economic Trinity" denote the same deity. However, this view refrains from identifying the precise nature of relations seen in the economy with the nature of the intra-trinitarian relations within the immanent trinity. This view is a re-statement of basic Christian theology, and thus offers no new insight into the Being of God. It avoids some of the extremes of twentieth-century trinitarian theology, as a result of the SRR of RR, particularly with relation to the theology of the cross. Ibid., 85–87. Rauser also offers a third possible reading. This is the "strict antirealist reading" (SARR). This is a reading in which "theological assertions about the Trinity are true within the Christian conceptual framework, and there is no sense in working outside this framework. The antirealist reading makes sense of the Rule as neither trivial nor (obviously) false. And so, to affirm that 'The "economic" Trinity is the "immanent" Trinity and that the "immanent" Trinity is the "economic" Trinity *is* to affirm that there is no intelligibility to positing a world beyond the economy of revelation in which God is not triune . . . All language of the 'immanent Trinity' is thus in fact language of the economic Trinity for there is no sense of conceiving God apart from this revelation." Italics are Rauser's. See Rauser, "Rahner's Rule": 90–91.

14. Sanders helpfully defines these two groups of interpreters, their relationship to Rahner's Rule and to one another. For Sanders, the radicalizers, are "those who argue that the 'is' in Rahner's Rule should be interpreted as a 'strong identity' between economic and immanent Trinity. Even within this grouping of thinkers, there is a considerable range of opinion. If we were to subdivide the category further, we would have to distinguish between those who are prone to dissolve the immanent Trinity into the economic without remainder, and those who continue to hold to the doctrine of the immanent Trinity so long as it is strictly identified with the economic in one way or another. Both are treated as radicalizers. Radicalizers and restricters . . . adopt the strategies they do in order to preserve different core values in their theologies." Sanders, *The Image of the Immanent Trinity*, 83–84. The "restricters" on the other hand, may be seen as those who are responding to the SRR of RR. "While the axiom itself drew very little criticism, its radicalization in the hands of . . . interpreters attracted much interest and concern. First in response to Schoonenberg and Küng, and more recently in response to LaCugna, a growing number of theologians have begun to urge caution in the interpretation of Rahner's Rule. Where the radicalizers saw Rahner as making a good start but not going far enough, the restricters see Rahner (or the radicalizers) as already going too far . . . Most of the thinkers treated under the heading of 'restricters' are happy to affirm Rahner's Rule and to pursue its implications throughout their work, so long

known as the "restrictivist" approach has also been called the "methodological" and "epistemological" reading of Rahner's Rule. Coppedge employs the language of "methodological" and "ontological" to differentiate two approaches to the Rule. He favors the "methodological" approach, which is the one taken by those whom Sanders would designate as "restricters." Coppedge writes: "It is probably best to see Rahner's insight as a methodological one, so the economic Trinity is understood as revealing the ontological Trinity. To take his rule in an ontological way might blur the distinction between the being of God and the doing of God. If that should happen the focus is on what God does in relation to creation and leads to a functional understanding of the Trinity. The result would be not enough attention given to the relationship of the triune God within himself."[15]

What Coppedge designates as "methodological" is equivalent to what others have called the "epistemological" interpretation of RR. A representative of the epistemological approach to RR states this view as: "*The ontological Trinity is the ground of being for the economic Trinity and the economic Trinity is the ground of cognition for the ontological Trinity.*" The rationale underlying this statement is that "one needs to acknowledge the ontological Trinity as the ground of being for the economic Trinity. If it were not for the ontological Trinity, there would not be the economic Trinity. The ontological Trinity that might be completed by the economic Trinity is not the ontological Trinity in *sensu strictu*. Only when there is the ontological Trinity is there the economic Trinity through which we can recognize and understand God."[16]

There has been confusion about how to interpret the Rule within Roman Catholic circles since Rahner penned it,[17] and Evangelical

---

as certain misinterpretations of the axiom are exposed and repudiated . . . The axiom must be somehow qualified, or its implications qualified, or at the very least there must be a great exercise of caution in dealing with it." Sanders, *The Image of the Immanent Trinity*, 123. Sanders also notes that of the two schools of thought on the interpretation of RR, the SRR or "radicalizing" group of theologians has most fully worked out and developed the outcomes of their interpretation of RR. Ibid., 84.

15. Coppedge, *The God Who Is Triune*, 114.

16. Lee, "The Relationship between the Ontological Trinity and the Economic Trinity," 106–7 (italics are Lee's.).

17. Roman Catholic commentator Battaglia writes: "it is not clear as to how Rahner wants his audience [which is primarily Roman Catholic] to understand this *Grundaxiom*. Is he claiming that the economic Trinity helps us *know* about the immanent Trinity (an epistemological principle) or is he saying that there is a *strict identity*

theology has not been exempt from this phenomenon. Evangelical theology has not ignored the role of RR within the "trinitarian renaissance" of the twentieth century. On this topic Kärkkäinen (who is a contemporary Evangelical theologian working on the Trinity) states that, "what is exciting about the current trinitarian renaissance is that questions and issues old and new are being re-visited and re-examined. Far from being an archaic doctrine, the Trinity has proven itself to be a source of vital debate and spiritual renewal."[18] In the context of explicitly speaking about RR, Kärkkäinen makes clear the priority of the correct understanding of RR when he says, "While a number of issues are being debated in contemporary trinitarian theology . . . at the heart of the discussion stands the question of the relationship between the economic and the immanent Trinity."[19] For Kärkkäinen, the importance of the interpretation of RR is not limited to the economic/immanent question alone: "The centrality of the issue is accentuated by the fact that the way one attempts to resolve this question is based on and has implications for several other key topics such as how to establish the oneness of God and how to defend the freedom of God."[20]

Rauser's three possible readings of RR, and the two possible readings by Sanders (above), point out the fact that a neat division of the

---

between them (an ontological statement)? It would appear that interpreters of Rahner have taken up both options, as his *Grundaxiom* is able to be read in both ways . . . The distinction between epistemological and ontological interpretations is important because it has a direct bearing on the kinds of conclusions we can draw about God's own life from a consideration of our salvific experience of God." Battaglia is himself very emphatically opposed to the SRR of RR, because "this position [the strict identity thesis] renders the immanent Trinity and the whole doctrine of appropriations otiose as it claims that our experience of God transposes into our knowledge of God *ad intra*. Hence, the 'vice versa' (*umgekehrt*) aspect of the *Grundaxiom* is problematic." For Battaglia the collapse of the immanent Trinity in to the economic Trinity entailed by the ontological reading of RR "is at odds with the whole tradition, both Latin and Greek, which clearly maintains the distinction between *theologia* and *oikonomia* . . . The proper roles in the economy are still the work of the *one* God *ad extra*, and do not define the immanent divine relations." Battaglia, "An Examination of Karl Rahner's Trinitarian Theology," accessed October 22, 2008 (italics are Battaglia's). For its reformulation by prominent Roman Catholic theologian, David Coffey, see O'Byrne, *Spirit Christology and Trinity*, 173 ff.

18. Kärkkäinen, "The Trajectories of the Contemporary 'Trinitarian Renaissance,'" 21.

19. Ibid., 18.

20. Ibid.

readings of RR into either an epistemological or an ontological reading is insufficient for Evangelicals because their foundations have not been demonstrated by Scripture. Rauser's LRR is equivalent to Sander's "restrictivist" view, which affirms a strong epistemological connection between the economic and immanent Trinity. However, what Sanders labels as the "radicalizing view" has many permutations—more so than Rauser's SRR and SARR.[21] This observation reveals the fact that theologians have not yet settled on one universally persuasive understanding of RR. Moreover, there is the need for a fresh language to express the God-as-God to world relationship, and vice versa.

Given the situation of an inadequate language, and the fact that in practice "interpreters of Rahner's Rule have tended to divide into two camps: those who believe in a strong identity of immanent and economic Trinity and those who would qualify that identity by positing a prior actuality of the immanent Trinity."[22] This study will assess the viability of the SRR of RR because of its great significance for many Evangelical theologies of the Trinity and its entailments for Christian faith and practice.

The SRR is argued with great conviction by some very influential Evangelical theologians. This is surprising, since from a "global perspective," "most theologians, apart from LaCugna (and possibly Moltmann, but for different reasons), are saying that while Rahner's Rule can be affirmed *epistemologically*, it cannot necessarily be affirmed in terms of the absolute identity of the economic and immanent Trinity."[23] Despite this, the employment of the SRR of RR is evidenced in the works of Ware[24] and Letham.[25] Letham's central tenets are explored below as representative of those who take the SRR as their guide for the theological interpretation of Scripture.

Letham's work affirms SRR as follows: "[Rahner's] main thesis, connecting and identifying the economic Trinity and the immanent Trinity, is vital *when appropriately understood and applied*. If the axiom is held to reflect the fact that God's self-revelation as triune in the work of creation, providence, and grace is a true revelation of who he is eternally,

---

21. The SARR refers to the "strict anti-realist reading" described in footnote 13.
22. Olson, "Wolfhart Pannenberg's Doctrine of the Trinity," 197.
23. Kärkkäinen, *The Triity: Global Perspectives*, 230 (italics are Kärkkäinen's.).
24. Ware, *Father, Son and Holy Spirit*; Grudem, ed. *Biblical Foundations for Manhood and Womanhood*.
25. Letham, *Trinity* ; Letham, "Does the Son Submit to the Father?"

then it expresses a truth at the heart of the Christian faith."[26] Letham has been careful to avoid some of the more extreme so-called trinitarian implications reached by others who take the SRR of RR. That is, Letham manages the one-ness/three-ness issue of the Trinity by holding both these aspects of God's life together.[27]

Letham's own "Vital Parameters" of trinitarian theology are instructive of the influence of the SRR on the core of his trinitarianism. These "vital parameters" are: (1) *"One being-three persons, three persons-one being,"* (2) *"The three persons are homoousios,"* (3) *"The three persons are irreducibly different from one another,"* (4) *"There is an order among the persons,"* (5) *"A doctrine of the Trinity that is to be faithful to the Bible from which it emerges must give equivalent expression to each of the above parameters."*[28] It is noteworthy that the minimum parameter for a trinitarian doctrine includes point 4: the necessary order amongst persons of the Trinity. That this is such a significant point in Letham's trinitarian theology is revealed by the fact that Letham is heavily critical of theologies with no clear fixed order within the Trinity. For example, he says that Moltmann's non-hierarchical social doctrine contains "no fixed order, between the three [persons of the Trinity], for their 'relationship' . . . is that of mutual, reciprocal love in freedom. There is emphatically no subordination." In Letham's view, the root and consequence of this theology could not be more serious: "This follows Moltmann's complete rejection of lordship and authority."[29]

Examples of contemporary Evangelical theologians who employ the LRR include Giles,[30] and Erickson. Erickson's work is discussed at length as an example of the trinitarian theology underlying, and entailed by, the use of the LRR of RR.

Erickson is a major proponent of what is described by the LRR of RR. He is one of the most influential Evangelical theologians of the second half of the twentieth century in North America. This is largely

---

26. Letham, *Trinity* 296 (italics are Letham's.).

27. Ibid., 307–9.

28. Ibid., 381–83 (italics are Letham's).

29. Ibid., 305.

30. "As a 'restricter' I take Rahner's Rule to speak of a correlation between the economic and immanent Trinity, not identification . . . In taking this approach I follow in the steps of Athanasius and the Cappadocian Fathers from the early church and Congar and Kasper from our own time," Giles, *Jesus and the Father*, 256.

through his basic introduction to theology, *Christian Theology*,[31] and other writings. As noted above, together with Letham's *The Trinity*, Erickson's body of work, including *Christian Theology, God in Three Persons*,[32] *God the Father Almighty*,[33] *Making Sense of the Trinity*,[34] and *Who is Tampering with the Trinity?*[35] makes him one of the two most significant conservative Evangelical theologians writing on the Trinity.[36] Erickson is a social trinitarian, who takes the LRR of RR. He sums up his own view of the nature of the relations within God the Trinity as follows:

> The Trinity is a communion of three persons, who exist and always have existed in union with one another and in dependence on one another . . . They share their lives, having such a close relationship that each is conscious of what the other is conscious of . . . Each is essential to the life of each of the others and to the life of the Trinity. They are bound to one another in love, *agapē* love, which therefore unites them in the closest and most intimate relationships. This unselfish, *agapē* love makes each more concerned for the other than for himself. There is therefore mutual submission of each to each of the others and a mutual glorifying of one another. There is complete equality of the three.[37]

Erickson's approach to the issue of the relationship between the economic and immanent Trinity and the interpretation of Rahner's Rule is via the LRR of RR. He states that it is a mistake to identify "too closely the economic (the Trinity as manifested to us in history) with the immanent Trinity (God as he really is in himself)."[38] In terms of Jesus' relationship to God the Father in the economy of salvation: "[t]here has been . . . temporary subordination of one member of the Trinity to the other, but this is functional rather than essential. At the same time, this unity and equality do not require identity of function. There are certain roles that distinctively belong primarily to one, although all participate in the

---

31. Erickson, *Christian Theology*.
32. Erickson, *God in Three Persons*.
33. Erickson, *God the Father Almighty*.
34. Erickson, *Making Sense of the Trinity*.
35. Erickson, *Who Is Tampering with the Trinity?*
36. Kärkkäinen, *The Trinity: Global Perspectives*, 214.
37. Erickson, *God in Three Persons*, 331.
38. Erickson, *Making Sense of the Trinity*, 90.

function of each."³⁹ Therefore, for Erickson the LRR of RR is employed as an epistemological principle with an attendant metaphysical identity statement. He writes: "there is a rather obvious sense in which we can say that the immanent Trinity and the economic Trinity are the same. That would be metaphysical identity, whereby there are not two different Trinities. The epistemological identity is something different, however. While the economic Trinity is certainly part of the immanent Trinity epistemologically, it does not exhaust it."⁴⁰ Though Erickson's expression of his point has been made in such a way that it has drawn critique for its lack of clarity,⁴¹ what he is driving at is clear given his social trinitarianism. Erickson's social trinitarianism requires a means to establish the unity of the triune God. This is achieved by means of shared divine love and knowledge, and an interpenetration-interdependence relationship.⁴² This interdependent and loving unity determines Erickson's appropriation of Rahner's Rule. Because for Erickson there can be no inequality in this relationship, notions such as the begottenness of the Son by the Father, and the spiration of the Holy Spirit by the Father and the Son, cannot entail either subordinationism nor causation. This is because the Son and the Spirit are as much God as the Father is: the term 'Son' is about 'likeness' to the Father, not derivation, further, the Spirit is "just God himself in the innermost essence of his being . . . His very life-element."⁴³

For Erickson, therefore, terms such as "begetting" and "spiration" are not to be understood with an immanent referent, rather, they must be taken to refer to events in the economy rather than events within God. For example, Erickson denies the eternal begotten-ness of the Son by the Father because he believes that statements in passages such as John 1:14, 18; 3:16, 18; Heb 11:7 and 1 John 4:9 refer to events in salvation history alone. He writes: "I . . . propose that there are no references to the Father begetting the Son or the Father (and the Son) sending the Spirit that cannot be understood in terms of the temporal role assumed by the second and third persons of the Trinity respectively. Further, to speak of one of the persons as unoriginate and the others as either

---

39. Erickson, *Three Persons*, 331 (italics Erickson's).
40. Erickson, *Christian Theology*, 362–63.
41. Kärkkäinen, *The Trinity: Global Perspectives*, 230.
42. Erickson, *Three Persons*, 222–28.
43. Ibid., 301–3.

eternally begotten or proceeding from the Father is to introduce an element of causation or origination that must ultimately involve some type of subordination among them."[44]

Erickson claims to follow B. B. Warfield's lead in his appeal to Scripture as the basis for his argument. Erickson argues that the Bible employs a variety of titles to the persons of the Trinity because there are a variety of relationships to one another. These persons are also in differing relationships to those who speak of them, therefore they are named in a number of name orders such as Son-Spirit-God or Father-Son-Spirit. He holds this view against a position that entails a limited set of intra-trinitarian relations at the core of the witness about God in the economy of salvation. Further, for Erickson there is a lack of evidence for God's essential taxis in the Bible. He argues this as follows:

> the Father-Son-Spirit order is thought to be normative [by those who take the opposing view] . . . what is remarkable, however, is the lack of uniformity of this pattern in the New Testament. Indeed, occasionally the reverse order occurs, as in 1 Corinthians 12:4–6: 'There are different kinds of gifts, but the same Spirit. There are different kinds of service, but the same Lord. There are different kinds of working, but the same God who works all of them in all men.' Another example is Ephesians 4:4–6, a passage whose content quite closely parallels the 1 Corinthians 12 passage . . . Yet there are passages in which even the reverse order is not preserved. An instance would be the Pauline benediction in 2 Corinthians 13:14: 'May the grace of the Lord Jesus Christ, and the love of God, and the fellowship of the Spirit be with you all.'[45]

Erickson also draws upon Warfield's covenantal view in which any general pattern in the relationships between the persons of the Trinity in redemption is recognized as an outworking of an eternal covenant within God. The redemptive patterns seen in the economy of salvation are the result of a willed "convention, an agreement among the persons of the Trinity, a 'Covenant' . . . According to this, a distinct function in the work of redemption is voluntarily assumed by each of the members."[46]

The christological consequences of Warfield's and Erickson's views include a covenantal hermeneutic and a covenantal view of the will of

---

44. Ibid., 309.
45. Ibid., 300.
46. Ibid., 303.

God and God the Son in particular. The covenantal hermeneutic involves understanding that "[t]he incarnation, in which the Son takes a creaturely nature into union with himself, definitely involves the Son in a consequent subordination, and this must be taken into account in interpreting passages that seem to affirm subordination."[47] The covenantal view of the will of God and God the Son in particular entails the perspective that "the person of the Trinity who became incarnate and thus took upon himself the responsibility of dying an atoning death did so voluntarily, in conjunction with the decision of the other two persons . . . On these grounds, the will of the Father to which he so clearly was subject was at that point the will that the Father asserted on behalf of the Trinity, but it was the will in which the Son had participated, in the original decision."[48] The pneumatological implication is alike: "[s]imilarly, the work of the Spirit—calling to remembrance the words of Jesus, directing persons' thinking toward him, and glorifying him—was the result of a decision in which the Spirit had participated."[49]

Erickson's trinitarianism consistently affirms the LRR of RR because it also builds upon Pannenberg's proposal for self-distinction, which upholds distinction and equality amongst the persons of the Trinity. Self-distinction amongst persons of the Trinity is based upon the reality that the personhood of the Father, Son, and Holy Spirit depend on each other for their distinction as persons. He states this as follows:

> Wolfhart Pannenberg points out that Jesus distinguished himself from the Father. His whole message was that the name of God should be hallowed by accepting and living his lordship. He said that the Father was greater than he (John 14:28), and that his words were not his own but the Father's who sent him (v. 24). He would not allow himself to be called "good teacher" because "no one is good but God alone" (Mark 10:18). While the Arians and the Socinians drew from this the conclusion that the Son was not fully divine, this is taking the sayings further than one should. These statements do, however, argue for the distinctness of personhood or of consciousness of the Son from the Father. The Son is only Son because of his distinction from the Father. Similarly, however, the handing over of the rule by the Father to the Son and the handing back of this by the Son

---

47. Ibid.
48. Ibid., 309–10.
49. Ibid., 310.

to the Father constitute the distinction of the Father from the Son. Pannenberg means by self-distinction that the one who distinguishes himself from another defines himself as also dependent on that other. Similarly, there is a self-distinction that constitutes the Spirit a separate person from the Father and the Son and relates to them both . . . It does seem . . . that there is a distinctness of consciousness capable of originating thoughts and relationships among the members of the Trinity. The way in which each refers to the other, and interacts with the other, suggests a greater multiplicity of identity than has sometimes been thought of in trinitarian theology.[50]

Gunton and Volf are two other theologians who have maintained that each person of the Trinity depends on the others for their own particularity. Gunton wrote "Both persons and things are . . . substantial particulars and rendered such by the patterns and relations that constitute them what they distinctively are: with God in the first instance and with other temporally and spatially related particulars in the second."[51] For Volf, trinitarian *perichoresis* entails the presence of one person within each of the others: "One divine person is what it is, not simply in virtue of being distinct from the others but in virtue of the presence of the other two persons in it. The Father and the Spirit are always 'in' the Son; to be the Son is to be indwelled by the Father and the Spirit."[52] The

---

50. Ibid., 226–27.

51. Gunton, *The One, the Three, and the Many*, 203.

52. Volf recently set this statement in the following context: "There are two related ways to think about this intimate connection between the divine three who are indivisibly one. First, when God acts 'toward the outside'—creating, redeeming, and bringing the world to completion—God's acts are undivided, inseparable. Every act of one person of the Trinity is caused by all three. If this were not the case, then, as Augustine put it, 'the Father [would do] some things, the Son others and the Holy Spirit yet others.' And this would be utterly unacceptable. It would verge on polytheism. The second way the divine persons are tied together is their mutual indwelling, or . . . *perichoresis*. Again as Augustine put it, 'they are always in each other' and never 'alone'; One divine person is what it is, not simply in virtue of being distinct from the others but in virtue of the presence of the other two persons in it. The Father and the Spirit are always 'in' the Son; to be the Son is to be indwelled by the Father and the Spirit." Volf then draws out two particular consequences of this: "1) in terms of the identity of divine persons, you cannot simply say: 'to be one is not to be in the other' as you can say of creatures, including human beings. When it comes to God, 'not to be the same' does not mean 'to be other,' and 'to be other' does not mean 'not to be the same' . . . 2) in terms of the activity of persons, you cannot say that the act of one is the act of one person alone, as you must say of human beings. When it comes to God, in the act of one person, all three

point at which Erickson may appear to move away from a LRR of RR towards some kind of anti-realist conclusion is when he leaves himself open to the interpretation that he proposes that the titles "Father," "Son" and "Spirit" only refer to the economy of salvation.[53] That Erickson argues for this is not clear from the citation given by Kärkkäinen, though he upholds the principle that any person of the Trinity could have become incarnate.[54]

For Erickson, the christological and ecclesial outcomes of his LRR thesis are significant. In particular he notes the obedience of God the Son in the economy of salvation, the example this sets for his disciples, and the "equality" of those who belong to the church of God the Trinity.[55] Thus, Erickson essentially draws out both an *imitatio Christi* and an *imitatio trinitas* from his LRR of RR. He thus adds the *imitatio Christi* to the view of those who hold that the SRR primarily leads to an *imitatio trinitatis*. Ironically, Erickson's use of the *imitatio trinitatis* appears to stem from the SRR of RR rather than from biblical warrant, whereas his appeal to the *imitatio Christi* is grounded in biblical passages such as Phil 2:5–11.[56]

EVANGELICAL THEOLOGY AND THE SRR OF RR

Evangelical theology will be greatly served by continued thoughtful assessment of the adequacy of the SRR and the LRR approaches to RR. Evangelical theology claims that Scripture is the foundation for belief and

---

always act because they are always 'in' that person. When human beings act together they join forces, each acting separately toward a common goal (as when three persons are pushing a car). It is different with God. The three divine persons never need to join forces because when one acts, the other two are in that person and act through it." Volf, "Allah and the Trinity," 22–23. See Volf's new work, *Allah: A Christian Response*, 2011.

53. Kärkkäinen cites Erickson, *Christian Theology*, 362–63. However, this reference does not warrant Kärkkäinen's conclusion.

54. Kärkkäinen, *The Trinity: Global Perspectives*, 230. If Kärkkäinen was correct, in terms of the significance of this for the interpretation of RR, Erickson may appear to be straying into a form of antirealism and thus adopting the strict anti-realist reading (SARR) of RR. However, a more accurate representation of his thought on this consequence of his original and overarching LRR of RR is that he is a realist about God's self, yet not about the names.

55. Erickson, *Making Sense of the Trinity*, 89–91.

56. Ibid., 87–89.

practice: it is the *norma normans*. Scripture is "the product of an asymmetrical double-agency. Scripture is God-breathed (*theopneustos*)."[57] Its role in Evangelical theological methodology is that of a touchstone. The use of the concept of a touchstone here functions as a "metaphor for Scripture's theological function in the life of God's people. A touchstone is a piece of quartz that can be used to test, for example, whether a piece of ore is really gold or merely fool's gold. Scripture as the Word of God is the norming norm (*norma normans*)."[58] Consequently, for Evangelicals all other norms for theology need to be confirmed by, and conformed to, the Bible. Non-scriptural norms such as RR, and its various readings, should relate to the Bible in a ministerial capacity and serve Scripture. This is significant for the role of Scripture in assessing theological proposals and traditions including ones that determine interpretation. Regarding theological proposals, Evangelical theologian Cole states that the Bible must undergird proposals if they are to be valid: "If a putative doctrinal proposal is textless—that is to say, it lacks biblical support—then it may be held as a speculative possibility but not as a candidate for a non-negotiable conviction expressing the faith."[59]

For Evangelicals, axioms for the interpretation of Scripture, such as RR, are appropriate only as follows: "Of course, other authorities such as tradition, reason, and experience are operative in Christian theology and life. But these lesser authorities are ruled norms (*norma normata*). In any conflict between authorities the appeal to Scripture is paramount since it is the touchstone and rules the others."[60] A sound and consistent Evangelical theology will determine the validity of a norm such as the SRR of RR. This will naturally be carried out via a Scriptural test. This is so especially since RR's usual use includes employing it as a norm *over* Scripture.[61] Furthermore, it is a norm that, in turn, determines Scripture's

---

57. Cole, *God the Peacemaker*, 26.
58. Ibid., 27.
59. Ibid.
60. Ibid.
61. Evidence for this includes theologians who deliberately adopt this norm (explicitly or implicitly) in their approach to deriving trinitarian theology from the Scriptures. Some believe this approach enables direct application of the doctrine to discipleship. For example, Bruce Ware begins his work *Father, Son and Holy Spirit* with the following statement: "The focus of our study of the Trinity will be to examine especially the ways in which the Father, Son and Holy Spirit *relate to one another*, how they *relate to us*, and what *difference this makes in our lives.*" Ware, *Father, Son and Holy Spirit*, 14–15 (italics

own message about who God is. What could be more foundational to theology than such a message? Surely any Evangelical use of RR, especially the very popular SRR approach, cannot go untested by Scripture.

Given the nature of Evangelical theology (above), it is astounding that though many Evangelicals employ the SRR of RR as a norm for Scripture, they have not carried out a sustained scriptural test of this norm. Thus, we are at present in a situation in which some Evangelicals have unquestioningly taken on an extra-biblical rule as their norm for interpreting Scripture, without seeing whether or not this rule is consistent with Scripture in the first place. There is thus a significant lacuna in present day Evangelical trinitarian theology. Without a biblical test of the SRR of RR, Evangelical theologians are employing an unsubstantiated, "text-less" norm for the theological interpretation of their Bibles.

The central problem that accompanies this approach is that theological proposals and debate amongst Evangelicals on trinitarian issues have no effective foundation stone, and no touchstone, as long as this problem continues. Therefore, the theological construals that stem from various interpretations of RR cannot ultimately be substantiated to the satisfaction of a truly "Evangelical" view, because the first-order scriptural questions have not been asked. In addition, trinitarian debates will not be settled by appeals to Scripture when it is normed by a questionable rule.

The focus of this book is whether or not the SRR of RR stands up to the witness of Scripture. Does it withstand an exegetical critique? The concerns underlying this work include the kind of Christology that may emerge from the use of the SRR of RR. To anticipate the conclusions of argument to come, the SRR of RR may struggle to sufficiently reckon with the nature and significance of the incarnation. According to the Bible, the fact of the incarnation entails "God plus," therefore there is a strong view of the humanity of Christ, and the economy of salvation in which his life is lived must be taken into account.[62] The theological issues related to the SRR of RR for an Evangelical theology stem from how one handles these two central points.

Further prominent theological issues which arise from the SRR of RR include: the basic question of the possibility of drawing conclusions about the immanent Trinity from the economic Trinity; the manner and

are Ware's).

62. Milne, *Know The Truth*, 147.

extent to which people may build social and ethical models from an understanding of how God relates within himself eternally and from how he relates to the world; maintaining God the Son's *homoousion* with God the Father; whether there is an essential analogue to the subordination of God the Son to God the Father in the economy of salvation; the extent of divine condescension by God in the incarnation of God the Son; the nature of God's freedom from creation and vice versa; and whether this particular application of RR (whereby it is the primary trinitarian hermeneutical norm) flattens out Scripture's witness to God's personal involvement and works in the economy of salvation.

REVIEW OF THE LITERATURE

Evangelical theologians have not carried out a thoroughly scriptural assessment of the SRR of RR. This is surprising given the widespread use and critique of RR as a theological norm. There is no known major published work which has as its central concern the exegetical viability, or otherwise, of any of the readings of RR. Direct attention to this foundational aspect of the use of RR is only occasional, and each particular author's reading of it is often assumed to be valid *a priori*. Though critique of the SRR is often secondary to the main work of the author who carries out the critique, the following points have been highlighted as problems with the SRR of RR: it stems from epistemic confusion,[63] category confusion and a logical mistake;[64] it results in the loss of the essential Trinity and thus the loss of the freedom of God and of creatures;[65] it leads to speculative, unfounded, yet highly influential theologoumena;[66] the use of the SRR has the effect of obscuring the clarity and evangelistic potential of the Christian faith;[67] it misunderstands the nature of language;[68] a multiplicity of christological issues may arise from its use, including monothelitism, monophysitism, or nestorianism,[69] there may

---

63. Erickson, *God in Three Persons*, 309.
64. Thomas F. Torrance, *Trinitarian Perspectives*, 79. Webster, "Trinity and Creation."
65. Molnar, *Divine Freedom and the Doctrine of the Immanent Trinity*, 1–25, 63.
66. Ormerod, *The Trinity*, 18–19, 29.
67. Ibid., 14, 29.
68. Erickson, *Three Persons*, 306–7. Also Ormerod, *The Trinity*, 126.
69. Ormerod, *The Trinity*, 128, 30–31.

be deleterious metaphysical entailments of its use;[70] lastly, its methodological usefulness may be questionable because it is unable to withstand the theological criterion of coherence.[71]

The closest anyone has come to testing the SRR of RR via Scripture is in the work of Jowers.[72] He investigated "whether the intra-Trinitarian relations reflected in the economy of salvation always correspond to the [taxis] of the immanent Trinity as this [taxis] is envisioned by Rahner."[73] Thus, Jowers was seeking to test Rahner's axiom via one of Rahner's own criteria for trinitarian theology. Rahner's criteria was taken to be his own belief that a fixed order of relations within the economy of salvation is the necessary reflection of a fixed order of relations within the taxis of the immanent Trinity. By virtue of assessing Karl Rahner's own theology, Jowers also implicitly proposed to test the Rule against a second criterion: the Western Christian view of the relations within the Trinity *ad intra*. Though Rahner's own theology is vague at times in relation to Western orthodox theology, he is a strict filioquist. Thus, in his study, Jowers brings his test into conversation with traditional Western theology by employing as his test case God the Father's anointing of Christ by the Holy Spirit in the Jordan (Matt 3:16–17; Mark 1:10–11; Luke 3:22; John 1:32). In Jowers' view, if he could show that the display of relations between the persons of the Trinity in the economy of this event could be reconciled with Rahner's understanding of the taxis, then Jowers' study would lend credibility to what essentially amounts to the SRR of RR.[74] However, "if the pattern of intra-Trinitarian relations displayed in Christ's anointing . . . cannot be reconciled with what Rahner considers the orthodox understanding of the intra-Trinitarian [taxis] . . . it appears

---

70. McCall and Yandell, "On Trinitarian Subordinationism."

71. Ormerod, *The Trinity*, 18.

72. Jowers, "A Test of Karl Rahner's Axiom."

73. Ibid., 423.

74. A clarification is required at this point: though Jowers' work is helpful in many respects, we must note that this thesis does not take Jowers' view on the baptism of Jesus. We disagree with Jowers' view that the baptism of Jesus is a baptism by the Holy Spirit. This event is best understood as an anointing and commissioning of Jesus in line with the OT patterns and expectations for a Davidic King and prophet. Most significantly, there is nothing in the text that makes it clear that Jesus was baptized by the Spirit.

that either Rahner's axiom or his own, mildly Latin Trinitarianism must be false."[75]

Jowers' intent is commendable in that he attempted to demonstrate the integrity (or otherwise) or Rahner's own theology by means of a scriptural test. The work of Jowers invites more exegetical investigation. Jowers did assess various views on the immanent correlate to the trinitarian relations witnessed in the anointing of Jesus. However, he did so via patristic antecedents, apocryphal writings and Rahner's own theology. Therefore, Jowers' test may not be sufficiently exegetical in order to satisfy the Evangelical criterion of the Bible as the foundation of all theological assessment.[76]

Though no attempt to test RR with the witness of Scripture is available, works relevant to a scriptural test of the SRR of RR may be grouped into four categories. These are firstly recent contributions to trinitarian theology that demonstrate the need for a scriptural assessment of the SRR of RR;[77] secondly works which outline the various approaches to RR;[78] thirdly, works which critique and attempt to restate the SRR of RR;[79] and fourthly works on Luke-Acts, including some specific studies in this area, which examine the Trinity, or the works and persons of the Trinity.[80]

---

75. Ibid., 423.

76 Neither did Jowers strongly substantiate his own position on the anointing of Jesus via a scriptural basis.

77. Sanders, "Chalcedonian Categories for the Gospel Narrative."

78. Sanders, *Image of the Immanent Trinity*; Rauser, "Rahner's Rule."

79. Kasper's work is a prominent example of an attempt to restate RR. "If . . . the axiom which states the identity of the immanent and economic Trinities is not to lead to the dissolution of the immanent Trinity instead of to its substantiation, this identity must not be understood along the lines of the tautological formula A= A. The 'is' in this axiom must be understood as meaning not an identification but rather a non-deducible, free, gracious, historical presence of the immanent Trinity in the economic Trinity. We may therefore rephrase Rahner's basic axiom as follows: in the economic self-communication the intra-trinitarian self-communication is present in the world in a new way, namely, under the veil of historical words, signs and actions, and ultimately in the figure of the man Jesus of Nazareth. The need is to maintain not only the kenotic character of the economic Trinity but also its character of graciousness and freedom in relation to the immanent Trinity and thus to do justice to the immanent mystery of God in (not: behind!) his self-revelation." Kasper, *The God of Jesus Christ*, 276. For the original restatement see Kasper, *Der Gott Jesu Christi*, 336.

80. Johnson, "Ripples of the Resurrection in the Triune Life of God; Anderson, *"But God Raised Him From the Dead"*; Rowe, "Biblical Pressure and Trinitarian

THIS BOOK

Thesis

The thesis of this book rests on the clarification of three theological implications of the narrative of Luke-Acts that resist the SRR of RR as grounds for constructing a doctrine of the triune God. These are: (1) the nature of Jesus' messianic vocation in the economy of salvation; (2) a fluidity in the trinitarian relations and works between God the Father and God the Son; and (3) a fluidity in the trinitarian relations and works between God the Son and God the Holy Spirit. Analysis will show that a SRR of RR does not comport with the witness of Luke-Acts. In addition, we shall point out that possible theologies that emerge if the SRR of RR were applied to Luke-Acts are highly problematic. Therefore, we will conclude that a SRR of RR is an untenable theory because it cannot include Luke-Acts within the boundaries of its data. This significantly undermines the usefulness of the SRR of RR as a conceptual tool. *In a nutshell we argue that the use of the SRR of RR as a tool for constructing a doctrine of the essential Trinity based upon the economy of salvation, fails exegetically.*

Research Methodology

The purpose of this book is to bring the SRR of RR into conversation with the witness of Scripture, specifically Luke-Acts. As such, this work is a scriptural test of a theological norm. It is an explicitly Evangelical work. Many of the methodological assumptions behind the test to be carried out are indebted to Erickson's "Criteria for assessing alternatives."[81] Erickson has written on testing theological alternatives, and provided solid criteria for assessing theological proposals. These criteria are described below, followed by the relevance of each criterion to testing the SRR of RR against the narrative of Luke-Acts. The usefulness of such a scriptural test of the SRR of RR rests on the degree to which this comports to Erickson's various criteria for assessing a theological proposal.

Erickson's criteria are: (1) *Consistency criterion*—A negative criterion, which does not guarantee that the proposal is true. However, if the proposal is not logically consistent (in other words, is contradictory)

Hermeneutics"; Rowe, "Luke and the Trinity."

81. Erickson, *Who Is Tampering with the Trinity*.

then it cannot be as stated.[82] (2) *Coherence criterion*—This looks at the "actual intermeshing of the elements in a theory . . . [c]oherence means that the truth of certain propositions is established by a logical connection with other propositions in a set."[83] (3) *Applicability criterion*—This deals with the issue of whether or not what is stated is an accurate representation of reality: "A proposition is ultimately justified by being shown to be taught by the Bible. In terms of the issue of applicability, the question becomes how well the theory relates to the elements in the Bible that it claims to represent."[84] (4) *Adequacy criterion*—On this criterion Erickson writes: "if applicability is the ability of a theory to portray suitably and accurately what it purports to represent, then adequacy measures the extent of the data that a theory can depict. Here the criterion is that a theory that can explain a larger percentage of the data is superior to the one that can deal only with a smaller segment."[85] (5) *Personal criterion*—This criterion often has priority in the minds of the people who adopt a given theory, and who have personal subjective motivations.[86] (6) *Pragmatic criterion*—This pertains to the effects the theory has on the life of the individual and wider society, the "affective or functional results."[87] (7) *The status of the conclusion*—This is a highly significant criterion for strong theories. A strong theory will emerge over competing theories because it can account for more evidence. However, at the same time it will not claim to take all the data into account. The benefit of this approach, which Erickson calls the "comparative-evidence approach," is that it "frees us from the ludicrous practice of trying to rebut every argument against our view or trying to show that every smidgeon

---

82. Ibid., 88.
83. Ibid., 90–91.
84. Ibid., 95.
85. Ibid., 99.
86. "[C]ompeting theories may be assessed in terms of how the signs constituting them relate to the knower of the theory or interpreter of the facts . . . in terms of the sequence in which people come to adopt a given viewpoint, this element often has priority. An idea or theory or system is adopted because it meets a particular need or gives meaning to life. It is satisfying on a subjective, personal basis. Then, one moves outward from there, as questions arise as to whether there is actual objective reality to what has proved subjectively meaningful. Epistemologically, however, rather than biographically, it must take a subsidiary place to other considerations." Ibid., 103.
87. Ibid.

of evidence supports it."[88] We shall return to Erickson's criteria, as they apply to our analysis of Luke-Acts, at the conclusion of this work.

Why Luke-Acts?

One of the most significant issues in the relationship between trinitarian studies and their interaction with the Bible has been that the trinitarian witness of the Gospel of John has often been emphasized at the expense of that of the Synoptic Gospels. There has been an historical imbalance in preference of a "procession model" of the Trinity drawn from an overstatement of some aspects of John's Gospel, in which Jesus comes from above, from the Father, into the plane of history.[89] This historic tradition needs to be complemented by the "return" model of the Synoptics (and the "return" aspects of John's Gospel, such as John 17:5), whereby in the economy of salvation, Jesus returns to glory with God the Father.[90] This book will work to redress this historic imbalance by working from the narrative of Luke-Acts, making a valuable synoptic contribution to trinitarian theology: a contribution which accounts for nearly 1/3 of the New Testament. Furthermore Luke-Acts can rightly be treated as an integrated, united document written by the same author.[91]

The primary aim of the record of the economic activities of God in Luke-Acts is to reveal God's salvific work, not the essential

---

88. Ibid., 105.

89. Evidence that this is the case may be taken from Letham, Ware and Sanders. Each of these three Evangelical theologians who write on the Trinity give a priority to the gospel of John in their works. The Scripture index in Letham's *The Holy Trinity* lists references to John's gospel a total of 102 times; Matthew, Mark and Luke are referred to twenty-nine, seven, and twbty-one times respectively. In Bruce Ware's *Father, Son and Holy Spirit*, the Gospel of John is referenced in the Scripture index forty-two times—and some are referenced multiple times. Matthew, Mark, and Luke are referenced fourteen, six, and fifteen times respectively, with little multiple referencing. That is, the Gospel of John is referenced more than the sum total of references to the Synoptic Gospels in both the works of Letham and Ware. Younger Evangelical theologians are not exempt from this trend. Sanders' new work on the Trinity, *The Deep Things of God*, refers to John's Gospel nineteen times in the Scripture index, whereas Matthew, Mark, and Luke are referred to a total of nine, one, and five times.

90. Coffey, *Deus Trinitas*, 33 ff.

91. Tannehill, *The Narrative Unity of Luke-Acts*. For recent debate on this see the following article and the responses to it: Rowe, "History, Hermeneutics and the Unity of Luke-Acts."

relations within himself.[92] However, according to Rowe,[93] Fitzmyer,[94] Buckwalter,[95] Hull,[96] Woods,[97] and Mowery,[98] the fact remains that the narrative of Luke-Acts demands a trinitarian reading. This reading is warranted by several episodes in the narrative, none more clearly than Jesus' anointing. In this event, Jesus' "I-thou" relationship with the Father is revealed (Luke 3:22b). This relationship obtains significance in conjunction with the fact that Jesus understood himself as Lord (Luke 20:42–44) and early Christian proclamation acknowledged him as such (Acts 2:25–36). However, a binitarian reading will not suffice, because as we shall will endeavor to outline, the identity of the Holy Spirit in Luke-Acts requires a trinitarian reading of this document. As the one who confirms Jesus' identity, the Spirit is revealed to be a separate personal agent in the anointing event (Luke 3:22a), a personhood confirmed both in Luke (4:1) and in Acts (5:4,9). It is therefore defensible to explore the economic relations between the Father, Son and Holy Spirit as found in the narrative of Luke-Acts with a trinitarian understanding.[99]

The Significance of this Project

The significance of this project relates to both trinitarian theology and to Evangelical theology. First, with reference to trinitarian theology, this project seeks to provide an original scriptural assessment of RR and address a lacuna in present Evangelical scholarship. Second, this book raises awareness of the theological (particularly the christological) issues that are at stake if one employs the SRR of RR or a view with great affinities with it.

This project also aims to enable Evangelical trinitarian studies to take a step forward in assessing extra-biblical norms in a manner that is more scripturally informed. The acceptance or rejection of the SRR of RR would then be carried out with greater integrity as Evangelicals

---

92. Marshall, *Luke: Historian and Theologian*, 92.
93. Rowe, "Luke and the Trinity," 4.
94. Fitzmyer, *The Gospel according to Luke*, 1:227.
95. Buckwalter, *The Character and Purpose of Luke's Christology*, 173–205.
96. Hull, *The Holy Spirit in the Acts of the Apostles*, 173–74.
97. Woods, *The 'Finger of God,'* 253.
98. Mowery, "God the Father in Luke-Acts."
99. Morgan, "Unity and Diversity in New Testament Talk of the Spirit," 12–13.

apply a scriptural test to it. Therefore, this work is a contribution to self-avowed, consistent Evangelical trinitarian theology.

The Shape of This Study

Chapter 2 will open by underscoring Rahner's significance as a theologian in the twentieth century. The philosophical nature of his theology, and particularly his theology of grace, will be noted as a way into Rahner's view on the Trinity and the penning of his norm. The trinitarian context in which Rahner himself posits his *Grundaxiom* will be explained. The method for outlining his trinitarianism will demonstrate the connectedness and interdependency between Rahner's doctrines of grace, the incarnation and the Trinity. This interconnectedness may be stated as follows: Rahner's trinitarian theology is an "anticipatory" trinitarian approach that employs grace as the structure for understanding the Trinity in the light of the incarnation. Prominent theological trinitarian and christological issues will be on view throughout this chapter. These are significant for those who seek to adopt any aspect of Rahner's trinitarian thought including this *Grundaxiom*. Following this analysis we shall describe Rahner's Rule and conclude that Rahner's own interpretation of the norm aligns with the SRR.

In chapter 3 the exegetical critique of the SRR of RR from Luke-Acts begins via a description of the messianic nature of Jesus' actions as he related to God the Father and God the Spirit in the economy of salvation. This exegetical work will demonstrate that Jesus' actions in the economy of salvation were not merely the expression of inner-trinitarian eternal relationships. Rather, God the Son's actions were accommodated to his earthly mission. Specifically, the aspects of Luke-Acts which challenge the SRR of RR are firstly, that Jesus' work in the economy of salvation takes place within Jesus' state of humiliation, not his glory; secondly, the shape of the messianic role which determines Jesus' actions in the economy of salvation is the reason behind Jesus' obedience to God the Father. Further, Jesus' humanity in the economy of salvation has a veiling effect upon his essential glory; in addition, given his anticipated eschatological work and revelation, Jesus' work in the economy of salvation is an incomplete revelation of who he is. Lastly, Jesus' own knowledge is limited by virtue of his humanity, therefore, his knowledge of the actions of God the Father in particular cannot be taken as a representation of the essential relationship between the first and second persons of the Trinity—otherwise, the Son *prima facie* is not omniscient.

In chapter 4 we shall explore aspects of the Father-Son relationship in Luke-Acts and the significant problems these pose for the use of the SRR of RR. This chapter will be divided into two parts. In the first part of this chapter we shall outline areas in which the narrative of Luke-Acts resists the logic of the SRR of RR when this is applied to the text. Examples of the problematic theology that would emerge from the application of the SRR of RR to Luke-Acts includes, for example, *if the SRR of RR is applied to the fact that God the Father* may be understood as being *subordinate to God the Son's will in at least one instance (Luke 10:22) this could be taken to mean that* there is a succession of reversed subordinations between the Father and the Son's wills in Luke's Gospel. Another example of a difficult theology that could stem from the application of the SRR of RR to Luke-Acts involves the ascension. The emerging theology raises the question of the relationship between the ascension of God the Son and God's being, especially if the sending of the Son into the economy of salvation is taken to be a reflection of the begetting of the Son in the trinitarian taxis. In addition, the SRR of RR is resisted by the narrative of Luke-Acts because there is fluidity of actor and action in terms of both God's *ad extra* revelation and soteriological works in Luke-Acts between God the Father and God the Son. This fluidity is compounded by the fact that Luke-Acts presents a profound continuity between the persons of God the Father and God the Son.

Chapter 5 deals with the resistance offered against the SRR of RR by the relationship between God the Son and God the Spirit in Luke-Acts. Luke-Acts' record of the economic relations between God the Holy Spirit and God the Son is also problematic for a SRR of RR. Firstly, we will offer the conclusion that the economic relations between the Son and the Spirit show a fluidity of actor and action that may well resist any strict appropriation of relationship or role as per the SRR of RR. Further, this chapter will present three exegetical conclusions from Luke-Acts, which if interpreted via the SRR of RR, would necessarily result in problematic theological outcomes. These exegetical conclusions from Luke-Acts are that: the Spirit, together with Mary, is responsible for the conception of Jesus and his entry into the world of humanity; Jesus experiences a double reception of the Spirit; there is a reversed subordination in the economic relations between God the Son and God the Holy Spirit. These are valid conclusions from Luke-Acts. However, if the SRR of RR were applied to these conclusions, then the following problematic theological conclusions may possibly arise. The first would be that God the Son might appear to be dependent upon the Spirit for his existence. Secondly, the employment of the SRR of RR could yield eternal analogues to the end that the theological conclusion from these may be that there is an instability within God's taxis which would preclude any definitive statement about God's inner relations. Thirdly, the use of the SRR of RR could result in a theological proposal that either there is a God with an unstable relational essence, or a two tiered God in terms of the relations between persons of the Trinity.

2

The Rahnerian Background

IN THE INTRODUCTORY CHAPTER we saw that there are several ways that RR has been interpreted. This chapter shall explore Karl Rahner's trinitarian theology, and its underpinnings. The question we ultimately seek to answer is, which of the major readings of Rahner's Rule is the most congruent with Rahner's own view? In doing this, we will highlight Rahner's significance for twentieth-century theology, and provide Rahner's primary theological views as the context for RR. We will also pinpoint and highlight some issues within his own trinitarian theology that should be a warning to those who seek to apply the SRR of RR as a theological norm.

In outline, this chapter will firstly provide biographical details about Rahner's immediate impact and the issue of his legacy. Secondly, we will describe the foundational role of philosophy and the outworking of the concept of grace in Karl Rahner's transcendental methodology. Thirdly, an outline of Rahner's doctrine of the incarnation will be provided in view of his theology of grace, which will reveal some pressing systematic issues. These issues stem—it will be argued—from the fact that Rahner's theology of grace pre-determines the shape, content, and interpretation of the incarnation, and by extension, his trinitarian theology. Following an outline and critique of various trinitarian and christological issues that arise from Rahner's theology of grace, the fourth section of this chapter will detail Rahner's proposal known as "Rahner's Rule," and Rahner's own interpretation of this norm. The chapter will conclude with a discussion of concerns raised by Rahner's exposition and defense of his norm.

KARL RAHNER: A TITAN OF TWENTIETH-CENTURY THEOLOGY

Karl Rahner (1904–84) has been described as "the theological titan of the twentieth century."[1] This description is warranted, as Rahner's friend and fellow one-time Jesuit student Johann Baptist Metz stated: "Karl Rahner renewed the face of our theology. Nothing is now as it was before him . . . Even those who criticize him are fuelled by his insights, insightful and moving perceptions about the world of life and faith."[2] Kärkkäinen describes Rahner's Roman Catholic and universally catholic significance:

> If John Zizioulas is the present leading Eastern Orthodox theologian, the late Karl Rahner is the main figure in recent Roman Catholic theology. No other twentieth-century Catholic theologian exercised such a universal influence, not only within the confines of the largest church in the world—about one half of all Christians belong to the Roman Catholic Church—but also ecumenically. Rahner's contribution to the Second Vatican Council (1962–65), the formative council that decisively set the Roman Catholic Church on the path of *aggiornamento*, renewal and modernization, has been unsurpassed.[3]

During his own lifetime, Rahner's impact was both immediate and enormous. His activities included his role as a *peritus* at Vatican II (where he worked in partnership with Joseph Ratzinger, the current Pope Benedict XVI), lecturing, writing, and editing.[4] On the sheer volume of his work, Marmion states: "His literary output was prodigious—even by 1974 it had reached almost 3,000 publications, including translations."[5] He was a polarizing and sometimes controversial figure during his lifetime. For example, working together with Benedict XVI did not mean theological agreement. Benedict has stated this very starkly: "Through

---

1. Egan, " Rahnerian Response"; Egan, "Theology and Spirituality," 13. (Italics are Egan's).
2. Metz, *Den Glauben*, 13.
3. Kärkkäinen, *Christology*. (Italics are Kärkkäinen's).
4. Egan, "Rahner, Karl," 449–51.
5. Marmion, "Some Aspects," 3.

the work together it was clear to me that Rahner and I, despite agreement in many results and wishes, lived theologically on two different planets."[6] Ratzinger explained the low significance of Scripture and the church fathers for Rahner when he enlarged on what he meant by his "two different theological planets" analogy:

> His theology was—despite the reading of the Fathers of his early years—stamped entirely by the tradition of Suarezian scholasticism and of its new reception in the light of German idealism and of Heidegger. It was speculative and philosophical theology in which Scripture and the Fathers, in the last analysis, played no great role, and in which the historical dimension was of only minimal significance. I, on the other hand, from my education was quite stamped by Scripture and the Fathers and by an essentially historical thinking. The whole difference between the Munich school, through which I had passed, and Rahner's became clear to me in those days [of Vatican II], before the parting of our ways became visible from the outside.[7]

Rahner's approach, in contradistinction from Ratzinger's, may have affected his legacy. As we are dealing with the current use of his norm in Evangelical circles (now well after Rahner's death) the issue of Rahner's legacy is more pressing than his lifetime accomplishments. One might surmise that if Rahner's theology is seen as having a great enduring value, then perhaps his trinitarian norm deserves the significant appropriation it has experienced in Evangelical theology. However, despite the popularity of RR, Rahner's theology, the theological presuppositions that underlie the *Grundaxiom*, have been found to be lacking by some. In the foreword to a volume of collected of essays proceeding from the 2009 conference "Karl Rahner: Theologian for the Twenty-First Century?," Siebenrock writes:

> In 2000 George Weigel praised the historic achievement of Karl Rahner, but suggested that Rahner's time, the time of dialogue, is over and now the time of mission is beginning. The future of the Church was not "Rahnerian"; the theology of Hans Urs von Balthasar was more suited to the missionary time of the Church. The American . . . accurately remarked that the last 25 years of the Roman Catholic Church has been marked by the theology of Hans Urs von Balthasar, as this corresponds more closely to

---

6. Ratzinger, *Aus meinem Leben*, 131, cited in Corkery, "Rahner," 86.
7. Ratzinger, *Aus meinem Leben*, 131, cited in Corkery, "Rahner," 87.

the basic theological line of Pope Benedict XVI. This is the same Benedict XVI who once wrote that he and Karl Rahner lived in different theological galaxies.[8]

Despite this contextual appraisal, Siebenrock has great hopes for Rahnerian theology. He continues: "this [Wiegel's] historical dismissal of the work of Karl Rahner is disputed . . . I am firmly convinced that the real future of Karl Rahner's theology is still to come. The Church long term cannot communicate in primarily aesthetic categories its hope for and against modernity. Rahner's approaches will gain a new efficacy . . ."[9]

On the other hand, there are grounds for believing that Rahner's "project" may have little lasting impact. Kilby describes why this may be the case:

> if Rahner is read as offering a grand system of theology, which beginning from the idealist-inspired philosophy methodically applies an anthropological turn and a transcendental method to the various questions of theology—if Rahner is seen in other words as systematically adopting the presuppositions of modernity in order to make Christianity presentable to the modern world—then it is not unreasonable to regard him as in danger of seeming, once the word "post-modern" comes to be mentioned, passé.[10]

For Endean, Rahnerian theology has little future for a different reason. Though Endean believes that Rahner's theology does have intrinsic value in itself, he notes that "the post-Conciliar experience shows us that it is not possible for a church to sustain itself on the tentative, questioning theology offered by Rahner, particularly as the subcultures that nourished him and many of his readers crumble."[11]

So what is the value in Rahner's theology? A positive view of Rahner's legacy is that it is an enduring theology because it meaningfully engages a fallen world with God's grace and being. Görres captures this well:

> What makes Rahner's theology different from other theologies? It seems to be that he develops a special way of thinking along with others. He tries to penetrate deeply into the perspective of others,

---

8. Siebenrock, "Foreword," xi–xii.
9. Ibid., xi–xii.
10. Kilby, "Karl Rahner," 104.
11. Endean, "Rahnerian Theology," 293.

> to understand why . . . any other person thinks the way they do, and why they feel the way they feel . . . Rahner found consoling and helping words for countless minds that were confused and for hearts that were wounded. He opened and made attractive a way that had been closed for legions of people injured by the church and disappointed by God; he found a way to a bloody history, to a suffering Gospel, to a burdened church.[12]

However, some significant English-speaking interpreters of Rahner doubt the enduring value of the material content of Rahner's theology. For example, Karen Kilby limits the value of Rahner's work to its function as a role model for other theologians. Kilby articulates this low view of his theological content but high view of the possibilities Rahner demonstrated as follows: "What is most significant about Rahner . . . is not in fact any systematic application of the transcendental method or anthropological turn, but instead the way in which he demonstrated the possibility of doing theology which is simultaneously faithful and creative, a theology which is genuinely immersed in the tradition and also genuinely open to the difficulties and insights of the contemporary world."[13]

Endean appears to argue for a similar living value to Rahnerianism; however, he believes that this value will not be found in the academic world, rather it will be fruitful in the sphere of practical human relationships.[14] There is a sense in which Rahner has a living legacy in Evangelical theology as evidenced by the widespread use of the SRR of RR. However, given these questions about Rahner's legacy from those who are closer to his theology than Evangelicals, it behooves us to look carefully at the inner structures of Rahner's theology and their contribution to his trinitarian theology.

---

12. Görres, "Wer ist?," 80.

13. Kilby, "Karl Rahner," 104.

14. He writes: "the future of this [Rahner's] theology probably lies with people rather than theologians . . . in a narrow, professional sense . . . The future of his approach to theology will lie . . . largely in the practical sphere, as people find Rahner a helpful source for the theological interpretation of different life situations." Endean, "Rahnerian Theology," 293.

THE METHOD BEHIND THE RULE

Transcendental Philosophy

Rahner did not like the idea of "identifying his own method," nor did he share the common preoccupation with the question of methodology.[15] In addition, he was a very complex writer, and at times, contradictory and unclear.[16] However, his methodology and *a priori* assumptions are revealed as his philosophical transcendental method, which focuses on the human subject.[17]

Rahner's philosophy is described as "transcendental" because it refers to the "a priori correlation between the meaningful and the constitution of its meaning . . . this correlation is called 'transcendental' in so far as the knowing subject necessarily 'transcends itself,' i.e., has already escaped from an imaginary Cartesian interiority and is always in a state of relatedness to possible objectivity as the a priori basis for knowledge."[18] However, there are limits to this transcendence, as it always takes place within the finitude of the human condition.[19] This preoccupation with humanity itself contributes to Rahner's philosophical approach being described as an "*anthropologische Wende.*"[20]

Rahner's transcendental theology developed in two stages. The first was the philosophical stage (1934 to 1941), which included the works *Geist in Welt* (1939) and *Hörer des Wortes* (1941). The second stage involved extending the transcendental insights into theology and thus re-expressing Roman Catholic theology with relation to the epistemic insights gained from his re-interpretation of Thomism.[21] *Geist in Welt* is the work in which Rahner most clearly outlines and deals with methodological issues.[22] This work tries to draw together Maréchal's[23]

---

15. Rahner, *Theological Investigations*, 11:68–69.

16. Egbulefu, "Theologie und Ausdrucksmittel: Bemerkungen zum Denken Karl Rahners."

17. Jorgenson, *Christologies*, 36.

18. Sheehan, "Transcendental," 32.

19. Ibid., 33.

20. Eicher, *Anthropologische Wende*.

21. Sheehan, "Transcendental," 29.

22. Ormerod, *Theologies*, 111. See how this is reflected in Rahner, *Foundations*, chapter 1.

23. Jorgenson, *Christologies*, 39; Muck, *Transcendental Method*, 38–39.

reinterpretation of Aquinas' epistemology,[24] and the philosophy of Kant and Heidegger. As a philosophical work, *Geist in Welt* employs the language of metaphysics, despite the affinity between its language and the language of psychology.[25] Rahner's foundation in *Geist in Welt*, and his overall philosophy, is what Sheehan calls "the classical metaphysical axiom, *operari sequitur esse*: operations are conditioned by and constant with the ontological structure of the operator."[26] The methodological and substantive significance—especially for the SRR of RR—of this approach is that once one is aware of what a person *does*, we can state what they *are*.[27] Therefore, once one knows what a person is, then the limits of human experience may be stated with relation to the various aspects of objects available for that person to know.[28] This delimitation of metaphysical *experience* draws on Kant.[29] Sheehan outlines the aim and anthropological outcome of Rahner's exploration in *Geist in Welt*:

> [Rahner] analyses and interprets the operation of predicative knowledge—the act of correctly judging that predicate P pertains to subject S . . . Rahner's analysis is focused on a central text in Aquinas' epistemology (Summa Theologica, I, q.84, art.7), and for the most part remains within the philosophical world view and language of medieval scholasticism . . . However, Rahner's *interpretation* of that analysis . . . propels his project . . . into the modern . . . refusal of any metaphysics that makes pretensions to direct knowledge of other worldly entities. For Rahner the human spirit is, for better or worse, stuck in the world with no escape; and the range of objects available to human experience—including metaphysical experience—is always and only material.[30]

---

24. Ormerod, *Theologies*, 103–4. Di Noia, "Human Transformation," 115.

25. Ormerod, *Theologies*, 104, 07.

26. Sheehan continues: "Or in another iteration, *quails modus essendi talis modus operandi*: an entity's way of being determines its way of acting." Sheehan, "Transcendental," 30.

27. Note that this simple assumption which lies behind the SR of RR appears at an early stage of his work.

28. Sheehan, "Transcendental," 30.

29. Ibid., 30.

30. Italics are Sheehan's (ibid., 31). Therefore, it is no surprise that in his theology Rahner seeks to minimize the role of miracles in Jesus' ministry, nor is it surprising that Rahner is also unsure about the specific events and nature of the resurrection. See Molnar's lengthy and astute discussion of the incarnation and resurrection in Rahner's theology, Molnar, *Incarnation*, 45–80.

With regard to the role of philosophy in Rahner's project, our position is the "semi-foundationalist view." This approach takes the stance that philosophy was an integral aspect of Rahner's theology, rather than merely a means for his theology.[31] Philosophy did have priority over theology in Rahner's thought because it provided the conceptual and linguistic tools for his theology, as well as his foundational assumptions about God, humanity, and the world.[32]

The prioritization of philosophy in *Foundations of the Christian Faith* explains why this work has very few biblical references within it. Though its lack of direct biblical interaction may be considered to reflect "the power of tradition," it actually reflects Rahner's scant direct use of the Bible in his theological methodology.[33] In fact, Roman Catholic commentator Joseph O'Leary believes that in *Grundkurs des Glaubens* (*Foundations of the Christian Faith*), "it became clear that his [Rahner's] metaphysical system risked becoming an obstacle rather than an aid to thinking biblical faith . . ."[34]

When Rahner summed up his transcendental theological program, he never appeals to the Scriptures directly despite appealing to multiple distinct sources of authority. He summed up his method as follows: "Dogmatic theology today has to be theological anthropology . . . Such an anthropology must . . . be a transcendental anthropology."[35] Transcendental anthropology involves "the necessity of considering every theological question from a transcendental view point."[36]

---

31. Jowers, *Axiom*, 1–34; Siebenrock, „Tranzentale Offenbarung:☒

32. For the contrary view see Dych, *Karl Rahner*, 32.

33. However, "such a philosophical approach is firmly entrenched in Catholic tradition. It is a mark of the power of that tradition that Rahner is able to produce such a profound reflection on Christian faith while making only scant direct reference to Scripture." Ormerod, *Theologies*, 104.

34. O'Leary, "Rahner and Metaphysics," 23.

35. Rahner, "Nature and Grace," 316.

36. Ibid., 316.

Rahner's Key Philosophical Assumptions and Their Significance for His Trinitarian Theology

Rahner's Epistemological Outlook Determines an Experiential Foundation for What Can Be Said about God

The natural consequence of the philosophy outlined in *Geist in Welt* is the belief that unless the traditional approaches to the doctrines of God and revelation are radically re-envisioned, they will be found to be irrelevant.[37] Rahner's stress on history and the way in which people find meaning is highly significant for his theology. According to Rahner, human dependence on the events within the world of experience determines the logic and possibilities for revelation and its meaning. In particular, Rahner's theology of the incarnation (more anon), which only allows for the Son to become incarnate, stems firstly from Rahner's "correlation focused theory of meaning" (a *Bedeutungslehre*) outlined in *Geist in Welt*.[38] God's self-communication is quasi-formal in that it reveals God as he really is: God's own being is communicated.[39] That is, "[God's] self communication occurs not because of a mere efficient causality, a consequence of created grace (as the Scholastics argue), but rather on account of a 'quasi-formal' causality, a term . . . to explain that grace is not extrinsic to nature but is none other than the indwelling of the triune God in the human soul, a bestowal of God himself."[40] God the Son's relations with other persons of the Trinity in history must therefore be exactly as they are for God the Son within God's immanent self. In one of his most significant pieces of writing, Rahner expressed the following view:

> Jesus is not simply God in general, but the Son. The second divine person, God's Logos, is man, and only he is man. Hence there is at least *one* "mission," *one* presence in the world, *one* reality of salvation history which is not merely appropriated to some divine person but proper to him. Here we are not merely *speaking* "about" this person in the world. Here something occurs "outside" the intra-divine life in the world itself, something which is not a mere effect of the efficient causality of the triune God acting as one in the world, but something which belongs to the Logos

---

37. Sheehan, "Transcendental," 31.
38. Ibid., 32–33.
39. Rahner, *Trinity*, 35–36, 100–101.
40. Battaglia, "An Examination."

alone, which is the history of the one divine person, in contrast to the other divine persons.[41]

The dependence on the economy of salvation history for a person's knowledge of God naturally leads to RR, and, in particular, the SRR. For Rahner, the fact that the economic Trinity *is* the immanent Trinity and vice versa is logically understood in the strongest way possible.

For Rahner, the Modes of God's Revelation Are Primarily Determined by the Ontological Structure of People, Thereby Creating Tension with God's Decision to Reveal Himself in a Specific Manner

Rahner's assumption that the possibilities for theology have been predetermined and limited by human experience and human nature has many out-workings.[42] These include the surprising outcome that God himself, and the possibilities within God, are not maximally determinative for theology. Thus, by virtue of reducing the possibilities for human knowledge to the limited range of the material world (because the spiritual world is taken to be beyond the range of human knowing and being),[43] Rahner has laid out the necessary conditions for his *Grundaxiom*. By this axiom (RR), human beings must know not only the taxis of the immanent Trinity, but also the meaning of God's taxis as he is in himself from his actions within the world. This in turn reflects the concern of *Geist in Welt*, which he later re-stated as: "We must explicitly deal with the a priori conditions for knowing a given subject of faith; and this reflection must determine the concepts we use to describe the theological objects."[44] This key *a priori* assumption is at the forefront of his mind in *Foundations of Christian Faith*. He asks: "What kind of a hearer does Christianity anticipate so that its real and ultimate message can even be heard?"[45] This question reflects the fact that for Rahner there is a fittingness between the hearer and the Christian message.[46] A two-way

---

41. Italics are Rahner's. Rahner, *Trinity*, 23. See also Rahner, *Trinity*, 24–25, 30–33, 64. Also Rahner, *Foundations*, 118–20, 28–29.
42. Sheehan, "Transcendental," 30.
43. Italics are Sheehan's. Sheehan, "Transcendental," 31.
44. Rahner, "Nature and Grace," 316. See also Rahner, *Foundations*, 131.
45. Rahner, *Foundations*, 24.
46. Hübner, "Nichtchristliche."

relationship is in view here: the hearer displays fitted-ness for the gospel, and the gospel is fitted to the subject.[47]

Rahner thus appears to have over-prioritized the human structure and limitations of knowing, such that God and all possibilities inherent within himself must be reduced to his work in the world. Ultimately, one is confronted with the realization that Rahner's foundational assumption is that God must conform himself to us. That is, in Rahner's view, the divine condescension at the incarnation is a condescension that makes sense of human experience and the search for meaning. The incarnation is primarily viewed with regard to the individual human and what they can make of it.[48] Whilst it may be commendable that in Rahner's theology the recipients of the incarnational work are recognized as the focus of God's work, in doing so the theo-centric foundation of the incarnation is lost. Moreover, it is highly significant that though there is still a focus on what God is doing *in* the world (rather than merely *for* the world), this is ultimately expressed as God's *becoming* in the world. This will be explored below.

The Vorgriff

In *Geist in Welt*, Rahner argues that people only seek to find that of which they have a prior awareness. This prior awareness, or pre-apprehension, is what Rahner refers to as *Vorgriff*.[49] *Vorgriff* is thus a pre-grasp of knowledge.[50] Kilby provides an excellent summary of Rahner's view of the *Vorgriff*: "Whenever we apprehend some particular object, or will some finite value, Rahner maintains, we never merely recognize or

---

47. Ormerod, *Theologies*, 107.

48. "Rahner insists upon a Christology that begins with anthropology . . . Theological anthropology presupposes and explicates Christology . . . Rahner's thought allows anthropology a kind of heuristic priority, but in the end, we discover that it is Christology that is its entelechy. Rahner's theology admits both the possibility and the necessity of something like a point of contact, but all language of this fashion presupposes the structure of nature and grace, in which nature is internal to grace. Grace creates the possibility for something like nature which serves as the condition for its expression. Rahner thereby asserts the necessity for a point of contact. The point of contact is, as one might expect, human experience . . . experience has both categorical and transcendental dimensions." For the point of contact see, TI, 17, 54. For the categorical and transcendental aspects of experience see Vaceck, "Developments," 36–39. Cited in Jorgenson, *Christologies*, 136.

49. Jorgenson, *Christologies*, 37.

50. This is debated. Sheehan, "Transcendental," 37. Ormerod, *Theologies*, 111.

choose the particular, but are always at the same time reaching beyond it towards the whole of being, and it is only because of this reaching beyond that we are in fact able to recognize or choose the individual finite object. Furthermore, in reaching towards the whole of being we also reach towards God."[51]

The *Vorgriff* is basic to Rahner's theology. For example, Rahner begins his work *Geist in Welt* with "Man questions."[52] This questioning "presumes something of a pre-apprehension of that which I question . . . Questioning, in effect, presumes an awareness of that which I seek. I would not seek that of which I was unaware. The pre-apprehension of what is to be known is identified as the *Vorgriff*. All knowing takes place against the 'horizon'; everything I know is finite is finite only by its necessary limitation against the infinite . . ."[53]

In Rahner's theology, the *Vorgriff* "becomes in a sense the place where human beings and God meet, and therefore central to Rahner's theological anthropology. It plays a critical role in Rahner's understanding of grace and of revelation, in his attempt to work out the significance of the incarnation and the intelligibility of the hypostatic union . . ."[54]

A key aspect of Rahner's methodology with reference to the *Vorgriff* is that it leads to a position where he correlates people with God's being. As a result, he states that it is only when a person gives up their self-sufficiency that they are united with the things known.[55] The entire-self-giving in a relationship of knowledge is expressed and developed in Rahner's use of the *Realsymbol*, where God the Father expresses himself in the Logos, and only becomes himself in perfect knowledge as he expresses himself in the other. The "other" are beings who are united to, but separate from himself. We shall return to the theology of the *Realsymbol*, its Arian affinities, and the fact that it undermines "Rahner's Rule," in the section Issue 1: panentheism (more anon).

---

51. Kilby, "Philosophy," 129.

52. Rahner, *Spirit in the World*: xlix–lv.

53. Otto Muck,, 'Verleiche von Heidegger,' 263. Cited in Jorgenson, *Christologies*, 37 n.

54. Kilby, "Philosophy," 129.

55. Karl Rahner, *Geist in Welt*, 79–80. Cited in Jorgenson, *Christologies*, 38.

A Transcendental Theology of Grace: Where Grace and Philosophy Embrace

The centrality of grace in Rahner's philosophical theology,[56] leads to "philosophical anthropology," as an apt description of his theological project.[57] Rahner provides the grounds for correlating the transcendental human structures with the Christian message as follows: "If moreover, the horizon of human existence which grounds and encompasses all human knowledge is a mystery, and it is, then man has a positive affinity, given at least with grace, to those Christian mysteries which constitute the basic content of faith."[58] Therefore, one can safely state that, for Rahner, grace is the bridge from philosophy and into theology. This must be held in tension with Rahner's employment of grace, which builds upon his philosophical-epistemological insights. Most importantly, a theology of grace is ultimately the employment of the mystery of God's self-communication as the unifying concept in his theological project. This self-giving of God to the world is not static, it is rather, "the divine self-gift evolving in history from creation to covenant to incarnation to vision and unfolding a 'world of grace.'"[59]

Rahner's view of grace must be carefully understood. By means of altering the traditional focus of the question of God's grace, Rahner did not strictly follow Vatican I's view of the relationship between grace and knowledge. He turned to history and historical reality as the context in

---

56. Sosa Silézar rightly captures Rahner's theology of grace as follows: "Human beings exist in the natural order of the world, however, this is founded upon a super-natural knowledge which is directed towards transcendence. Every person has a supernatural vocation which is given with existence itself. From there it follows that grace (which is always present as a gift) is at the central and most intimate place of each human existence. Grace is thus situated as the central and constitutive element of the human subject, and not outside the human being. This grace determines the person's knowledge, freedom, and the totality of their life." My translation of the original which reads: "El ser humano existe en el orden natural pero fundado sobre un cimiento sobrenatural que tiende hacia la trascendencia. Todo hombre tiene una vocación sobrenatural que le viene dada con su existencia misma. De ahí se sigue que la gracia como oferta está siempre presente en el centro mismo y en lo más íntimo de cada existencia humana. La gracia se sitúa, entonces, no fuera del hombre sino como elemento constitutivo y central del sujeto. Esta gracia determina su conocimiento, su libertad y la totalidad de su vida." Translation is mine. Sosa Silézar, "La teología de la gracia en el pensamiento de Karl Rahner," 141.

57. Ormerod, *Theologies*, 104.

58. Rahner, *Foundations*, 19, 136–37.

59. Duffy, "Experience," 43.

which to discuss the relationship between nature and grace, thus moving the question away from the relationship between nature and grace with respect to revelation. Rahner's position is similar to Lubac's as he tries to avoid both intrinsicism and extrinsicism.[60] Rahner stated that the possibility for revelation from God lies within people as a result of God gracing human nature, because the "supernatural existential" is God's work of grace in people.[61] Therefore, human beings already share in a natural structure as freely determined by God, which makes them open to accept the gift of God himself in grace.[62] Thus, "as an explanatory term the supernatural existential wants to affirm . . . the reality of grace . . . that it is a constituent part of our historical existence . . . If grace is a supernatural existential . . . God is closer to us than we are to ourselves."[63] Rahner's theology of grace in the supernatural existential has enormous consequences for his understanding of revelation and human fallen-ness, and the work of the one who becomes incarnate.[64] From this point of departure, Rahner then proceeded to draw upon Pauline and Johannine language of the indwelling of God's Spirit in order to posit that God universally indwells all people through the mode of quasi-formal causality.[65] Hence, God communicates through history in space and time,[66] rather than in so-called extrinsic transcendental revelation.[67]

In summary, the outline above has demonstrated that in Rahner's theology he employs the category of grace to reinforce what he has said philosophically about the limits of human existence and the search for meaning, with particular reference to history. Grace determines the orientation of human beings to, and the possibilities of, the presence of God in human history through the Spirit and the Son. Therefore, Rahner's understanding of grace undergirds his theological methodology and

---

60. Keppler, "Begnadung als Berichtigte Froderung? Gedanken zur Bedeutung des übernatürlichen Existentials in der Gnadenlehre Karl Rahners."

61. Rahner, *Foundations*: 240–41. See also Dych, *Karl Rahner*, 36.

62. Dych, *Karl Rahner*, 36.

63. Ibid., 37.

64. The supernatural is actually "already a share in God's grace or divine self-communication, which allows us to hear the Word of God, which is God, the truly divine Word, and not to reduce it to a merely human word." Ormerod, *Theologies*: 108–9.

65. Rahner, "Some Implications," 320–22.

66. Rahner, *Foundations*, 268–69.

67. Given this, one naturally asks: what is the content of the revelatory self-communication of God? Dych, *Karl Rahner*: 43.

dictates the parameters of what will, and what will not, be said about both the incarnation and the Trinity.

THE INTERCONNECTEDNESS OF GRACE, INCARNATION, AND THE TRINITY

Jorgenson rightly states that "[i]n Rahner's theology, Trinity, Incarnation and grace are identified as the three fundamental doctrines of the Christian faith."[68] Though this is true, Rahner himself related these three to each other in an even stronger fashion: they are not only functionally related but fundamentally related. In *The Trinity*, he stated that both the doctrines of grace and Christology *are* doctrines of the Trinity.[69] The interconnectedness of these three doctrines for salvation is especially clear when one bears in mind that grace provides the necessary conditions for human experience and knowledge,[70] in the light of the incarnation, and thereby anticipates the trinitarian shape of salvation.[71] The inter-relatedness of these three doctrines is based on God's self-communication with the world via quasi-formal causality.[72] This is captured as follows: "The topic of grace correlates soteriology to Christology insofar as Christology and grace are both instances of trinitarian engagement with the world. Both are expressions of the self-communicative character of the triune God."[73] The incarnation is the clearest moment within the "the movement of that nameless mystery which is the vehicle of all understanding," towards humanity.[74] Beyond the fact of the interconnectedness of these theologies, the significance of this clustering of grace, incarnation and the Trinity is highly important. For example, as far as the identity of God is concerned, the gravity of self-communication in grace, incarnation and the Trinity is as follows:

68. Jorgenson, *Christologies*, 85.

69. "[A]s is evident from our basic axiom, Christology and the doctrine of the grace *are*, strictly speaking, doctrine of the Trinity." Italics are Rahner's. Rahner, *Trinity*, 120.

70. For the categorical and transcendental aspects of experience see E. Vaceck, "Developments," *Irish Theological Quarterly*, 42.1 (1975) 36–39. Cited in Jorgenson, *Christologies*, 136.

71. Vass, "Homage to Karl Rahner."

72. Rahner, "Symbol," 245.

73. Jorgenson, *Christologies*, 136.

74. Rahner, "Incarnation," 105–20.

> In order to understand the various texts about the distinction of the Spirit from the Father and the Son and about his "procession" we must . . . repeat what we said about the Son. The starting point is the experience of faith, which makes us aware that, through what we call "Holy Spirit," God (hence the Father) *really* communicates *himself* as love and forgiveness, that he produces this self-communication and maintains it by himself. Hence the Spirit must be God himself. The reality of revelation history is . . . distinct from the Father who gives and the Son who mediates. We demonstrate this according to our fundamental trinitarian axiom, through the fact that the concrete Christ distinguishes this gift from himself not only with respect to God (the Father) but also with respect to those who receive the Spirit.[75]

RAHNER'S CHRISTOLOGY

The organic nature and consequences of Rahner's theologies of the Trinity and grace will become even clearer (below) as both Rahner's descending and ascending christologies are outlined.

Descending Christology: God's Movement of Self-Communication towards the World in the Incarnation

In Rahner's thought, "descending" Christology must start with the self-expression of the Father in the Logos. The self-expression of God is logically fundamental to the self-communication of God. This is clearly enunciated in Rahner's concept of the *Realsymbol*. God expresses himself as symbol, which is ontologically united to what is expressed and as such differentiates the symbol from a mere sign. Rahner underscores the necessity of the symbol for the expression of a being's nature: "all beings are by their nature symbolic, because they necessarily "express" themselves in order to attain their own nature."[76] Not only is self expression essential to being, self-expression *in another* is essential to its own existence, and to the existence of the other: "the symbol strictly speaking (symbolic reality) is the self-realization of a being in the other, which is constitutive of its essence."[77] The significance for trinitarian theology

---

75. Italics are Rahner's. Rahner, *Trinity*, 67–68; Jorgenson, *Christologies*, 136.
76. Rahner, "Symbol," 224.
77. Ibid., 225; Kress, *Rahner Handbook*, 43. An avenue for further research may be

is that the only way in which God the Father can be the Father is in the act of generating his own image in the Son, as plurality within the unity of God is not accidental (i.e., a composite of elements) but, rather, based on necessary casual relations.[78] The perfection that God achieves in terms of plurality within unity occurs when he creates within himself subordinate inner-moments of love and knowledge. Thus God achieves his perfection via his inner missions in love whereby "a spiritual being achieves perfection and self-possession by the gift of itself to another," and in knowledge where "the spiritual subject achieves perfection by positing within itself an object distinct from itself."[79]

Rahner established a logical sequence of being-in-relation from God the Father through to the incarnation. The first step in this chain of ideas is the assumption that the Logos carries out the same roles in the self-expression of God in the economic Trinity as in the immanent Trinity. That is, the outward expression of the Logos is derived from, and congruent with, the self-expression of God's being within himself.[80] However, it needs to be noted at this stage that Rahner's qualifications with regards to the immanent and economic self-expression of God in the Logos carry no true weight in the actual outworking of his theology.[81] The Logos is therefore "a real symbol of the Father, i.e., the Son, is a reality within the Godhead distinct from the Father and yet inwardly posited by the Father through his generative act of self-knowledge. Thus the Son is the perfect expression of the reality of the Father."[82] Rahner states that the Logos is "the word of the Father, his perfect 'image,' his imprint, his radiance, his self-expression."[83]

---

constructing a viable description of the oneness of God as three co-inherent symbols of himself.

78. To anticipate the work of chs. 3–5, we shall argue that exegesis of Luke-Acts leads to the conclusion that causal relations in the economy of salvation (understood within a context of divine perichoresis and simplicity) will only be applied to God the Son as he is particularized as Messiah. This particularization in the economy of salvation—which entails some degree of ontological change—is not found to be viable when applied to the Father and the Spirit in an ontological sense as they have no creaturely reality to be particularized.

79. Gelpi, *Life and Light*, 9–11.
80. Rahner, "Symbol," 231.
81. Ibid., 236–37; Sanders; *Image*, 76–77.
82. Gelpi, *Life and Light*, 10–11.
83. Rahner, "Symbol," 236.

The next point in the sequence that follows on from the fact that the Logos is the real symbol of the Father is that two elements must be theologically retained within the life of the Trinity. These are, firstly, "the Word-as reality of the immanent divine life-is 'generated' by the Father as the *image* and *expression* of the Father." Secondly, "this process [of generation] is necessarily given with the divine act of self-knowledge, and without it the absolute act of divine self-possession in knowledge cannot exist."[84] Having made these points, Rahner emphasizes that the logical consequence of what he has stated is that the Son alone could be the expression, and thus the self-possession, of the Father.[85] The Christology is thus a descending Christology in which Christ has his identity from God the Father's expression of himself towards the world in the Logos as his symbol. This in turn captures and completes the identity of the Father. We shall continue to explore the foundations of Rahner's trinitarianism as we now turn from an outline of Rahner's descending Christology to his ascending Christology.

Ascending Christology: Christology from the Direction of the Humanity of Christ towards God

Rahner's ascending Christology is expressed in such a way as to make it clear that the history of revelation, salvation and grace "reaches its goal and climax in Jesus Christ."[86] The incarnation is the climactic moment when humanity is most open to God. This openness is defined as self-abandonment towards God. It is an abandonment which "is done in the strictest sense and reaches an unsurpassable pitch of achievement, when the nature which surrenders itself to the mystery of the fullness belongs so little to itself that it becomes the nature of God himself."[87] Christology is the link between Rahner's understanding of nature and grace on one hand and his Christology on the other.[88] This Christology takes place within the universe as a dynamic entity; with God at the centre. Ormerod states that in this view of the universe there is an ongoing process whereby, "matter continually seeks to express itself in even

---

84. Ibid., 236.

85. One wonders why, if one is going to argue against the bounds of tradition, these things said of the Son cannot also be said of the Spirit. Rahner, "Symbol," 236.

86. Rahner, *Foundations*, 176.

87. Rahner, "Incarnation," 110.

88. Ormerod, *Theologies*, 178ff.

higher, more complex forms. In this process, spirit is not something superimposed upon matter from above, but is matter become conscious of itself and the cosmos."[89] Within the evolving universe, finite beings are transformed or "complexified" via a process of "active self-transcendence," whereby beings evolve beyond their current default state to a higher state.[90]

God's being and work is intimately involved in this process of active self-transcendence, as this process is understood "as taking place by the power of the absolute fullness of being [God]."[91] Thus the incarnation is not understood as a downward movement alone (from God to the world below), but is rather the outworking of a movement within universe, culminating in an upward movement of knowing and loving. Rahner wrote: "In Jesus the self-transcendence of the human spirit reaches its ultimate fulfillment and breaks through into the divine."[92] Ormerod argues that "this should not be seen as an 'achievement' of Jesus, in some adoptive sense, but as God's definitive self-communication in Jesus. Creation as a whole is seen by Rahner as a deficient mode of God's self-communication, which then reaches perfection in the incarnation."[93] Walter Kasper and Hans Urs von Balthasar recognized the diminished nature of Rahner's Christology. They believed that Rahner's anthropological Christology led to an ideology or philosophy rather than Christology proper. For Kasper, what actually takes place in Rahner's theology is that "Jesus Christ is set in a predetermined scheme of reference, and that the eventual result of the . . . diminution of faith is a mere philosophy or ideology."[94]

Three questions about Rahner's ascending Christology are appropriate at this juncture. Firstly, does Rahner's Christology break with the creedal and scriptural affirmation of a strong separation between God and creation? Secondly, if, within a dynamic view of Christology, salvation is the historical outworking of the "final and definitive validity of a person's true self-understanding and true self-realization in freedom

---

89. Ibid., 110.
90. Ibid., 110.
91. Rahner, *Foundations*, 185.
92. Ormerod, *Theologies*, 110.
93. Ibid., 110.
94. Kasper, *Jesus*, 18.

before God,"⁹⁵ how can this be sustained with reference to Christ as savior and statements regarding Jesus' salvific work in the Bible and in the historic Creeds? A third question is a plea for clarification: could Rahner show that the distinction between creation and recreation, and common and special grace, are not blurred by his ascending Christology? Further, Rahner's Christology may lack a sufficient universal Christ-event that brings about definite change. This may be because Rahner may have unintentionally reduced Christology to being history's climax instead of being the grounds of a climax that began (and is yet incomplete) in the incarnation, life, death, and resurrection of Christ. Therefore the drama of redemption is swallowed up by mere historical process, and we are left with history without a story to tell.

Rahner's emphasis on the revelatory function of history leads him to configure his Christology as an "ascending Christology," which begins with understanding the "historical Jesus."⁹⁶ Significantly, this does not mean that the incarnation is the point of departure for Christology, rather it is the life of Jesus. On the other hand, the benefits of Rahner's focus on the Jesus of history has three implications: firstly it avoids Gnosticism and Docetism, thereby providing a reasonable basis for faith, secondly "real history" mediates real faith: without history there can be no real basis for faith, thirdly it affirms the incarnation.⁹⁷ Despite these positive aspects, Rahner's focus on history leads him to appropriate many of the historical-critical views about the limits of what may be known about Jesus.⁹⁸ Thus we conclude with Ormerod that for Rahner, the incarnation is merely an heuristic tool for an "open ended method" in which the incarnation is only peripheral to, and not foundational nor necessitated by, most of Rahner's reflections on this topic.⁹⁹ The fact that the perceived problems presented above are possibly found in such a significant theologian should be a concern to the wider church as it seeks clarification on how to deal with Rahner's trinitarian norm.

---

95. Rahner, *Foundations*, 39–40.
96. Rahner, *Foundations*, 177.
97. Dych, *Karl Rahner*, 50–1.
98. Ibid., 52.
99. Ormerod, *Theologies*, 111.

CRITIQUE OF THE TRINITARIAN AND CHRISTOLOGICAL OUTCOMES OF RAHNER'S THEOLOGY OF GRACE AS A BACKGROUND TO RAHNER'S RULE

Issue 1: A God-World Relationship That Tends towards Panentheism

The God-world relationship in Rahner's theology is bound up with God's own self-utterance, which is a condition that God must meet to achieve self-perfection.[100] Two consequences of this theology become may require further investigation. Firstly, it may be the case that God's aseity is compromised as he necessarily requires that which is not himself in order to become himself. God the Father is dependent upon creation to become himself.[101] In addition, with reference to the Logos, given that the humanity of the Christ is the self-expression and self-actualization of the Logos, then the Logos, too, is dependent upon creation.[102] DiNoia believes that this problem in Rahner's theology stems from a departure from the tradition in terms of God's freedom.[103] The way in which this departure interacts with his theology of grace and the incarnation raises "the specter of a necessitarian account of divine action." Di Noia draws these various elements together as follows: "Given a description of the processions in terms of the ontology of the symbol in combination with an insistence on the strict identity of the economic and immanent Trinity, Rahner's trinitarian theology risked a pattern of explanation in

---

100. Rahner states: "We . . . now define man . . . as that which ensues when God's self utterance, his Word, is given out lovingly into the void of god-less nothing." Rahner, "Incarnation," 116.

101. For arguments to give warrant for the panentheism charge, see Cooper, *Panentheism*. For a discussion on the aseity of God and Rahner's theology see Molnar, *Divine Freedom*.

102. Rahner, "Symbol," 225, 38–45.

103. DiNoia believes that Rahner's trinitarian theology, the SRR of RR, "involves too tight an identification of the missions and processions. In this conceptuality, the trinitarian processions and missions are explicated in terms of concepts of self-expression and self-possession. This conceptuality can suggest that the Trinity really could not really be itself independently of the orders of creation and redemption . . . Rahner insisted on the tradition that the external missions of the Trinity are extensions of the processions. But in traditional theology, these missions were understood as freely chosen actions, described in terms of efficient causality." Di Noia, "Karl Rahner," 129. On the tradition of the unity of God, see the fruitful contribution of Bruce Marshall. Marshall, "Unity," 19ff.

which the free actions of creation, incarnation, and grace could be seen as necessary extensions of God's self-expression and self-possession."[104]

Rahner's apparent panentheism also receives a contribution from another aspect of his methodology. Namely, it is that aspect which is a spiraling argument in which the "knowledge of the human subject, whatever its source, can be further verified by human experience and hence has an independence from that source." Significantly, this leads to a "circularity," which "is a further example of how subject and object mutually condition one another."[105] This dialectical, mutual conditioning, also found in Rahner's view is a panentheistic view in which the world is necessary for the ontological expression of God's being and God's continuing development.

This dependence is the final point in a sequence of points that follow on from the fact that the Logos is the *Realsymbol* of the Father. He writes: "the Word-as-reality of the immanent divine life-is 'generated' by the Father as the *image* and *expression* of the Father;"[106] and secondly, "this process [of generation] is necessarily given with the divine act of self-knowledge, and without it the absolute act of divine-self possession in knowledge cannot exist."[107] Having made these points, Rahner emphasizes that the logical consequences of what he has stated is that only the Son could be the expression and thus the self-possession of the Father. The Word carries out the same roles in terms of the self-expression of God both in the immanent and economic Trinities, as the outward expression of the Logos is derived from, and congruent with, the self expression of God's being within itself. The underlying thought is as follows:

> a being realizes itself in its own intrinsic "otherness" (which is constitutive of being) . . . as its derivative and hence congruous expression, it makes itself known . . . it could be shown that the two extremes of this extension, the manifest visible "figure" on one hand . . . and the "essence" which gives rise to the figure on the other hand, make us the full sense of the concept. For how does the figure-forming essence of a being . . . constitute and perfect itself? It does so by projecting its visible figure outside itself

---

104. Di Noia, "Karl Rahner," 129.
105. Ormerod, *Theologies*, 108.
106. Rahner, "On the Theology of Symbolic Reality," 236.
107. Ibid., 236.

as its symbol, its appearance . . . which allows it to be there, which brings it out to existence in the world: and in doing so, it retains it—"possessing itself in the other." The essence is there for itself and for others precisely through its appearance . . .[108]

Given these statements and their underlying suppositions, it is clear that in Rahner's theology God is dependent upon the world for the fruition of his selfhood. The parallel between Rahner's and Hegel's views of God's movement in "becoming" has been noted by Pearl: "So, both Hegel and Rahner seem to begin with the exigency of Being to move from itself (thesis) to 'otherness' (antithesis) as a movement in its self-realization (synthesis)."[109]

God's "becoming in the world" is evident in Rahner's theory that the actual identification of the economic and immanent Trinity (the SRR of RR) means that "one cannot have one without the other—no Father and Son without the incarnation, no God without the world . . . the rule implies what Hegel taught—that it is essential for the immanent Trinity to actualize itself in history as the economic Trinity."[110]

More pointedly, Rahner argues that humanity is essential to who God actually is: "God himself is man and remains so for all eternity . . . Man is for all eternity the expression of the mystery of God which participates for all eternity in the mystery of its ground."[111] As a result, the created order is drawn into God. The reverse also occurs where God is drawn into the essence of the created order as "the innermost life,"[112] and is "immediately interior" to the universe via the animating work of his Spirit.[113] Given these points, one cannot deny that Rahner's theology has strong affinities with theologies that are labeled as panentheistic. This influences his doctrine of the incarnation to the point where it is fair to say that for Rahner, this is an inevitable event in the eternal life of God. Rahner draws the destiny of God and the destiny of humanity together in his view of the cosmos as it relates to the incarnation. In

---

108. Rahner is inconsistent as he continues: "in the 'analogous' measure, of course, in which a being is there for itself and for others according to its own measure of being." Rahner, "Ontology," 231.

109. Pearl, "Dialectical Panentheism," 119.

110. Cooper, *Panentheism*, 225.

111. Rahner, "Evolutionary View." Cited in Cooper, *Panentheism*, 225.

112. Rahner, "Evolutionary View." Cited in ibid.

113. Rahner, "Evolutionary View." Cited in ibid.

the incarnation both God and humans move towards what they must become, hence Rahner's focus upon God's own self in salvation history, and the use of the SRR of RR as a norm for interpreting Scripture.

The trinitarian outcome of Rahner's panentheism, taken together with his theology of grace and the incarnation, is that the works and relations of God the Trinity in the economy of salvation are the starting point for the knowledge of God. Zaragoza clarifies the tight links between grace, Christology and Trinity in Rahner's theology. He writes:

> Based upon the intention and christological key of the hypostatic formula from Chalcedon, and based upon his own conception of grace, Rahner elaborated his theology of the trinitarian mystery within a desire to think without dichotomies in the God-world relationship. This respect for humanity and for the world, a respect which seeks to comprehend a united reality in unity but without the cost of reducing everything to its final pure identity . . . That is why Rahner is opposed to continuing to conceive God theologically from *a priori* categories of substance or essence. God is Father, Son, and Holy Spirit. God is in himself Trinity. Only in this manner is he one, and not in virtue of an monistic abstract substance. The treatment of the Trinity therefore must not begin with a metaphysical consideration of this *one substance* in order to be able to think our way to the *One God*, rather, one must begin from the basis of the Trinity itself and how it has manifested itself in the economy.[114]

A preferable starting point would be the complete "whole Bible" scriptural revelation of God's attributes revealed in his actions and words. When these two aspects of the revelation of God's being are taken in tandem with his personal actions in history, they temper how a norm such as RR is applied. This issue is further explored in chapters 3, 4, and 5.

114. The original Spanish reads: "Desde la clave cristológica de la fórmula hipostática de Calcedonia y basado en su propia concepción de la gracia, Rahner elaboró su teología del misterio trinitario desde este intento de pensar sin dicotomías la relación Dios-mundo. Este respeto por el hombre y por el mundo que busca comprender la realidad en unidad pero no al costo de una reducción de todo a la pura identidad final . . . Por eso Rahner se opone a seguir concibiendo teológicamente a Dios a partir de la categoría de substancia o esencia. Dios es Padre, Hijo y Espíritu Santo. Dios es en sí mismo Trinidad. Sólo así es uno y no en virtud de una única substancia abstracta. El tratado sobre la Trinidad no debe partir entonces de la consideración metafísica de esa *substancia una* para poder pensar al *Dios uno,* sino que debe partir de la Trinidad misma tal como ella se nos ha manifestado en la economía." Translation is my own, italics added in one instance. Zaragoza, "Communión trinitaria," 267.

Issue 2: Subordinationist Affinities in Rahner's Christology.

Rahner's apparent panentheism ultimately leads to a position that has affinities with christological subordinationism. God the Son is the subordinate means of God the Father's self-fulfillment and communication with, and within, the world. Rahner's theology finds itself in a theological bind at this point, as the second person of the Trinity (as the *Realsymbol*) must be the only self-expression of the Father, if the Father is to be the Father. The Trinity is thus composed of relations that require the world for their expression. Therefore, the very structure and being of the Trinity is dependent upon the world.

In the manner in which this is articulated, Rahner's perspective is somewhat reminiscent of the Arian position, which according to R. P. C. Hanson includes at its core "the inferiority of the Logos to the Father ... for a communication, and particularly for an Incarnation, to take place at all."[115] There are various significant connections between humanity and the Logos-humanity relationship. These are systematically (in terms of the interconnected breadth of theology) problematic and may therefore diminish the credibility of the SRR of RR. Firstly, the logic of Rahner's *Realsymbol* runs as follows: "the Father is precisely the Father insofar as he utters himself in the Logos, who is distinct from but in union with him. The Logos or the Word is the image of the Father ... The Logos is the eternal symbol of the Father-God. Jesus is the historical symbol of the Logos."[116] Secondly, humanity itself results from the self-expression of the Logos.[117] Rahner's theology holds that Jesus' own humanity is actually intrinsic to who the Logos is when he expresses himself in the world. Therefore, it is not something assumed, as an alien nature that must be united to the Logos.[118] Instead, humanity is the *Realsymbol* of the Logos who is in turn the real symbol of the Father. Thus Sanders is right to say that given the *Realsymbol*, the "humanity of Christ, and more generally human nature, is the grammar of God's self-communication."[119]

---

115. Hanson, *Arian Controversy*, 100.

116. Kress, *A Rahner Handbook*, 43.

117. The affinity between the Logos and humanity is stated by Rahner as follows: "human nature is not a mask ... assumed from without, from behind which the Logos hides to act things out in the world, From the start it is the constitutive real symbol of the Logos himself." Rahner, *Trinity*, 33.

118. Rahner, "Incarnation," 116. Rahner, *Foundations*, 225.

119. Sanders, *Image*, 77.

Therefore, the metaphysics of Rahner's symbolism may give a diminished role to the true humanity of Christ. Doud provides the following insightful critique: "Rahner only develops the Logos, as *Realsymbol*, eternally ready to become man. For this reason Rahner's Christology of *Realsymbol* fails to convey his larger Christological intention of asserting the full manhood of Jesus. [This] onesidedness . . . causes him to jeopardize the humanity of Christ and relapse into monophysitism . . ."[120]

The consequence of the above may be that the uniqueness of Christ's own humanity appears to be diminished, especially Christ's mediatorial role (which was so important to Rahner).[121] A response to this is to ask how the Word, whose *Realsymbol* is the grammar of God's self-communication, is in any sense *autotheos*? Is he not essentially, and functionally, a subordinate means of the Father? The overall impression given by Rahner appears to call into question the *homoousion* of God the Son, via his prioritization of God the Father over the Son.

The significance of Jesus' diminished humanity for the SRR of RR is that the humanity of Christ is afforded little weight in qualifying the relationships between the persons of the Trinity in the economy of salvation. The corrective would be to provide an ontological and salvation-historical basis to Jesus' Messianic role.

Issue 3: Is Rahner Correct in his View that Only God the Son Could Have Become Incarnate?

There is a strong "classic" answer to this question. In his *Summa Theologica*, St. Thomas Aquinas asks "whether each of the trinitarian persons could have assumed human nature," (III.q3, art.5). His answer is in the affirmative: "Whatever the Son can do, so can the Father and the Holy Ghost. Otherwise the power of the three persons could not be one." Aquinas proceeds to state that either the Father or the Holy Spirit could have become incarnate.[122] In III.q3, art.8 Aquinas deals with the question: "whether it is more fitting that the Person of the Son rather than any other Divine Person should assume human nature." His answer is that it is more fitting for the Son to become incarnate.[123] Lombard

---

120. Doud, "Rahner's Christology," 148.

121. Egan, "Rahnerian Response."

122. Thomas, *Summa Theologica*, Vol. 48, "The Incarnate Word" IIIq3, art.8 obj 2; see divine power and personal properties in IIIq3, art. 5, reply.

123. See Athanasius' view of the fittingness of the incarnation of the second per-

also held that any person of the Trinity could become incarnate. His treatment of this question is very brief, demonstrating that he took his answer as self-evident.[124]

Openly deviating from Lombard and Aquinas, Rahner affirmed the exclusivity of the incarnation of the second person of the Trinity.[125] Arguing that "the Logos is really as he appears in revelation, that he is *the one* who reveals to us (not merely one of those who might have revealed to us) the triune God...."[126] Thus, according to Rahner, it was not only fitting for the Son to become incarnate, but it was necessary because were it not so, then the revelatory aspect of the incarnation would lose integrity.[127] He assumed that if any person could have become incarnate, then all that people could know of God from Jesus would only be based on Jesus' words alone.[128] Further, for Rahner, if there were no necessary relationship between the second person of the Trinity and the incarnation, "there would no longer be any connection between 'mission' and the intra-trinitarian life... That which God is for us would tell us absolutely nothing about that which he is in himself, as triune."[129] Thus, Rahner employed the rhetoric of *reductio ad absurdum* to argue against the humanity of Christ being a mere clothing of his divinity. He writes:

> A "functional Christology" asks not what are the natures of Christ, but what he means for us and what he does for us. May one not suspect all the same that it contains the traditional

---

son of the Trinity. This view holds to fittingness, without subordination. Weinandy, Athanasius.

124. Peter, Silano, and Pontifical Institute of Mediaeval Studies, *Sentences, Book 3*, Dist. 1, ch. 2 "Whether the Father or the Holy Spirit could have become incarnate or could do so now," 5. It must be noted that Bonaventure held a similar view. He believed that: "[t]he incarnation was brought about by the Trinity... and the union occurred... not of any [divine] Person indifferently, but of the Word alone." However, the reason for this is that it is fitting for the creator to be the recreator. "In this way, just as God had created all things through the Word Not Made, even so He restored all things through the Word Made Flesh." Bonaventure states that God could have saved in other ways, but this manner was more fitting than any others. It is important to note that this fittingness is not based in natures or relationships amongst persons of the Trinity. Bonaventure, *Breviloquium, IV.2.2*.

125. Rahner, *Trinity*, 11.
126. Ibid., 30, see also 11, 23, 28–29.
127. Ibid., 28.
128. Ibid., 28, 37.
129. Ibid., 30.

"ontological" Christology, if it is thought out radically enough? Completed in such a way, could not this functional Christology, while preserving its proper character, open up the faith of many, who for fear of the "mythology" which they wrongly suspect to be present, would otherwise never find the way to the faith? The official theology of the Church is not monophysite. But monophysite misapprehensions have often affected the faith of individual Christians, who see the "human nature" of the Word as scarcely more than a uniform or a puppet for the Godhead, something that only looks towards us, but does not look to God in the freedom of dialogue? Could not these attitudes be corrected by a truly "functional" theology?[130]

Ironically, this is a clear result of his trinitarian axiom, as God relates to and within himself in the economy as in the immanent Trinity. Thus the relations in the economy are merely the same as they have always been, with the sole exception that these are clothed in flesh in Jesus. Rahner's view of Jesus' flesh does not require the fullness of humanity as demanded by a true incarnation. Interestingly, the German word for incarnation, "Menschwerdung," describes this issue more clearly as the incarnation is not merely God-in-carne. In the "Menschwerdung," the incarnation entails God taking on human-ness, thus, this human-ness naturally demands a change in how God relates to himself, as the humanity of Christ now has to be taken into account in the inter-trinitarian relationships in such a way that a human will (not just flesh) must be obedient to God. In practice, however, Rahner's axiom detracts from the incarnation because it asserts that God the Son's relations with the other persons of the Trinity in history must be exactly as they are for God the Son within God's immanent self.[131]

Thus, the extent of the condescension of God in the incarnation, and salvation history as the context for the incarnation, may have a reduced place Rahner's theology. These reductions occur because Rahner's theology does not prize the learnt obedience of God the Son in the sphere of human existence. This learnt obedience is clear in both Jesus' own life and apostolic preaching on his life. Jesus' own life will be

---

130. Rahner, "Exegesis," 51.

131. Rahner, *Trinity*, 24–25, 30–33, 64. See also Rahner, *Foundations*, 118–20, 28–29. Rahner, argues that "the Logos is really as he appears in revelation, that he is *the one* who reveals to us (not merely one of those who might have revealed to us) the triune God . . ." Rahner, *Trinity*, 30, also 11, 23, 28–29.

covered at length in chapter 3 of this book, therefore, at this stage only a few examples from the NT will be taken as illustrative. For example, in Acts 8:32–33, Isa 53:7–8 is quoted in order to align the humble obedience of Jesus to the contours of the Messianic mission he had received. Reflecting upon Jesus' behavior during his trial and death, Luke quotes Isaiah: "Like a sheep lead to the slaughter, and like a lamb silent before its shearer, so he does not open his mouth. In his humiliation justice was denied to him . . . For his life was taken away from the earth." In the book of Hebrews (Heb 2:10; 4:15; 5:7–10; 7:26, 28b), the author makes explicit the connections between the themes of Jesus' suffering and his learnt obedience as essential aspects to his salvific role seen in Acts 8:32–33. In particular, Heb 5:7–10 crystallizes and clarifies this nexus. Heb 5:7–10 reads as follows: "In the days of his flesh, Jesus offered up prayers and supplications, with loud cries and tears, to the one who was able to save him from death, and he was heard because of his reverent submission. Although he was a Son, he learned obedience through what he suffered; and having been made perfect, he became the source of eternal salvation for all who obey him, having been designated by God a high priest according to the order of Melchizedek." This point is underlined in Heb 7:28b (which we have italicized) that states that "God's word of oath has appointed . . . a Son who *has been made perfect* forever."

A further critique may be that Rahner's theology could have benefitted from giving more dogmatic weight to Jesus' words in John 17:5 ("So now, Father, glorify me in your own presence with the glory that I had in your presence before the world existed"). These words strongly suggest a pre-incarnation relationship between the Father and the Son that is different from that which Jesus had with the Father in his incarnational vocation of obedience. Thus Rahner does not sufficiently deal with the two "states of Christ": his humiliation and glorification. These states capture the change in both Jesus' status, and his relationship to God, in the incarnation and resurrection, as stated in Phil 2:5–11, particularly verses 7–9, "but emptied himself, taking the form of a slave, being born in human likeness. And being found in human form, he humbled himself, and became obedient to the point of death . . . Therefore God also highly exalted him . . ." Again in this passage we see the interconnection of Jesus' mission, suffering and obedience to God. A fuller view of the full significance of these aspects of Jesus' life would have contributed to the robustness of Rahner's theology.

Issue 4: Divine Simplicity Is Called Into Question by Positing that the Son Has a Power That the Father Does Not.

One result of Rahner's argument that only God the Son could become incarnate, is that Rahner implicitly attributed a divine power to the Son which is not attributed to the Father or the Holy Spirit. Rahner therefore appears to have inadvertently undermined God's simplicity and *perichoresis* despite his overarching concern to hold to the unity of God. Rahner's theology of the *Realsymbol* means that if God the Father is to express himself, it must be in the form of the Word, who is his perfect expression. Indeed, it can only be the Word who becomes incarnate, as the second person of the Trinity is the Father's *Realsymbol* expressed in time and space.

Rahner could only argue for his *Realsymbol* theology in the context of the unity and one-ness implied for God by his language of a "distinct manner of subsisting" as a replacement for trinitarian "person."[132] This language and its attendant proposal is highly problematic for a supposedly personal conception of the trinitarian God. Bracken states Rahner's ironic turn away from the trinitarian "person" as follows:

> even though his understanding of the economic Trinity clearly reflects a heightened awareness of the strictly interpersonal relationships between God and man, Rahner hesitates to use the same interpersonal categories in his doctrine of the immanent Trinity. Throughout [*The Trinity*] . . . he calls into question the continued use by the Church of the term "person" to describe the reality of the Father, Son and Holy Spirit as distinct from their nature as one God . . . His own solution [to the one-ness in three-ness of God] is to substitute the phrase 'distinct manner of subsisting' for the word 'person,' so that he can state the mystery of the Trinity as succinctly as follows: the one God subsists in three distinct manners of subsisting; the Father, Son and Spirit are the one God each in a different manner of subsisting and in this sense we may count "three" in God; God as subsisting in a determined manner of subsisting (such as the Father) is "somebody else" (ein anderer) than God subsisting in another manner of subsisting but he is not "something else" (etwas anderes).[133]

Due to this rejection of the term "person," Rahner failed to deploy a key resource for trinitarian theology that avoids undermining God's

---

132. Rahner, *Trinity*, 74–76, 109–15.
133. Bracken, "Trinity?," 11–12.

unity. Phan writes: "Is not Rahner too dependant on the Enlightenment conception of 'person' as center of consciousness so that he is overly suspicious of the term in developing his trinitarian theology? Should one not make use of perichoresis, as Leonardo Boff has done, as the central concept for a theology of the Trinity?"[134]

Another problem raised by Rahner's use of "distinct manners of subsisting" is that it creates an internal inconsistency to the SRR of RR. Bracken notes that given Rahner's use of "person," he is open to the criticism that "if interpersonal categories are used to illuminate the relations between God and human beings in the doctrine of the economic Trinity, then the same interpersonal categories should be employed in his exposition of the immanent Trinity." The conclusion for the SRR of RR is that given Rahner's instance on "distinct manner of subsisting," means that his interpreters need to "question whether the term 'person' can be abandoned in favor of 'distinct manner of subsisting' without doing damage to the delicate balance between the economic and immanent Trinities."[135]

Issue 5: Rahner's Inconsistency in Holding Both the Realsymbol and the SRR of RR

As previously noted, Rahner's sequence of thought ultimately leads him to make the statement that only the Logos of the Father could have become incarnate. In this sense, the *Realsymbol* has led him to blur the immanent-economic divide. Thus Rahner merely follows the logic of his *Realsymbol* theology to its inevitable conclusion: the economic Trinity and the incarnation are the *Realsymbol* of the immanent Trinity. However, if we take Rahner's *Grundaxiom* strictly, whereby the immanent Trinity is the economic Trinity and vice versa, to what extent can we read the economic Trinity back into the immanent Trinity given Rahner's theology of the *Realsymbol*? Sanders noted that: "Rahner's Rule in its original form includes a 'vice versa,' and the logic of the *Realsymbol* cannot run in reverse: the immanent Trinity may express itself outwardly as the economic Trinity . . . But the economic Trinity can hardly be said to express itself ad extra in or as the immanent Trinity. . ."[136] Therefore,

---

134. Phan, "Rahner," 138.

135. Bracken, "Trinity?," 12.

136. Sanders, *Image*, 78. Rahner never explicitly comments on this to my knowledge.

ironically Rahner's foundational theology of *Realsymbol* undermines the full, bi-directional, application of his *Grundaxiom* to trinitarian relations. Rahner failed to notice that there is an "indirect reciprocity" built into the economic/immanent divide as a result of the incarnation.

What is powerful about the idea of "indirect reciprocity" as appropriated from Iredale, is that we can state that there is a moral motivation behind the fact that this phenomenon is present in a divine relationship and is "indirect" and not "direct reciprocity."[137] "Indirect reciprocity" captures the biblical notion of grace as outlined in John 3:16 and Phil 2:6–11. Given the importance of grace for Rahner, this point is worth expanding as a constructive critique.

One can maintain that in Scripture there are two relationships in which indirect reciprocity is on display. Firstly, the Father does not relate to the Son in the economy of salvation in a pattern that is returned in kind by the Son. That is, there is no direct reciprocal relationship between them. This reciprocity is indirect. The key is that what can be taken as essential to a true "indirect reciprocal relationship" is that there is a moral motivation for the non-reciprocal aspect of this relationship. Scripturally speaking, the moral motivation and action that accompanies it, is that the decision for the incarnation and the incarnation itself are motivated by the benefits for others. The incarnation entails a morally motivated act that alters the eternal reciprocal nature of the relationship between the Father and the Son when this is expressed in the economy of salvation. From Phil 2:6–11, we can say that the non-reciprocal "indirect relationship" between members of the Trinity in the economic sphere of God's activity and the relational variance this causes is due to the gracious work of God for and in the incarnation.

The second aspect of morally motivated "indirect reciprocity" in trinitarian relationships is the relational contrast between divine relations in the economy of salvation and those relations as they were in the immanent sphere prior to the incarnation. Though Rahner's conceptual theology underlying the incarnation is *linked* to the foundation of his trinitarian axiom, it ultimately disallows the vice-versa explicit in the Rule. Rahner never resolved this contradiction within his own theology; he simultaneously collapsed the immanent-economic trinitarian divide and held on to the *Realsymbol*.[138]

137. Iredale, "Indirect Reciprocity."

138. Rahner resolves this issue in part, as a response to a critique of his trinitarian

58   Trinitarian Self and Salvation

Battaglia points out that Rahner's theology of grace undermines the helpful role that the *Realsymbol* could play in safeguarding the collapse of the immanent Trinity into the economic in Rahner's theology. He suggests:

> Rahner's theology of the symbol, which he uses to explain the incarnation, also supports the distinction between the immanent and the economic Trinity. In grace, however, Rahner tends towards an identification of the economic and immanent Trinity through the operation of quasi-formal causality. That is, grace in the economy is none other than the self-donation of God where the graced person becomes as close to God as possible without removing the ontological difference between God and the creaturely recipient as grace is a "quasi" communication of the 'form' of God.[139]

Dallavalle notes that this problem is the result of the core inconsistency and contradiction between Rahner's anthropological theology of grace and his trinitarian pursuit. Her insightful comment, which notes parallel nullifying concepts in Rahner's theology, runs as follows:

> The axiom's "identification" of the economic and immanent Trinity and vice-versa also raises the question whether this situation of a world already constituted by the offer of self-communication has theological as well as anthropological resonance. As Rahner's description of the human situation *a posteriori* to God's gift drains such "created" things as pure nature and world history of meaning, is it not possible that this de facto situation also, in rendering 'moot' the notion of God untouched by self-communication, introduces the very modern possibility that the "immanent Trinity" is also a remainder concept?[140]

For Dallaville, the root of the problem lies in a theological bind:

> Particularly in the discussion of grace, Rahner seems caught between the economic starting point's epistemological focus and his commitment to the ontological distinctions of scholastic theology, distinctions which he will on one hand honor and on the other hand collapse in order to give full rein to his claim about

---

theology, in Rahner, "The Mystery of the Trinity." Rahner had ample opportunity to clarify his positions, such as in his response to critiques of his theology in Rahner, "Reflections." However, he remained unclear.

139. Battaglia, "An Examination."
140. Dallavalle, "Revisiting Rahner," 145.

the fullness of God's self gift. In a system so dominated by modern theological anthropology, the possibility of any "economic" sense to the notion of an ontologically distinct immanent Trinity expires. And while Rahner continues to assert the existence of such an ontologically distinct immanent Trinity, this assertion is belied by the fact that the immanent Trinity appears in his theological system precisely as does "pure nature": as a logical hypothesis employed only to be rendered moot by the theology of self-communication.[141]

Given these points above, we can say that these issues are very significant because when judged by the Erickson' criterion of coherence, we must say that Rahner's theology fails at this point.[142]

Issue 6: Rahner's Diminished Understanding of the "States of Christ"

Rahner's theology of the incarnation did not take into account the full significance of the changes in the Logos' relationships to the other persons of the Trinity in the economy of salvation. These changed states of affairs are entailed by what has traditionally been denoted as the "states of Christ." Both the Scriptures (in narrative and didactic sections) and the Niceno-Constantinopolitan Creed affirm the states of Christ. Rahner did not work this out across his theology, and therefore his theology may be interpreted to lack a thorough appreciation of the contours of the incarnation for a Christian theology of God. In contrast to Rahner's view, we would argue that the incarnation involved a change in the way in which God relates to himself as Trinity after God the Son took on human flesh. This is borne out in John's Gospel where Jesus prays with his pre-incarnate life in mind: "So now, Father, glorify me in your own presence with the glory that I had in your presence before the world existed" (John 17:5). The book of Hebrews articulates this change with reference to Jesus' testing in the economy of salvation: "For we do not

---

141. Ibid., 145.

142. Erickson, *Tampering*, 90–94. Sanders also notes the lopsided outcome of Rahner's theology. "At times, Rahner seems to be pushing the immanent Trinity out of the picture altogether, in favor of a concentration on the economic Trinity. In his *Foundations of Christian Faith*, for instance, the doctrine of the Trinity receives only scant mention [133–37], with no interest whatsoever in the immanent Trinity, while the economic structure . . . (Christology plus grace) gives the synthesis its shape. This development is the logical result of his argument that 'no adequate distinction can be made between the doctrine of the Trinity and the doctrine of the economy of salvation.' (*The Trinity*, 24)." Sanders, *Image*, 79.

have a high priest who is unable to sympathize with our weaknesses, but we have one who in every respect has been tested as we are, yet without sin" (Heb 4:15). The change in trinitarian relations which is demanded by Jesus' economic role is a stark contrast to a theology such as Rahner's, which ultimately holds that God the Son was merely taking on a veil of flesh through which he continues to relate with the other persons of the Trinity as he has for eternity. Ironically, Rahner's own view was the very view he attempted to reject: that the humanity of Christ is merely clothing on the divine Son of God.[143] However, his theology cannot avoid this problem, because given the low view of personhood which Rahner accords to the members of the immanent Trinity, it is no surprise that he lacks robustness in the personal relations of the immanent Trinity to which the economic roles and trinitarian relationships of Jesus can provide a strong contrast. Moreover, the use of "distinct manner of subsisting" instead of "person"[144] calls into question his whole project, which aims at human closeness with a personal trinitarian God. That is, "Rahner's somewhat impersonal definition risks undermining his overall theological project of declaring that God acts dynamically in free love to address the world personally in order to save it."[145]

RAHNER'S OWN EXPLANATION OF HIS TRINITARIAN AXIOM

When Rahner's Rule,[146] was first published in an English translation it read as follows: *"The 'economic' Trinity is the 'immanent' Trinity and the*

---

143. Rahner sought to restore the theology of the incarnation by the strict application of his Rule, whereby he stressed the revelatory nature of the incarnation by emphasizing that Jesus is the second person of the Trinity. However, the ironic outcome of Rahner's theology is that a reverse situation results from this methodological approach. In interpreting his axiom strictly, Rahner lost much of the depth and significance of the theology of the incarnation.

144. Rahner, *Trinity*, 74–76, 109–15.

145. Battaglia, "An Examination."

146. Interestingly, it was two Protestants who first coined the term "Rahner's Rule." They both cite each other as the originator of the term. For example, Peters says: "Borrowing the term from the work of Roger E. Olson, I first employed the name 'Rahner's Rule' to describe this principle in a series of articles titled "Trinity Talk" for the Theology Update column in *Dialog* 26, no.1 and . . . no.2 . . .". Peters, *God as Trinity*, 213, n.33.

'immanent' Trinity is the 'economic' Trinity."[147] This *Grundaxiom* [148] first appeared in *The Trinity*, a booklet that was originally published as part of a larger work: *Mysterium Salutis*, a multi-volume attempt by theologians to "recast every locus of Roman Catholic theology along consistently salvation-historical lines."[149] This begs the question: how did Rahner interpret his own rule? The answer is that Rahner's read his own rule strictly, his own view is the SRR of RR.[150] There three clues reveal this is the case.

The First Clue: The German Original

The original German wording which Rahner used to articulate his norm allows for no equivocation in terms of the how the economy of salvation was related to God's inner taxis. Rahner stated his Rule as: "The 'economic' Trinity is the 'immanent' Trinity and vice versa."[151] That is, not only is it true that "the economic Trinity is the immanent Trinity," but it is so *vice versa* with a stress on the economy of salvation. The theology behind the original wording of RR is enormously significant. This comes to light when it is compared to its translated form in English. In English it read: "The 'economic' Trinity is the 'immanent' Trinity and the 'immanent' Trinity is the 'economic' Trinity." The "*umgekehrt*" (vice versa) tightens this relationship more closely than the 'vice-versa' allows, as there can be no equivocation about the isomorphic[152] nature of the "*umgekehrt*." Dallavalle has also highlighted this "translation discrepancy" because as stated in the original German, it reveals that "it is highly characteristic of Rahner to emphasize that his focus is on

---

147. Rahner, *Trinity*, 22. (Italics are Rahner's).

148. By *Grundaxiom* theologians have meant the basis of the axiom as well as the axiom itself, rather than the axiom taken in isolation. That is, the *Grundaxiom* is RR itself but it also includes the basis of this norm within it.

149. Sanders, *Image*, 54.

150. Rahner, *Trinity*, 39.

151. The orginal German reads: "Die «ökonomische» Trinität ist die «immanente» Trinität und umgekehrt. Rahner, „dreifaltige Gott," 328. That is, the economic Trinity is the immanent Trinity and vice-versa.

152. "One system is isomorphic with another if there is a one-to-one representation or mapping of its properties associating them with another system. To say that there is an isomorphism between two systems is to say that they share the same structure." Blackburn, "Isomorphic," 200.

the real presence of the triune God in salvation history."[153] The methodological principle at work here is also found in *Foundations of Christian Faith*: "[T]he salvation and revelation-historical Trinity *is* the immanent Trinity." Significantly, the italics are Rahner's. Rahner follows this quote with his rationale for the isomorphic relationship between the immanent and economic Trinity: "because in God's self-communication to his creation through grace and Incarnation God really gives himself, and really appears as he is in himself . . . in both the collective and individual history of salvation there appears in immediacy to us not some numinous powers or other which present God, but there appears and is truly present the one God himself." [154] In this case the italics are also present in the original German.[155]

Second Clue: Rahner's Reasons for RR

Rahner's reasons for articulating the RR reveal that he not only held to RR, *but to the SRR of RR*. That his particular approach to his *Grundaxiom* was the SRR is clear when the reasons for the positive articulation of norm are outlined. Rahner's reasons for proposing his axiom all derive from the fact that he believed that the doctrine of the Trinity mattered.[156] For Rahner, three reasons in particular were central to the importance of this doctrine. Firstly, the Trinity is important for understanding salvation. It is essential to understand the Trinity if people are going to comprehend the structures of human beings and the experience of salvation. Jowers rightly paraphrases Rahner on why we should be interested in God's own life: "if the human experience of divine self-communication is an experience of the immanent Trinity as it eternally and necessarily exists in itself, *then the doctrine of the immanent Trinity in large part accounts for the peculiar structure of this experience and explains to a great extent the structures of human beings themselves,* whom God has created to be *the addressees of his self communication.*"[157]

By basing his trinitarian theology upon the human experience of God's economy of salvation, salvation itself became the key to trinitarian

---

153. Dallavalle, "Saving History," 79.
154. Rahner, *Foundations*, 136.
155. *Grundkurs des Glaubens*, 141. Cited in Dallavalle, "Saving History," 79.
156. Cf. Rahner, *Trinity*, 10–15, 39–40. Jowers, "Test," 423.
157. Ibid., 421–22. Based upon Rahner, *Trinity*, 88–89, 91–99. (Italics added).

theology, not neo-Scholastic proposals. Therefore, Rahner was consistent when he stated that the economy was "actually the whole of theology and . . . contains and reveals the immanent Trinity in itself."[158]

Secondly, Rahner believed that the Trinity should have immense practical consequences in Christian living. His concern was that trinitarian theology was isolated from the piety of most Christians: "Christians are, in their practical life, almost mere 'monotheists' . . . should the doctrine of the Trinity have to be dropped as false, the major part of religious literature could well remain virtually unchanged."[159] In response, Rahner stated that it is necessary to "try to make the doctrine of the Trinity fruitful for practical Christian living, given that the doctrine has a 'sitz im leben' and that the Trinity is of crucial importance for actual Christian life and spirituality . . . The teaching cannot even have the right 'speculative' content and form, unless it meets these demands in Christian life."[160]

Thirdly, Rahner claimed that if the economic Trinity was not in a strict correspondence to the immanent Trinity, then the reality of the Trinity is an enclosed reality which is distant from human beings: "It is as though this mystery has been revealed for its own sake, and that even after it has been made known to us, it remains, as a reality locked up within itself. We make statements about it, but as a reality it has nothing to do with us at all."[161] Rahner believed in a fundamentally interconnected relationship between God and the world. This interconnection was so strong that to reduce revelation to merely "putatively revealed propositions," is a failure to deal with the phenomenology of God in the world, and therefore words alone "cannot constitute the immediate means by which the immanent Trinity discloses itself . . ."[162]

The three motivations that underlie the SRR of RR are highly significant, especially for Evangelicals who employ RR as a norm for the theological interpretation of Scripture. It is crucial for Evangelical interpreters to note that though Rahner emphasized the economy of salvation as the key motivation and source for *Grundaxiom*, the economy

---

158. Rahner, 'Trinitätstheologie,' in *Sacramentum Mundi*, cited without page number by Jowers, "Test," 422.

159. Rahner, *Trinity*, 10–11.

160. Rahner, "Mystery of the Trinity," 256.

161. Rahner, *Trinity*, 22.

162. Jowers, "Test," 422; Rahner, *Foundations*, 87.

of salvation that he had in mind is *not* the biblical economy of salvation, rather it is a person's experience of grace. Evangelicals should be naturally cautious of a norm to which the Bible will be subjected. This is especially the case when the norm itself is not motivated, warranted, nor validated by the testimony of Scripture itself.[163]

Third Clue: Rahner's Assumptions Underlying a SRR

That Rahner's view of his RR was the SRR is quite clear when the assumptions behind this norm are outlined. Rahner's three theological (and trinitarian) assumptions that underlay the Grundaxiom are that firstly the relations between the persons of the Trinity are fixed. Significantly, Rahner stated that "these 'distinct manners of subsisting' should be seen as relative and standing in a determined taxis to each other (Father, Son and Spirit)."[164] Also, Rahner wrote, "we cannot say that the Son proceeds from the Spirit."[165] Furthermore, Rahner states that the persons within the Trinity are "opposed relativities ... concretely identical with both 'communications' ('processions') as seen from both sides."[166] Commenting on this last quote from Rahner, Jowers rightly recognizes the significance of this for Rahner's reading of his norm. Jowers states: "Any manifestation of the divine persons relating to each other, therefore, is *ipso fact* also a manifestation of the taxis in which the divine persons occur."[167] At several points in *The Trinity*, Rahner very clearly argues that the structure of the intra-divine relations corresponds

---

163. On this issue, see Adam, *Written for Us*, 12, 53–64, 134–37.

164. Rahner, *Trinity*, 112. Also "we cannot say that the Son proceeds from the Spirit." Rahner, *Trinity*, 117, n. 41. Furthermore, Rahner states that the persons within the Trinity are "opposed relativities ... concretely identical with both 'communications' ('processions') as seen from both sides." Rahner, *Trinity*, 73. Commenting on this last quote from Rahner, Jowers states: "Any manifestation of the divine persons relating to each other, therefore, is *ipso fact* also a manifestation of the taxis in which the divine persons occur." Jowers, "Test," 424. See Rahner, *Trinity*, 36, 88–89, 91–99. In these pages the structure of the intra-divine relations corresponds strictly to God's self communication and the human experience of them in the economy of salvation. This view is held in tension with the belief that there is change in God 'in another' in the incarnation. This could lead to the conclusion that his position on immutability is not a strong one, and, by extension that Rahner did not believe in a set order of relations within the Trinity. Rahner, "Incarnation," 114, n.3.

165. Rahner, *Trinity*, 117, n. 41.

166. Ibid., 73.

167. Jowers, "Test," 424.

strictly to God's self communication and the human experience of it in the economy of salvation.[168]

Rahner's second assumption is that the relational make up of the immanent Trinity constitutes an *a priori* law for the *ad extra* manifestation of the Trinity,[169] Rahner believed that divine self-communication "can . . . occur only in the intra-divine manner of the two communications of the one divine essence by the Father to the Son and the Spirit."[170] Rahner's conception of what this "intra divine manner" meant was which Rahner conceives is driven by very particular and unique theological beliefs. These include the idea that the second person of the Trinity must be the only self-expression of the Father, if the Father is to be the Father. The logic of Rahner's *Realsymbol* runs as follows: "the Father is precisely the Father insofar as he utters himself in the Logos, who is distinct from but in union with him. The Logos or the Word is the image of the Father . . . The Logos is the eternal symbol of the Father-God. Jesus is the historical symbol of the Logos."[171] In addition, because Jesus' own humanity is actually intrinsic to who the Logos is when he expresses himself in the world, humanity (including Jesus' humanity) is the *Realsymbol* of the Logos, who is in turn the real symbol of the Father. Thus, in the end, theology is really anthropology. Given this logic, the human nature and relationships with the Father and Spirit that Christ has in salvation history must correspond isomorphically with the pattern of relationships that the second person of the Trinity has with the Father and the Spirit within the inner life of the Trinity. This leads to the conclusion that Rahner's own theology assumes the SRR of RR.

The third assumption within Rahner's trinitarian theology confirms the second. This assumption is that only God the Son could become incarnate. In holding this view, Rahner openly deviated from Lombard and Aquinas because he affirmed an *exclusivity* of the incarnation of the second person of the Trinity.[172] He began his argument for this by holding that that "the Logos is really as he appears in revelation, that he is *the one* who reveals to us (not merely one of those who might have revealed

---

168. Rahner, *Trinity*, 36, 88–89, 91–99.
169. Jowers, "Test," 421.
170. Rahner, *Trinity*, 36.
171. Kress, *Rahner Handbook*, 43.
172. Rahner, *Trinity*, 11.

to us) the triune God . . ."[173] Thus, according to Rahner, it is not only fitting for the Son to become incarnate, but it was necessary because were it not so, then the revelatory aspect of the incarnation would lose integrity.[174] He assumed that if any person could have become incarnate, then all that people could know of God from Jesus would only be based on Jesus' words alone–and in Rahner's mind this is clearly unsatisfactory.[175] Further, for Rahner, if there were no necessary relationship between the second person of the Trinity and the incarnation, "there would no longer be any connection between 'mission' and the intra-trinitarian life . . . That which God is for us would tell us absolutely nothing about that which he is in himself, as triune."[176] Rahner was quite confident in his departure from tradition on this issue, a confidence that reveals his commitment to read the RR with the SRR. He charted his own course: "If one does not make this presupposition with Augustine [that any person within the Trinity could become incarnate], which has no clear roots in the earlier tradition and still less in Scripture, one need have no difficulty in thinking that the Word's being the symbol of the Father has significance for God's action *ad extra*, in spite of such action being common to all three persons."[177]

From the above, we can see that Rahner's approached his own axiom in the SRR manner.[178] Ironically, though, Rahner did not want to hold that Jesus' humanity was mere clothing for his divinity. This appears to be the result of his trinitarian axiom and the SRR approach he took to it. According to Rahner, God relates to and within himself in the economy as he does in the immanent Trinity. Thus the relations in the economy are merely the same as they have always been, with the sole exception that these are clothed in flesh in Jesus.

Unfortunately, this SRR of RR ultimately detracts from a full view of the incarnation because it asserts that God the Son's relations with the other persons of the Trinity in history must be exactly as they are for God the Son within God's immanent self.[179] Rahner argued that "the

173. Ibid., 30, see also 11, 23, 28–29.
174. Ibid., 28.
175. Ibid., 28, 37.
176. Ibid., 30.
177. Rahner, "Symbol," 236. Benner, "Augustine and Karl Rahner."
178. Rahner, "Exegesis," 51.
179. Rahner, *Trinity*, 24–25, 30–33, 64. See also Rahner, *Foundations*, 118–20, 28–29.

Logos is really as he appears in revelation, that he is *the one* who reveals to us (not merely one of those who might have revealed to us) the triune God . . ."[180] This is problematic from the standpoint of the New Testament, which highlights the extent of the condescension of God in the incarnation, and salvation history as the context for the incarnation. These are underappreciated in Rahner's theology.

The Western Filioquist Tradition.[181]

With reference to the Western Filioquist tradition, and its role as a norm for distinguishing persons of the Trinity, Rahner was a staunch supporter of creedal Roman Catholicism. In his essay "Exegesis and Dogmatic Theology," Rahner chides some Catholic exegetes for not remaining within the bounds of Roman Catholicism and for not serving the purposes of Roman Catholicism.[182] Rahner elaborates on the "rules of interpretation" to which he refers the exegetes:

> Catholic exegesis is a science of faith, not merely philosophy or the history of religions. It stands in a positive relationship to the faith and teaching authority of the Church. The doctrines and directives of this authority are not merely a negative norm for exegesis, a boundary not to be transgressed if one wishes to remain a Catholic. They are rather a positive intrinsic principle guiding research itself . . . it is your most radically proper task to show the real compatibility of your results with Catholic dogma and, fundamentally at least, with official, if not defined, Church doctrine . . . For you are Catholic theologians. You have exactly the same responsibility with regard to Church doctrine and the belief of the simple faithful as the theologian has.[183]

---

180. Rahner, *Trinity*, 30, also 11, 23, 28–29.

181. Though Rahner's own theology is vague at times in relation to Western orthodox theology, he is a strict filioquist. See footnote 129.

182. For example, Rahner reprimands the exegetes as follows: "you exegetes often forget that you are Roman Catholic theologians . . . forget, without denying it and rejecting it on principle, that you are engaged on a subject which is an intrinsic element of Catholic theology, and which must therefore observe all the rules which are in fact proper to Catholic theology." Rahner, "Exegesis," 34–35.

183. Rahner, "Exegesis," 35–36.

Critics of Rahner have pointed out that Rahner did not do extensively deploy the *Filioque*.[184] He simply assumed it as a fact,[185] because he believed that theology needs to be creedal.[186] This demonstrates that the mission of the Son into the world provides not only the material content of the SRR of RR but the mission of the Son as the *RealSymbol* of the Father provides the structure of the for trinitarian theology.[187]

CONCERNS RAISED BY RAHNER'S DEFENSE OF HIS RULE

What the SRR entails has been critiqued by many scholars, as extensively outlined in chapter 1. We shall deepen this list by concentrating on christological concerns. These include the loss of the biblical asymmetry between the economic and immanent Trinity, and its hermeneutical significance. Further scholars argue that Rahner's position entails a diminishing of the extent of the gracious condescension which occurs at the incarnation, and a diminishing of the extent of divine love,[188] and a diminishing of the events of the cross and resurrection.[189] The use of this

---

184. Ormerod, *Trinity*, 133–41. Battaglia, "An Examination."

185. Rahner, *Trinity*, 66, 83. Despite Rahner's acceptance of the *Filioque*, one must acknowledge that Rahner's definition of trinitarian persons and his low pneumatology undermine a full view of the *Filioque*. Coffey, "Trinity," 102 ff.

186. For example he wrote that theology should be based upon "the modest, sober clarity of the Chalcedonian formula." Rahner, "Current Problems," 150.

187. This structure is expressed in the *Filioque*. Therefore, Rahner's commitment to Western Filioquist tradition serves to strengthen the view that he took the SRR of RR because he understood the missions of the Son and the Spirit comported with God's inner life as demonstrated above.

188. This is ironic because the Trinity is upheld to present God as the ultimate model of love. Yet, a Trinity without condescension in the incarnation is a Trinity who loves to a different degree, and in a different manner, than a Trinity whose love includes the desire for, and act of, the incarnation on the behalf of others. If God is taken to love himself in the same manner in both his immanent self and in the economy of salvation, then God's love can be understood without the particular self giving character ascribed to it in Phil 2:5–11 as well as 1 John 4:9. This is a serious impoverishment of divine love. John 10:17 is of special note as post the incarnation the Father has an additional reason for loving the Son.

189. "[T]he *Grundaxiom* does not tell us much about how the event of the cross and resurrection of Jesus Christ bears on our understanding of the immanent Trinity, despite the fleeting reference to Jesus Christ as the 'absolute bringer of salvation,' ([*The Trinity*], 63). This is because Rahner's focus of the self-communication in the Word is on his incarnation, yet the incarnation appears to be disjointed from its intrinsic

norm has been held responsible for leading to, and assuming, an *imitatio Trinitatis* as the model for Christian life, which obscures the fact that the Bible instead presents an *imitatio Christi* as the norm for Christian service. Further, it has been argued that the SRR of RR undermines the fact that in the immanent Trinity the Logos participates in the one will of God *together with* God the Father and God the Holy Spirit, and that in the economy of salvation there are two wills within person who is the incarnate Logos.[190] Also, this norm has been charged with implicit subordinationism.[191] In subsequent chapters we shall see if these concerns

---

soteriological unity with the death and resurrection of Jesus Christ . . . in addition, Rahner's concern for soteriology jeopardizes the doxological character of theology; a trinitarian language must be found that is at once kerygmatic, meaningful, coherent, and prayerful, and not just explanatory." Battaglia, "An Examination of Karl Rahner's Trinitarian Theology." Phan asks the question with regards to the cross and its entailments for God's immanent life: "important questions beg for answers . . . given Rahner's Grundaxiom that the economic Trinity is the immanent Trinity and vice versa, how does the event of the Cross bear on our understanding of the immanent Trinity? Should one accept Von Balthazar's *theologumenon* of a supra-temporal 'event' of suffering love in the inner trinitarian life or Moltmann's bolder speculation on the cross as the breakdown of trinitarian relations?" Italics are Phan's. Phan, "Rahner," 138.

190. "The Third Council of Constantinople taught that there are two wills in the incarnate Logos, whilst the immanent Logos shares one will with the immanent Father and Spirit." Battaglia, "An Examination."

191. This is due to Rahner's *enhypostasia* Christology which allows a strict correspondence between the obedience of the Son in the economy to be read back into the immanent Trinity with the attendant ontological implication of subordinationism. Two Catholic theologians, reflecting on two different works by Rahner provide some significant insights on this issue. From Rahner's work, "On The Theology of the Incarnation," Coffey is right to draw the following alarming conclusion: "the divinity of Christ is not something different from his humanity, which is the achievement of God's grace, to which the human efforts of Jesus are subordinated." Thus, we have arrived "back at the point reached by the New Testament with its use of the functional language of salvation history. That is to say, the New Testament did not conceive the divinity of Christ as something different from his humanity: what it had to say about his divinity was a statement about his humanity: expressed in the language of salvation history, not philosophy. When philosophical language entered the scene with the translation of the gospel message into the categories of Greek thought, a wedge was driven between the humanity and the divinity of Christ, the classical expression of which was the Chalcedonian dogma. The problem began to be solved only with the introduction of the *enhypostasia*, which set the two natures of Christ in relationship. Surely, now that also philosophically it can be said that whatever is predicated of Christ's divinity is a statement about his humanity, we have come full circle. That I why I observed . . . that with Rahner's Christology the *enhypostasia* may well have attained the full potential of its development." Italics are Coffey's. Coffey, "Incarnation," 467–68.

are validated in so far as they comport with the SRR itself and the scriptural witness about the Trinity in Luke-Acts.

SCRIPTURE AS A SIGNIFICANT CRITERION FOR RAHNER'S THEOLOGICAL NORM

How do we decide if the SRR of RR is valid and useful? As we saw in chapter 1, Erickson provided a variety of criteria, one of which is particularly relevant here. Namely, the applicability criterion. To recall, that criterion runs: "A proposition is ultimately justified by being shown to be taught by the Bible. In terms of the issue of applicability, the question becomes how well the theory relates to the elements in the Bible that it claims to represent."[192] Despite Rahner's existential motivations for his norm, within the same work in which he states his axiom, Rahner appeals to the "whole sense of Holy Scripture" as one of the central authoritative theological criteria.[193] Though Rahner did not emphasize this often in practice, he was willing to critique official church doctrine that was not in harmony with the plain reading the Bible. For example, concerning Jesus' life-long beatific vision, he states that "Such assertions . . . seem at first sight to come into hopeless conflict with the data of Sacred Scripture, which speaks of a developing consciousness in Jesus (Luke 2:52), of a Lord who himself professes ignorance of decisive matters definitely part of his mission (Matt 24:36; Mark 13:32)."[194] Rahner desired a close relationship between Scripture and theology;[195] however, he may not have achieved this himself even though with reference to trinitarian theology he stated that the task of the theologian is to show the correspondence between dogma and the Scriptures. He wrote: "We could well show that the inter-trinitarian process and the mission of the Son and the Spirit for the work of redemption are so connected that the immanent processions have already been spoken of when the mission ad extra has been correctly presented, as is done in Scripture."[196]

192. Erickson, *Tampering*, 95.
193. Rahner, *Trinity*, 30.
194. Rahner, "Dogmatic Considerations," 241–42.
195. "For it is your job as a dogmatic theologian to use all available means for listening to the word of God wherever it is pronounced—and where better then in Holy Scripture"? Rahner, "Exegesis," 77.
196. Rahner, "Exegesis," 48.

Therefore, it is in keeping with the intent of Rahner's own theology to employ Scripture a very significant measure of the validity of his norm.[197] The role Rahner gave to the Bible is highly relevant to the present work, in that it establishes the methodological appropriateness of a scriptural assessment of RR by Evangelical theologians. However, there are points in Rahner's writings (other than *The Trinity*), which may cause one to doubt the appropriateness of assessing Rahner's Rule via Scripture in order to be fair to Rahner. Three questions can be asked of Rahner's understanding of the use of Scripture as a measure of this rule. Jowers shall be our guide. He has asked the following questions from an Evangelical point of view. These are: Did Rahner consider the Bible to be a "legitimate measure of the truth or falsehood of theological statements?"; "does Scripture constitute an appropriate norm for the *Grundaxiom* of Rahner's theology of the Trinity?"; Is the narrative of Scripture, which includes miraculous events, a fair context within which to assess Rahner's Rule?[198]

The answers, rightly given, are firstly that though Rahner had reservations about Scripture, he did consider it to have a decisive and normative role in theology. Secondly, the *Gundaxiom* was developed in order to do justice to the biblical witness to the Trinity, and to account for the biblical expression of the experience of the Trinity. Thirdly, the narrative of Scripture is Rahner's foundational witness to God's revelation despite its supernaturalism.[199]

Therefore, an assessment of the SRR of RR via the norm of Scripture is not an inappropriate task nor is it unjust to Karl Rahner himself. However, we must note that in practice Rahner did not test his norm

---

197. However, it must be noted that Rahner's position is not an Evangelical one in terms of the dogmatic weight accorded to Scripture in the overall project of theology. Rahner himself believed that, ultimately, the Church is the arbiter of what constitutes Christian theology "In the questions posed to theology to-day, it is inevitable that solutions should be weighed and tested whose compatibility with the authentic doctrine of the Church is not at once obvious and clearly ascertainable . . . It may be a long time before it can be seen that such an answer is unexceptionable from the point of view of the Church." Rahner, "Exegesis," 59.

198. Jowers, "Test," 432–33.

199. Ibid., 432–33. It is interesting to observe Rahner's distaste for the presence of supernaturalism in Scripture, by which he mostly refers to miracles. For the apologetic and theological reasons for Rahner's "demythologization" program see Barnes, "Demythologization," 26–32.

via Scripture, and if the SRR is tested by Scripture, the norm may be undermined (more anon).

CONCLUSION

Given the nature of RR, and the popularity of the SRR, this chapter has outlined Rahner's significance and legacy as a theologian, the grace-incarnation-Trinity matrix as the background to his Rule, the Rule itself, and Rahner's reasons for this axiom and the assumptions that underlay it. It was concluded that Rahner's reading of his axiom comports best with the SRR. Concerns raised by Rahner's exposition and defense of his rule pointed to a very original and peculiar theological method as the circumstance for RR and the SRR of RR. This formed the foundation for some problematic theology, which underlies the SRR of RR. In particular we have noted that a kind of christological diminution appears to be inherent in Rahner's trinitarian theology, especially given the SRR of RR. This may be due to Rahner's under appreciation of some biblical features of the incarnation, which we have previously highlighted. Namely, first, the learnt obedience of God the Son in the sphere of human existence (Heb 2:10; 4:15; 5:7–8; 7:28); secondly, the reality of a pre-incarnation relationship between the Father and the Son which is different from that which Jesus had with the Father in the economy of salvation (John 17:5); and thirdly the reality of the "states of Christ" which alter both Jesus' status and relationship to God given the incarnation (Phil 2:6–11).

It was also pointed out that Rahner did leave open the possibility of a scriptural engagement with his norm. Given this final point, in the subsequent chapters we shall pursue this line of thought in the service of Evangelical trinitarian theology. This scriptural test will determine the viability of the SRR of RR for Evangelicals. Indeed if it can be suggested that the SRR may be countered by Scripture, then the SRR would be problematical in for Evangelical theologians.

3

The Messianic Office of God the Son in Luke-Acts

THIS CHAPTER WILL ARGUE that the messianic office of Jesus, as presented in Luke-Acts, challenges a SRR of RR for a number of inter-related reasons. That is, the witness of Scripture presents very real problems for anyone wanting to apply the SRR of RR to the Bible. This is very significant for Evangelical readers of the Bible who desire a scriptural norm and approach to the doctrine of the Trinity. The aspects of Luke Acts which challenge the SRR of RR are that Jesus' work in the economy of salvation takes place within Jesus' state of humiliation, which is one aspect of the two states of Christ. Also, the very particular shape of the messianic role, which determines Jesus' actions in the economy of salvation is the reason behind his obedience to God the Father. Further, Jesus' humanity in the economy of salvation has a veiling effect upon his essential glory. Another challenge is posed by the fact that given his anticipated eschatological work and revelation, Jesus' work in the economy of salvation is an incomplete revelation of who he is. Lastly, there is a challenge to the SRR of RR comes from Jesus' knowledge is limited by virtue of his humanity, therefore, his knowledge of the actions of God the Father in particular cannot be taken as a representation of the essential relationship between the first and second persons of the Trinity.

This chapter will outline and treat each issue arising from the messianic nature of God the Son's work in the economy of salvation in the order outlined above.

JESUS' STATE OF HUMILIATION

The Gospel of Luke highlights both the beginning and the end of Jesus' earthly life in order to demarcate the uniqueness of this period of his existence. Jesus' earthly life is "enclosed" by the virginal conception, and his resurrection/ascension. These two events underscore the fact that Jesus' earthly life and ministry take place within what is referred to as his "state of humiliation" in dogmatics.[1] Lukan Christology describes Jesus' life *after* the resurrection as the "glorification" stage of his existence.[2] These two phases—"humiliation" and "glorification"—are deliberately employed by the author of Luke-Acts as two clearly separate periods.[3] These phases are the contexts that determine the interpretation of any of Jesus' relationships, works, and words, and have a determinative effect upon what may be said about Jesus theologically. This determinative effect extends to what may be said of the Trinity, and inner-trinitarian relationships in particular, based upon each stage of Jesus' life.

Jesus' relationships, words, and works from his birth to the resurrection should be interpreted in the theological context of his "humiliation." Thus, Jesus' relations to persons of the Godhead in his state of humiliation are not necessarily reflections of these relations as they were in his pre-incarnate glory, nor are they necessarily reflections of how these are in his state of post-resurrection glory. The author of Luke expects these phases of humiliation and glorification to be taken into account in Christology and the subsequent understanding of the identity of God. This is made clear by the introduction of the "humiliation hermeneutic" via the circumstances surrounding Jesus' birth. In Jesus' birth narratives the incarnation is presented in such a way as to accentuate the extent of the divine condescension of the Son. This is achieved by means of the contrast between the glory of God and the statements regarding Jesus' low birth status.[4] A massive stooping has occurred as a

---

1. Tatum, 143–44.

2. For example, Acts 1:6–11, which is an assumption account. "Whether Jewish or Greco-Roman, these assumption stories accentuate the elevated status of their subjects. Likewise, the ascension of Jesus functions to underlie the exaltation of Jesus." Parsons, *Acts*, 27. The theological purpose of the ascension is also matched by its literary function. "The narrator of Luke and Acts has employed the ascension narrative to bring closure to one narrative and provide entrance into its sequel . . . the exalted Christ, although absent as a character is present throughout the narrative" Parsons, *Acts*, 35.

3. Fitzmyer, *Luke*, 1:196.

4. Nolland's comments on 2:7 ("And she gave birth to her firstborn son and wrapped

The Messianic Office of God the Son in Luke-Acts 75

result of the divine initiative in the process of God becoming incarnate as a human being.[5] The recipient of Luke-Acts is expected to recognize that this witness to Jesus is about God the Son relating to the Father and Spirit from within a state of humiliation. The reader will therefore implicitly know that when Luke refers to these relationships, he is not referring to the relations within God *a se* aside from this condescension.

The condescension event conforms to the historical setting in which it takes place. History is a great focus of Luke's work.[6] Therefore, this historically conditioned condescension holds together two poles—pre-existence and historical conditioning. The author of Luke never loses sight that the One who comes into history is the One who precedes and transcends history. There are examples of holding both of these poles in tension. In these instances, the pre-existence of Jesus is set in a context that highlights the specific and concrete nature of the works he does in the economy of salvation. For example, when Jesus confronts the man with the evil spirit in Capernaum (Luke 4:34), the demons ask Jesus: "What have we to do with you, Jesus of Nazareth? Have you come to destroy us? I know who you are: the holy one of God." In this passage, we are lead to understand that Jesus comes from a heavenly realm to do

---

him in bands of cloth, and laid him down in a manger, because there was no place for them in the inn") are helpful: "The baby is wrapped in swaddling cloths as a mark of maternal care (Ezek 16:4; Wis 7:4). The best that can be managed for a bed is an animal's feeding trough . . . [I]t is most likely that Mary and Joseph have for accommodation the shared use of a one-room Palestinian peasant home. Because fitting everyone in is a squeeze, when the baby comes there is no spot for him in the room. A spot, however, can be found for him under the same roof by making use of a manger on an adjacent wall of the animal stall that formed part of such a peasant home . . . Those who know the identity of the child will be impressed by this paradox of divine condescension." Nolland, *Luke*, 1:111.

5. On Luke 2:12 ("This will be a sign for you: you will find a child wrapped in bands of cloth and lying in a manger"), Nolland writes: "What is given the shepherds as [a] sign is prepared for in the narrative at v. 7 'wrapped in swaddling cloths' . . . the sign is the manger baby (cf. 17). That the sign is certainly more than just the means of recognizing the child is indicated by the importance in v. 20 of what the shepherds have seen . . . what is signified by such a sign . . . is simply the humility of the divine condescension . . . It is likely that a first-century Hellenistic reader would find in the configuration created by good news (v. 10) concerning the birth of one who is to be savior and bringer of peace (v. 14) an echo of the language in which Augustus had been honored . . . The sign by which the shepherds are to recognize the Christ-child is a paradoxical one and probably signals the humility of the divine condescension: God allows his Christ to be without outward splendour." Nolland, *Luke*, 1:107–8, 12.

6. Meeks, "Assisting." Marshall, *Luke*.

a work in the economy of salvation. He is clearly divine and pre-existent: "seeing an advent of a pre-existent 'holy one' is . . . supported by the fact that this supernatural knowledge of Jesus is possessed by a demon . . . the tendency for Jesus to be recognized fully in the Synoptics only by demons," and is thus a pointer about Jesus' heavenly identity, his provenance from the heavenly realm, and his coming to carry out a specific work which in this instance is judgment.[7] Therefore there is a specific work to be completed in salvation history, carried out as the messianic deliverer figure who is conjoined with Jesus' divine status.[8]

The tension between Jesus' pre-existence and a specific work is also captured in passages such as Luke 19:10. There we read that Jesus said: "For the Son of Man came to seek and to save what was lost." This passage captures Jesus' provenance from the heavenly realm and draws upon Ezek 34:10–16 in terms of the new work this pre-existent One must do. In Ezek 34:10–16, we read that *God* says: "I will rescue my sheep . . . I myself, will search for my sheep, and will seek out my sheep and I will rescue them . . . I will bring them out . . . I will feed them . . . I myself will be the shepherd of my sheep . . . I will seek the lost."[9] Thus the pre-existent One does work which is conformed to fulfilling God's promises to save his covenant people in salvation history. The Spirit-anointing that Jesus received for the sake of this mission (Luke 3:21–22; 4:18–19) must be understood in this context.

The significance of this passage in terms of the SRR of RR is that it links, yet does not collapse, the pre-existence of Jesus into a specific saving role which is tied to the specific accomplishments of God in the face of the demanding needs of his people in history. History therefore particularizes the mission that the pre-existent One must accomplish— pre-existence and mission are thus held in tension. This tension between the life of God before creation and after it is also captured in the title used in the passage above: Jesus is "the Son of Man." This title is "the title

---

7. Gathercole, *Preexistent Son*, 152.

8. This interwoven Christology is found in the other Synoptic Gospels. For example, in Mark, the "paradox of Mark's Christology is Jesus is depicted in disparate fashions. He is portrayed as powerful and powerless, regal and rejected, victorious and victimized. This paradoxical portrayal is discernable in Mark's juxtaposition of Christological titles 'Christ' and 'Son of Man,' titles which form a mutually interpretive Christological spiral where one defines the meaning of another." Bird, "Jesus," 12.

9. That this work is God's work is further clarified by the fact that a mere prophet could not do this saving work. Gathercole, *Preexistent Son*, 169.

of majesty by means of which Jesus refers to himself 'in public' . . . in order to point to himself as 'the man' . . . (earthly, suffering, vindicated), and to assert his divine authority in the face of opposition."[10]

This tension places the burden of proof on radicalizers of RR to prove that the mission of Jesus is not strictly aligned with his saving work with reference to the particular needs of humanity and God's covenantal promises to Israel, and that this mission was instead only or primarily aligned with inner-trinitarian relationships.

In other words, if the SRR of RR is true, God's fulfillment of the covenant must be shown to be satisfactory and successful by means of the expression of the inner-trinitarian relations in history alone. If this were true, the consequences would be that the SRR of RR would displace the shape of Jesus' works of covenantal fulfillment as required by the nature of human sin and God's dealings with Israel. Thus the hermeneutical key of Jesus as the Messiah from Israel (Luke 24:26, 46) would be lost. This loss results because the SRR of RR's methodology places the divine rescue within the conceptual scheme of trinitarian relationships based around the incarnation. In this view, God's mission and its fulfillment does not include within it the depth of covenantal history. Therefore, the SRR of RR entails that human sin, the historic covenants, and prophecy, require nothing of the shape which Christ's work takes as God's mission in the economy of salvation.

There are other examples of passages that clearly present the two states of Christ, and also present the effect of these states upon Jesus' works and words. A representative sample of those clearly referring to his state of humiliation, and both the newness and interpretive significance of this condition for God the Son, include his development (Luke 2:48–52), anointing (Luke 3: 21–23), and transfiguration (Luke 9:27–36). In addition to these events, that Jesus calls his disciples to "carry their cross" as an obligation and conditional sacrificial demand, is instructive (Luke 9:23; 14:27; 23:26). This is to be their imitation of him who obeyed the qualifying demand to turn away from himself and live out a selfless way of being for the sake of others, which culminated in the passion (Luke 23:33). Indeed, according to Dunn, Jesus' unique application of Isa 53:12b ("he poured out to death, and was numbered with the transgressors, yet he bore the sins of many") with his own death in Luke 22:37 ("For I tell you, this Scripture must be fulfilled in me, 'And

---

10. Kingsbury, *Christology*, 168.

he was counted among the lawless,' and indeed what is written about me is being fulfilled") can only be rightly understood within what Dunn calls the "humiliation-exaltation motif."[11] Taking up the cross involves self-denial, not self-expression.[12] In the writings of both Luke and Paul, cross-bearing is a surrender to one's entire life to God.[13] Surely this implies an alignment of Lukan theology and the hermeneutic of incarnational condescension in Phil 2:6–11. Scott McKnight writes that because of Luke's emphasis on the downwards-then-upwards nature of the life, ministry, death, resurrection and glorified ascension of Jesus and his subsequent sending of the Spirit, "Luke's theology ought to be compared favorably with the primitive tradition behind Philippians 2:5–11."[14]

The state of Jesus' humiliation is reinforced by statements and actions that reveal Jesus' second transition—from "below" to a returned state of glory "above." Jesus himself gives the disciples this hermeneutical principle by which they are to understand him in Luke 24:26: "Was it not necessary that the Christ should suffer these things and enter into his glory?" Passages which clearly mark a new state of Christ in his "glorification," and its significance for understanding his identity and works in this context, include Jesus' resurrection (Luke 24), ascension (Acts 1:9), session (Acts 7:56–57), sending of the Spirit (Acts 2:33), and his appearance to Paul on the road to Damascus (Acts 9:4–6; 22:7–10; 26:14–18). In fact, Jesus' passion prediction in Luke all contain references which are deliberate redactions of Markan material on Luke's behalf. Luke establishes this contrast between the passion of Jesus and the glory which he will enter in Luke 9:22, whereby Jesus' suffering is held in tension with the confession that he is the "Christ of God" (Luke 9:20). The second passion prediction (Luke 9:44) immediately follows people being "astounded at the greatness of God . . . and amazed at all he [Jesus] was doing," as well as the transfiguration account which speaks of both Jesus' glory and his "exodus." The third passion prediction (Luke 18:31–34) begins the transition from the time of Jesus' miracles to the time of his

---

11. Dunn, *Jesus Remembered*, 811–12.

12. "Luke places cross bearing in the closest proximity to self denial; in 9:23 the two demands are juxtaposed, and in 14:27 Luke places it very close to the demand to 'hate . . . even one's life', in 14:26 . . . Luke understood cross bearing as an internal conflict, a conflict with one self." Bøe, *Cross-Bearing*, 222.

13. Bøe, *Cross-Bearing*, 225–26.

14. McKnight, *Jesus*, 363.

temptations and passion. This transition is highlighted in 19:37a, where the disciples praise God for Jesus' miraculous work (19:37a) yet shortly thereafter Jesus' own suffering occurs at that very place (22:39–53).[15] Thus, the accommodation of the Son of God to the work required of God in the economy of salvation plays a significant hermeneutical role in the theology within Luke-Acts. This should lead one to recognize that Jesus' life as recorded in the Gospel of Luke is mostly a record of God the Son in his state of humiliation. In our view, the SRR of RR does not sufficiently reckon with this fact.

THE MESSIANIC SHAPE OF JESUS' WORK

Divine relations between the persons of the Trinity in the economy of salvation are specifically brought about by the particular shape of the humiliation of God the Son. Specifically, this humiliation takes the form of a Messiah who is called to obedience to God the Father. As such a person, Jesus relates to the Father and the Spirit in a specific messianic manner which is, a newly-structured relationality. To hold the contrary opinion, namely that the trinitarian relations in the economy of salvation are the unrestrained self–expression of God's immanent taxis, is to lose sight of Jesus' vocation as Messiah and its significance for Christian theology.

A Messianic Vocation Determines Jesus' Actions in the Economy of Salvation.

The incarnation involves a change in the state of the second person of the Trinity, from pre-incarnate glory to a vocation which includes his vocational humiliation in the role of God's Messiah. The messianic nature of Jesus' role belongs to the earliest confessions of Jesus' identity. On this original Messiah-Christology, Dahl famously wrote: "Thus from the beginnings of Greek-speaking Christianity (within a few years of the crucifixion), the name 'Christ' as applied to Jesus must have been firmly established. But this presupposes that Jesus was already designated 'the Messiah' and 'Jesus the Messiah' in Aramaic speaking regions. To this

---

15. Flender, *St Luke*, 31–32.

extent the Christology of the primitive community from the very first must have been a Messiah Christology."[16]

Luke's primary purpose is to "present the events he narrates as the completion of God's saving purpose for Israel," which is achieved through a Messiah.[17] Michael F. Bird lays out the messianic perspective which is particular to Lukan theology. He writes:

> Unique to Luke-Acts is that Jesus is "Messiah the Lord" (Luke 2:11, 26; cf. Acts 2:36) and Messiah of God (Luke 9:20; 23:35 cf. Acts 4:26). Luke also wishes to show the continuity of the church with the promises of Israel and to demonstrate how the work of Jesus and his followers represents the fulfillment of these promises. The Lucan Jesus, then, is simultaneously the "leader and savior" of Israel, the Jewish "Messiah" (Acts 5:31, 42) and the "Lord" of all who believe in him including the gentiles (Acts 10:36; 19:10, 17; 20:21).[18]

Matera similarly states: "The central concept for identifying Jesus is *messiahship* . . . Of the many terms that Luke employs to identify Jesus, then, 'Messiah' is among the most important. Indeed one could argue that it is *the* title in reference to which all others are to be understood."[19]

Luke and Acts are best classified as a "salvation history" which centers on the role of the Messiah. At the outset of his first work, the overwhelming emphasis of Luke's '*Kindheitsevangelium*' (Luke 1:46–55, 68–79; 2:13–14, 29–32, 34–36) is to affirm that God is to be praised for sending a "Messiah-Savior."[20] That Jesus is the saving Messiah in response to sin is clear from the prominence of salvation terminology used in Luke's Gospel. Luke uses *sōzein* seven times in accordance with its use in Mark's Gospel. Also, "Luke uses the word in ten places in which there are no parallels in the other Synoptic Gospels. In addition, Luke uses *sōter* twice, *sōterion* twice, *sōteria* four times, *lutrousthai* once, *lutrōsis* twice, *apolutrōsis* once and *diasōzein* once, in no instance with parallels in the other Synoptics."[21] This Messiah-Savior is the Spirit-conceived

---

16. Dahl, *Crucified Messiah*, 37.
17. Dunn, "Book of Acts," 389.
18. Bird, "Jesus," 69.
19. Italics are Matera's. Matera, *New Testament*, 68–69.
20. Gryglewicz, "Die Herkunft der Hymnen Des Kindheitsevangelium des Lucas," 272–73.
21. Giles, "Salvation (I)," 10.

Son of God (Luke 1:32, 35), who must be understood "in terms of the eternal and eschatological throne of David (1:32f)."[22] Thus Luke strategically places a messianic hermeneutic at the outset of his entire narrative. This messianic hermeneutical expectation is reinforced by the fact that the author primarily presents Jesus as the Christ (Luke 24).[23] The messianic ministry is the key to understanding Jesus' fulfillment of Scripture through his ministry.

Jesus had to comport himself with God's work of exalting the humble (Luke 1:52),[24] and so was an obedient and humble messianic figure (Luke 22:42), and a new Moses (Deut 18:15; Luke 9:29–31). As the new Moses (Acts 3:22–23) and for the benefit of the people of God,[25] Jesus brings in a new revelation and a new way of relating to God.[26] He does so before entering his glory and receiving a new status before God.[27] Jesus' role reversal from above to below, great to lowly, was an entailment of his messianic responsibility. This responsibility, whereby he becomes a humble person for the sake of others, is illustrated by Jesus' role-reversing table-fellowship parables.[28]

The relationship between the messiah and the cross is significant for Lucan theology. Bird captures this well:

> the death of Jesus in Luke's Gospel comes as no surprise. Beyond the passion predictions (Luke 9:22, 43–45; 18:31–34) we have the personification of Jerusalem as the one who kills the prophets and stones those sent to her (Luke 13:34–35), the call to carry one's cross and follow Jesus (Luke 14:27), the parable of the wicked tenants depicts Jesus as a son murdered by the tenants of the vineyard (Luke 20:9–19), and at the Last Supper Jesus says that the bread is his body "given for you" and the cup is "the new covenant in my blood which is poured out for you" (Luke 24:14–23). For Luke, Jesus' death is not redemptive in and of itself, but is

---

22. Turner, "Jesus and The Spirit," 34.
23. Fitzmyer, *Luke*, 1:198–99.
24. Bock, *Luke*: 1:147; 1:867.
25. Dunn, "Book of Acts," 392.
26. Bock, *Luke*: 1:867.
27. Note the unfolding of this theme: Luke 9:44–45; 18:31–34; 24:18–21; Acts 3:18; 17:2–3. Green, *Luke*, 849, 32–35. The role reversal of God the master becoming God the servant is necessarily included within the messianic role of Jesus.
28. Green, *Luke*: 849.

part of the movement from suffering to exaltation that will effect the forgiveness of sins and dispensing of the Holy Spirit.[29]

The cross in Lucan theology, therefore, demonstrates that Jesus' actions in the world were conformed to God's radical fulfillment of OT expectations and promises, rather than the eternal trinitarian relationships. Jesus' messianic vocation involved a staurological demand. There was a script that Jesus had to follow, which was driven by salvation-history not inner-trinitarian relationality. McKnight writes: "From beginning to end, and not unlike the other Christian traditions, Luke-Acts emphasizes the divine necessity of Jesus' suffering as part of the scriptural plot in God's plan (Luke 1:1; 22:22, 37; 24:26–27, 44–49; Acts 2:25–28, 34–35; 3:17–18; 4:28; 8:35; 13:27). Jesus must die in Jerusalem, and his death there is the second exodus (9:31; 13:31–33)."[30] Indeed, the cross of the messiah can only be understood in terms of a scripted salvation history and its ongoing significance for salvation history.[31]

Even after the ascension, Jesus' life and ministry continues to be seen as messianic in line with the OT expectation of a Messiah. According to scholars such as Dodd, McKnight, and N. T. Wright, the premier passages which inform the Christian understanding of Jesus include: Gen 12:3; 22:18; Deut 18:15, 19; Pss 2; 8; 22; 31; 41; 42–43; 60; 80; 88; 110; 118; Isa 6:1–9:7; 11:1–10; 28:16; 40:1–11; 42:1—44:5; 49:1–13; 50:4–1; 52:13—53:12; 61; Jer 31:10–34; Dan 7: Hosea; Joel 2–3; Zech 9–14. This creative re-interpretation of Scripture is attributed to Jesus himself and his own self-understanding.[32] This view regarding the anticipation of Jesus in the OT is reflected in early Christian preaching in the book of Acts. For example, Peter's speech recorded in Acts 3:

29. Bird, "Jesus," 74–75.

30. McKnight, *Jesus*, 361–62.

31. For example, in Mark's Gospel the reader's cultural objections to a crucified messiah are overcome by the following points which draw from the narrative and its rhetoric: "(1) The story culminates in the cross as a redemptive event; (2) the Jewish hope for the arrival of the kingdom is fulfilled in Jesus' death and resurrection; (3) Jesus epitomizes the true servant-king; (4) Jesus' crucifixion does not count him as accursed by God. He is honored by being resurrected; and (5) Israel's messiah is the Son of Man, a mysterious figure who represents Israel and triumphs over the pagan beasts by suffering at their hands . . . one could add mark's messianic exegesis of the Old Testament to bolster the case." Bird, "Jesus," 14.

32. McKnight goes so far as to claim that N.T. Wright's Jesus and the Victory of God "can be seen as a fleshing out of Dodd's passages assigned to Jesus!" Wright, *Jesus*; McKnight, *Jesus*, 189–90, also notes.

12–26.³³ In this long speech, Peter speaks of God sending "the Messiah appointed for you, that is, Jesus, who must remain in heaven until the time of universal restoration that God announced long ago through his holy prophets" (Acts 3:20–21). Jesus' messianic role is shaped by the Moses archetype and promise, as well as the Abrahamic covenant (Acts 3:22–26), Davidic kingship (Acts 13:33–37), and the Isaianic universal hope (Acts 28:26–28). This messianic-hermeneutic is not limited to Peter and the beginning of the book of Acts, rather the book of Acts is bracketed by this view. In Acts 28:23, the final recorded speech of Paul closes the work with Jesus' messianic role defined as the One who ushers in the kingdom of God. Acts 28:23b tells us that Paul "explained . . . testifying to the kingdom of God and trying to convince them about Jesus both from the law of Moses and from the prophets." Schnabel draws out the significance of the messianic theme as follows: "the phrase 'the kingdom of God' is, in Luke's account in the book of Acts, a summary of the Christian message. Paul sought to convince his visitors that the crucified and risen Jesus is the Messiah and fulfills the meaning and the promises of the law and the prophets . . . some Jews 'were convinced' . . . they converted to faith in Jesus as the Messiah."³⁴ The messianic nature of Jesus and the basis of his person and mission are founded upon the God of the OT. Luke emphasized this in Paul's teaching in Acts 28:28. As Schnabel explains: "Paul links the quotation from Isa 6:9–10 about the hard-heartedness and stubbornness of God's people (Acts 28:26b–27) with allusions to Ezek 2:3–5 and Ezek 3:4–7 [as] . . . a prophetic indictment . . . with the hope of provoking the Jews in Rome to repent and believe in Jesus as the Messiah."³⁵

In Acts 28:31, a summary of Paul's final two-year ministry in Rome concludes the book of Acts with the following description of his focus: "proclaiming the kingdom of God and teaching about the Lord Jesus Christ with all boldness and without hindrance." This underlines the point that what one reads about Paul's teaching in Rome about the Messiah is what Luke records as Peter's proclamation in Jerusalem. Acts 2:36 reads: "Therefore. Let the whole house of Israel know with certainty that God has made him both Lord and Messiah, this Jesus whom you

---

33. Dunn, " Book of Acts," 388.
34. Schnabel, *Early*, 1269.
35. Ibid.

crucified."[36] The author of Luke-Acts employs the harmonized preaching of Peter and Paul to underline that the message of Jesus *as Messiah* is the central theological point of the Christian message, and its centrality is taught all over the world. In view of such a finale to Luke's work, we can see that together with the "*Kindheitsevangelium*" (Luke 1–2), it brackets Jesus' identity and work in the messianic work of God who fulfills his promise to his people, which is congruent with Jesus' own message (Acts 1:3: "After his suffering he presented himself alive to them . . . appearing to them . . . and speaking about the kingdom of God").[37]

Jesus' behavior towards God the Father and God the Holy Spirit in the economy of salvation is determined by three factors in particular: Jesus' state of humiliation, the messianic role; and the lowly nature of Jesus' incarnation. These factors stem from the assumption of a human nature by the second person of the Trinity, and the responsibilities and expectations placed on Jesus by God's plan and the human need for salvation. Only by fulfilling these will Jesus accomplish his mission in his deliberate state of humiliation. Because of the human nature assumed by the second person of the Trinity, a new way of trinitarian relating is brought about. Therefore, Jesus' behaviour in the economy of salvation is not taken to be an expression of the immanent baseline Father-ward and Spirit-ward relations of the second person of the Trinity. To do so would disregard the context of his ministry.

A great theological outcome of the approach taken here is a heightened awareness of God's grace. God the Son's humble and relationally demanding (divinely-speaking) mission reveals the depth and great extent of God's love for humanity through the magnitude of the incarnational stooping. Not only did this earthly mission entail divine condescension but also divine relational accommodation. This scriptural emphasis is lost to interpreters who take the SRR of RR, where the actions of God the Son in the economy of salvation are taken only to be an expression of a set of unchanged relations that have always been the case, and can only ever be the case, within the Godhead. Further, if one takes the accommodation of God to human capacity in his revelatory communication via the nature and words of Scripture, why would one disallow *a priori* the accommodation of God in his self-revelation to human beings? Given that the human condition towards which God is revealing himself

---

36. Ibid.
37. Dunn, "Book of Acts," 398–400.

is the same in both the case of Scripture and the incarnation, is not an accommodation appropriate in both instances? That is, it is *not* the case that humans are able to receive revelation from God's written accommodation, yet not able to receive it from his relational accommodation as a human Messiah.

In essence, the SRR of RR leads to a "weak" view of the humanity of Christ. Such a Christology is "weak" because of the low significance it accords to the implications of the human nature assumed by the second person of the Trinity.[38] The specific messianic particularity of Jesus' human nature plays a monumental role in Christ's life, and thus affirms a "strong" view of the humanity of Christ. This view needs to be maintained by a precise theology of the "*Communicatio Idiomatum*." A satisfactory model for this can only be one which holds that

> [t]he effects of the hypostatic union on the person are . . . threefold: the communication of attributes, of office, and of honour. In each case . . . the communication must be considered as only from the natures to the person, not from one nature to another. [This] . . . account of the *communicatio idiomatum* relies on a distinction between communication between natures and person and communication between the two natures. Properties of each nature may be meaningfully and rightly applied to the person, but properties of one nature may not be applied to each other . . . [the] great point is that the natures are different, and for there to be a real incarnation, and not a Eutychian mixing of natures leading not a *tertium quid*, the natures must remain distinct.[39]

By means of this view of the *communicatio*, a "strong" Christology maintains the significance of the humanity of Christ for both what may and *may not* be said of the immanent Trinity. A "strong view" avoids anti-realism on one hand, and collapsing or strongly aligning the natures of Christ into each other, and also collapsing the immanent into the economic Trinity, on the other hand. Such a strong view can be correlated with the LRR of RR.

It may be the case that the points made above have begun to be recognized by some Evangelicals who hold to the SRR of RR. In particular,

---

38. This occurs in the current debates on the eternal subordination of God the Son to God the Father. McCall and Yandell, "Trinitarian Subordinationism."

39. This view requires "[t]he deployment of the anhypostatic-enhypostatic distinction [as] . . . the only way of denying Nestorianism—insisting there is only one hypostasis of the incarnate Son." Holmes, "Reformed Varieties," 77–78. (Italics are Holmes').

Bruce Ware recently asked: "while Christ was (and is) fully God and fully man, how do we best account for the way in which he lived his life and fulfilled his calling—by seeing him carrying this out as God, or as man, or as the God-man?"[40] His answer is surprising in view of his previous works on the Trinity, which have accented the life of Jesus as directly correspondent to the lived-out life of God the Son (by means of taking the SRR of RR). Ware answers the question above as follows: "I would argue that the most responsible answer biblically and theologically is the last, 'as the God-man,' but that the emphasis must be placed on the humanity of Christ as the primary reality he expressed in his day-to-day life, ministry, and work."[41] What is most interesting about Ware's result is that in seeking to be "biblically responsible," he appears to have departed from the SRR of RR.

The Learnt Obedience of Jesus to God the Father

The obedience of Jesus[42] as God's faithful son is perhaps the central feature of the NT's basis for faith in Jesus as Messiah. Though Longenecker may overstate his case in the quote below, the force of his argument can be substantiated from the NT. He argues:

> the various terms and expressions used in the NT with respect to Christ are to be understood as pictorial representations . . . that

---

40. Ware, "Man Christ Jesus," 5. He repeats his position: "while he was fully God, and while this is crucial to understanding rightly his full identity, life, and the fulfilment of his atoning work, the predominant reality he experienced day by day, and the predominant means by which he fulfilled his calling, was that of his genuine humanity."

41. Ibid., 5.

42. We will take the following definition of obedience as our definition and rationale: "The 'obedience of Christ' (*obedientia Christi*) is a traditional category some use in discussing the significance of Christ's life and death. This category admits of two sub ones: the active obedience of Christ (*obedientia activa*) and the passive (meaning suffering) obedience of Christ (*obedientia passiva*) . . . How then are the faithfulness and obedience of Christ to be related? The obedience of Christ, so essential to atonement, I suggest, issued from his faithfulness . . . Faithfulness involves a belief as to the value of the word to be obeyed and/or the person to be obeyed. Though necessary belief as to value is still not sufficient. Faithfulness as an attitude issuing in action also requires a commitment to a person or task and that is maintained over time, especially in the face of testing. Paul describes the Roman Christians as those who had 'become obedient . . . from the heart . . . to the form of teaching to which you were entrusted . . .' (Rom 6:17 NRSV). The apostle was not interested in mere outward conformity. He also wrote in the same letter of 'the obedience of faith' (Rom 1:5 and 16:22, NRSV)." Cole, *God the Peacemaker*, 115–17.

stem ultimately from a basic conviction that has to do with the obedience, faithfulness, and sonship of Christ—with its corollary being the trustful obedience of the believer in response. In the case of Christ . . . all the titles ascribed to him in the NT and all the metaphors used in description of the nature and effects of his work are founded ultimately on the early Christians' conviction regarding the full obedience and entire faithfulness of Jesus of Nazareth, God's Son par excellence, with this complete filial obedience seen as having been exercised throughout his life and coming to ultimate expression in his death on the cross.[43]

The righteous obedience of Jesus to God as his Father is of paramount importance in the economy of salvation, especially given what occurred in the Fall in Gen 3:6 onwards, and the account of faithless Israel from Exod 32 through to Jesus own life, death and resurrection. Jesus' obedience to his Father is foundational to his Lordship and messianic role, as he is both the new Adam and the new Israel. Luke's mention of Adam in Jesus' genealogy highlights the importance of Jesus as the new Adam (Luke 3:37). The wilderness temptation account in the very next chapter points out that Jesus succeeded in the wilderness where Israel failed. He is thus the true human (Adam) and the true chosen one of God (Israel). Key events which highlight Jesus' obedience to the Father take place within a narrative setting where Jesus is expressly presented as God's "chosen one." These include the beginning of his ministry in Nazareth (Luke 4:18; cf. Isa 42:1–2), the transfiguration (Luke 9:35), the crucifixion (Luke 23:35, 38–39) and the session of Christ (Acts 2:32–36). In each of these instances Jesus is understood to be fulfilling and recapitulating the role of Adam and/or Israel. Jesus' obedience is the key to this re-capitulation, and thus Jesus' messianic obedience to God the Father is of special significance to Lukan theology. Even though Jesus' role as the suffering Messiah occurs within a trinitarian context, it primarily concerns God's saving activity through the Messiah, rather than God's relational triune self-expression in the world.

The importance of the double aspect of Jesus' obedience to the Father, representing both the true human and true Israel, has been noted by scholars such as G. A. Cole:

> The linchpin of the divine plan and the central figure in the divine project is God's faithful Son, Jesus Christ. This can easily be seen

---

43. Longenecker, "Foundational Conviction," 475. (Italics are Longenecker's).

in the fact that there are four accounts of his person and work in the canon of Scripture. No other biblical character is treated from so many angles. Even the synoptic gospels support this point. An outstanding characteristic of Jesus is that here is one who really does live by every word that proceeds out of the mouth of God. Adam did not, nor did Israel; yet this Son did.[44]

The overall flow of Luke's narrative witnesses to the fact that Jesus grew in knowledge, and that he learnt obedience to God in a new way (Luke 2:52). Luke employs a number of events to make this clear. Three testing stories play this role: the temptation in the wilderness, the testing on the Mount of Olives, and the temptation on the cross.

In the wilderness temptation narrative (Luke 4:1–13) Jesus is tempted to disobey God the Father three times, yet he remains faithful. During these tests, Jesus "recognizes the devil's strategy as an attempt to deflect him from his single-minded commitment to loyalty and obedience in God's service, and interprets the devil's invitation as an encouragement to question God's faithfulness. Israel had manifested its doubts by testing God, but Jesus refuses to do so (cf. Deut 6:16) . . . By facing these tests and proving his fidelity, Jesus has demonstrated unequivocally his faithful obedience to God and thus to engage in ministry publicly as God's Son."[45]

For the purposes of our study at hand we must ask: Does Jesus overcome the Devil because the obedience he displays is merely a duplication of the obedience he gives God the Father within the inner-trinitarian life? The answer is "No." This is no mere duplication because Jesus had to demonstrate obedience to God the Father in a way that was simply not possible prior to the incarnation. In the temptation in the wilderness and the following temptations, the manner and degree to which God the Son incarnate needed to be faithful to God the Father's character and demands would be impossible within the divine *taxis* if it were required aside from creation. Created beings, and the typology which arose from God's particular history with humanity through Israel, only exist in the sphere of creation. As Jesus' faithfulness to God entailed obedience as the Messiah, this new situation required an expression of new obedience of God the Son to God the Father in an environment that is *ad extra* to the divine life.

44. Cole, *God the Peacemaker*, 103.
45. Green, *Luke*, 196.

Jesus' prayer on the Mount of Olives (Luke 22:39–46) is "what in the Synoptic Gospels is presented as Jesus' last great spiritual struggle before enduring the agony of the cross—with, in particular, the Evangelists' focus on his response of obedience."[46] At the outset of our exploration of this account, and any theology stemming from it, we must necessarily acknowledge that there is deep mystery here due to a multiplicity of overlapping theological issues including the nature of temptation and the necessity of Jesus' actions and attitudes as God (i.e., divine goodness). Jesus' agony and anguish during this time of prayer are highlighted by all the synoptic authors, especially Luke: "Though the details of the Gethsemane experience differ somewhat in the three Synoptic Gospels (e.g., Matthew: 'he fell down on his face'; Mark: 'he fell down on the ground'; Luke: 'he knelt down'; also note Luke's addition of an angel being sent to strengthen him and his sweat being 'like great drops of blood') . . . the Evangelists agree in focusing on Jesus' attitude of complete obedience . . ."[47] There is no bypassing the fact that Jesus' obedience to the Father was difficult, and a new relational condition between him and God. His prayer reveals both his struggle in the decision process for obedience to the Father, and also his actual act of obedience. In Luke 22:44 Jesus famously shed "sweat like great drops of blood" as he prayed more earnestly what he had prayed in verse 42: "Father, if you are willing, take this cup from me; yet not my will but yours be done." Jesus' obedience to his Father was costly yet sure: "Jesus' prayer in verse 42 shows that he also desires to escape testing . . . But Jesus' request is preceded and followed by acknowledgement that God's will must prevail."[48] Obedience was a necessary aspect of Jesus' work in order that salvation could be extended to the world.[49]

One cannot overstate the significance of the fact that this account of obedience entailed a new situation in which God the Son had to be obedient to God the Father in a new way. God the Son carried out his specific messianic obedience to God the Father, an obedience which was impossible outside the context of creation and salvation history: "In some situations the divine will must be realized through suffering and

---

46. Longenecker, "Foundational Conviction," 486.
47. Ibid.
48. Tannehill, *Luke*, 324.
49. Gander, *L'Evangile*, 953–55.

death. Jesus is now in such a situation."⁵⁰ The depth of Jesus' anguish was such that he required strengthening by an angel. Though this may have helped him in his suffering, his great travail continued through to his crucifixion.

Supremely, it is on the cross itself where Jesus displayed ultimate obedience to God the Father. Luke purposively redacts Mark's account of the mockery of Jesus in order to highlight this point.⁵¹ A catena of verses within the short record of Jesus' crucifixion drive home and highlight the point that Jesus continued to obey God on the cross. A multitude of voices attempt to shame him and tempt him to live up to his claimed and perceived special status and so rescue himself from the cross. The plurality of voices tempting him to release himself from the mission of God include the voices of the rulers: "He saved others—let him save himself if he is Christ of God, the Chosen One;" (23:35b); the soldiers: "If you are the King of the Jews, save yourself!" (23:37) and lastly the criminal: "Are you not the Messiah? Save yourself and us!" (23:39). The taunts by the leaders in particular are ironic as they sarcastically wallow in their success, for in their minds they "have stopped Jesus."⁵² This could not be further from the truth, as the fact is that Jesus' purposeful endurance on the cross leaves no doubt that even in "the midst of this dreadful experience, Jesus remains true to his own vision: God is still his Father . . . even in this extreme situation."⁵³

Following the mockery of those around him, the crucified one cried out: "Father, into your hands I commit my spirit" (Luke 23:46). The narratival thrust in Luke's Gospel accentuates the Son turning towards God the Father in trust.⁵⁴ This relational direction is part of a narrative complex that includes various active movements on Jesus' behalf towards his Father.⁵⁵

---

50. Tannehill, *Luke*, 324.
51. Nolland, *Luke*, 1146–48.
52. Bock, *Luke*, 2:1852.
53. Nolland, *Luke*, 1148.
54. Fitzmyer, *Luke*, 1:193.

55. These movements are "different ways of describing Jesus' 'departure' (*exodus*, Luke 9:31) or his transit to the Father through suffering, death, burial, resurrection, and exaltation to glory (one effect of which will be the outpouring of the Holy Spirit)." Fitzmyer, *Luke*, 1:195.

The Messianic Office of God the Son in Luke-Acts 91

The author of Luke's Gospel does not follow Matthew and Mark in portraying Jesus as abandoned on the cross: "Luke is careful to present Jesus in a state of communion and openness with the Father rather than the turmoil and anguish so dramatically presented in Matthew and Mark's gospel."[56] Instead, in Luke, Jesus commits his life into God's hands, which is the equivalent of committing himself to God's power.[57] This commitment to God on the cross cannot be divorced from Jesus' entire life of obedience. That is, if one is going to employ the SRR of RR to the narrative of Luke-Acts, then one must apply it to the whole narrative and not selectively. One cannot interpret the cross using the SRR of RR on one hand, and yet on the other hand not interpret the entirety of Jesus' life in this manner. The integrated nature of God's plan and Jesus' mission means that there must be consistency in christological and trinitarian interpretation.

The active and passive obedience of Christ must be held together as aspects of the one office of Jesus as Messiah. Thomas F. Torrance understood the necessity of holding together everything Jesus did for humanity under the rubric of his obedience to the Father: "When the Son of God came into this world He laid hold of our humanity which had gone astray and corrupted itself. He the Holy and Sinless One assumed our 'flesh of sin' in order that He might heal it, turn it back to God, and restore it to communion with him. And that is what he did all through his life from His birth to His death, through His wonderful obedience and faithfulness to God He bent our perverted humanity back to the divine will."[58]

In view of the above, it is clear that in order to uphold a SRR of RR that adequately deals with the scriptural testimony of the obedience of Jesus to God the Father on the cross, such an exegete would have to deny the new experience and struggle of Jesus on the cross. In order to make a case for such a denial, the exegete has to argue that both the nature and extent of Jesus' obedience to the Father was one that was: (1) already present and (2) lived out, in an isomorphic manner, in the inner-trinitarian life. To deny the newness and great obedient effort of Jesus on

---

56. Bibb, "Characterization," 159, 61.

57. Ps 30:25; see the pattern of entrustment in Luke 12:48; Acts 14:23; 20:32. Johnson and Harrington, *Luke*, 379. Exod 3:8; 7:4; 15:6; 1 Sam LXX Ps 9:35; 30:15 Johnson and Harrington, *Luke*, 340.

58. Torrance, *When Christ*, 73. Torrance, *Trinitarian Faith*, 152.

the cross would be a great loss, and would greatly weaken and detract from Luke's Christology and call to discipleship (for example, Stephen's speech and martyrdom in Acts 6:8—7:60).

It is clear that the *missio Dei* is paramount for the author of Luke. Jesus the Messiah's obedience to God the Father is driven by the necessity of this plan.[59] However, though many revelatory and salvific events during Jesus' ministry include references to God, Jesus and the Holy Spirit,[60] it is clear that the focus of these passages is not for the trinitarian taxis to be expressed in the world. Rather, it is God's covenantal activity in response to, and in the context of, the fallen situation of the world. This determines that God save *people* in a particular way. That is, God saves as the Trinity *pro nobis*, and not solely as the relational self-expression of the Trinity. Therefore we can say that the work of God the Trinity is accommodated to the shape of the world in which salvation takes place. As such, an accommodation takes place. The significance of this point is that the way—the "what" and "how"—Jesus lived in the economy was not a mere reduplication of the immanent relations within God. It was altogether a new situation.

The uniqueness of this situation is highlighted by the canonical witness to the process of Jesus learning a particular kind of obedience. This is found in passages such as John 17:1–3 and Heb 3:16; 5:8. Hebrews 5:8 is particularly striking: "Although he was a Son, he learned obedience through what he suffered."[61] The entailment of this obedience is set forth immediately in Heb 5:9: "and having been made perfect, he became the source of eternal salvation to all who are related to him in obedience."[62]

---

59. Luke 1:1; 22:22, 37; 24:26–27, 44–49; Acts 2:25–28, 34–35; 3:17–18; 4:28; 8:35; 13:27.

60. Lee, *Transfiguration*: 79.

61. On this verse Ellingworth states: "The present verse . . . probably implies a contrast between his eternal status on one hand, and the learning process of Christ's earthly life on the other . . . the likely meaning is 'Although he has (eternally) the status of (God's) Son.'" Ellingworth, *Epistle to the Hebrews*, 293. O'Brien states: "Hebrews makes it clear that suffering, and death are fully compatible with Jesus' status as the eternal Son, and are an essential part of his saving work (see v. 9)." Note that O'Brien does not say that Jesus' suffering based upon obedience is an essential part of Jesus' *nature*, rather it is essential to his *work*. O'Brien, *Letter to the Hebrews*, 200.

62. A vocational understanding of this obedience and perfection is required by the text, rather than a trinitarian one. O'Brien highlights the nature of Jesus suffering: "As in the earlier reference (2:20), the perfecting of Christ is best understood in vocational terms, for it describes the process by which he was made complete or fully equipped

These verses and the narrative of Luke make it clear that the work of God the Son in the economy of salvation entails his learning obedience to God the Father in new ways through new challenges. Stated another way, it would be unnecessary for the second person of the Trinity to learn obedience to God the Father in the economy of salvation if within the inner-relational life of God, the eternal Son had always been obedient to God the Father in such a manner.

Given Luke's theology of a Messiah-in-salvation-history, one must admit the point that the trinitarian economy cannot be merely a reflection of the trinitarian taxis if the weight of history of salvation is going to be taken into account. If an interpreter applies a SRR of RR to the Bible, there will be a loss of the significance of biblical history, the extent of the active obedience of the second person of the Trinity as the Messiah, and the significance and degree of God's condescending grace to human beings.

All three of these concerns are captured and highlighted in what is an apex of the entire Lukan story, though it ironically seems like a great "ditch"—Luke 23:42–44. Here Jesus prays: "Father, if you are willing, remove this cup from me; yet, not my will but yours be done. Then an angel from heaven appeared to him and gave him strength. In his anguish he prayed more earnestly, and his sweat became like great drops of blood falling down on the ground." The fact that God the Son required an angel to strengthen him demonstrates the degree to which God the Son has stooped for the sake of saving his people. Surely this is an inversion of God's relationship to created beings. To argue that *a priori* there can be no inversion or change in terms of God's relationship within himself in this inverted economy of salvation fails to take into account the facts of Jesus' abasement.

---

for his office. Here his being 'perfected' is the result of his learning obedience through what he suffered, with all this involved—his offering up prayers and petitions with loud cries and tears, and his reverent submission to God on the basis of which he was heard and delivered out of the realm of death (v. 7). Put simply he is 'qualified' as the unique deliverer through his death and heavenly exaltation." O'Brien, *Letter to the Hebrews*, 202. We note therefore, that Jesus was not qualified to be the agent of salvation via the reduplication of the obedience which was previously expressed in eternity between the persons of the Trinity. For the Paul's view on the Messianic nature of Jesus' work, see Fee, *Pauline Christology*, 532 ff.

Case Study: Gethsemane

If the SRR of RR is applied to Jesus' struggle for obedience to God the Father on the Mount of Olives, this struggle would result in a "battle of wills" between Jesus and God the Father or a "battle" between the natures of the one person Jesus Christ. Thus either a trinitarian or christological problem is created.

Jesus' obedience to God the Father on the Mount of Olives also brings the SRR of RR into question. Jesus' words and internal struggle at the Mount of Olives raises the issues of how to relate the will of Jesus as the Son incarnate to that of God and/or God the Father. The tension in this narrative is heightened by Luke, the author, who allows this event to be developed with the conditions of the presence of the angel and Jesus' suffering in Luke 22:42–44. The tension between Jesus and God the Father in this narrative is very strong.[63]

If this passage were to be interpreted strictly according to the SRR of RR it would arguably lead to a tri-theistic theology that posits that within God there are competing wills—the will of God the Son and the will of God the Father, and thus God's simplicity and monotheism would be denied. In addition, the christological conclusion would be that the human and divine wills in the one person of Jesus are not engaged with one another. These theological conclusions undermine the biblical focus, which is on the logic of the salvation history of God being for us himself, in Jesus' whole life as Messiah.[64]

The relationship between the will(s) of Jesus and the will of God the Father, and the will(s) and natures of Jesus, have been the cause of much debate and theological nuance from the Arian debates onwards and through Medieval thought.[65] Essentially, the history of the interpretation of the story of the Mount of Olives serves as a case study of what can happen if the SRR of RR is applied to God the Father and Jesus' relationship without much biblically informed thought. Indeed the history of interpretation reveals that an orthodox interpretation of this event

---

63. Bovon, *Evangelium Nach Lukas*, III/4: 302.

64. Jesus' "special relation of the human nature of the Logos as its creative origin is . . . the condition of the possibility of the incarnation," an "individual human life, a union [with the Logos] . . . the form of a life history in which this relation [to God the Father] unfolded. The process of this history is the concrete form of the human reality of Jesus. Only here does he have identity as a person." Pannenberg, *Systematic Theology*, 2: 386.

65. Madigan, *Passions of Christ*, 90. (Emphasis is Madigan's).

required some nuance beyond the mere SRR of RR. Madigan sums some of the hermeneutical maneuvers taken in the Christian past to avoid the unorthodoxy inherent in the use of a hermeneutic which is assumed in the SRR of RR:

> Ambrose declares categorically that "as a man" Christ prayed and it . . . seemed obvious that Christ prayed for himself. For Hilary, this would have sounded like a dangerous concession to "Arianism," and he went so far as to assert that the desire of his human will was not affected . . . Essentially, Peter Lombard, Thomas, and Bonaventure all agree that Christ did not doubt, did not fear, did not ask for the removal of the cup with his rational will but, rather, with some inferior "natural" human will which could contain, discipline, and finally reorder the anxieties which were brewing in the nether regions of Christ's will. In this sense, if only in this sense, there was a perfect "concord" of wills. Christ's will is not in utter conformity with the Father's will from the point of view of *what* is willed (*in volito*) but in *ratione volendi*—that is, in how Christ willed. If there is no identity in the thing desired, there is an ordered concord of wills.[66]

Hugh of St. Victor struggled with the question of Christ's wills. William Placher sums up Hugh of St. Victor's argument from *On the Four Wills of Christ*, as follows: "not only did Christ have a divine will and a human will, but his human will was divided into a will of reason, a will of piety, and a will of the flesh or a sensitive will. Thus, in a case like this [struggling on the Mt. of Olives] he would understand (will of reason) that, yes, he must die on the cross, and accept (will of piety) conformity to God's wishes, while still, at an emotional level not wanting to die."[67] Placher then adds the comment: "Such a multiplication of wills may just complicate the issue . . . but in its cumbersome way it captures something true about Jesus' situation."[68] This biblical and historical case study demonstrates that approaching salvation history with an unmodified SRR of RR is problematic for theology proper and for Christology. That is, the humanity of Jesus and its significance for his person in salvation history resists the SRR of RR.

---

66. Ibid., 90. (Italics are Madigan's).
67. Placher, *Mark*, 209.
68. Ibid., 209.

JESUS' VEILED ESSENTIAL GLORY

Beyond providing the context within which Jesus' works are to be interpreted, the incarnate state of the humble Messiah includes, and results in, a "veiling" of Jesus' essential divine nature.[69] This effect needs to be taken into account as its significance is not incidental to what can be known and said about who Jesus is in himself, and who the triune God is in himself. The hermeneutical caution provided by Jesus' human nature, with reference to Jesus' life being lived out in the state of his humiliation, is re-affirmed at Jesus' baptism (Luke 3:21–22) and at the transfiguration (Luke 9:27–36). At both times, the disciples received an insight into Christ's true glory; a glory veiled by his flesh. At the outset we notice that both the baptism of Jesus and his transfiguration reveal that there is more to the divine identity of Jesus and God than salvation history reveals.

For Luke, the *shekinah* glory of God has descended to the earthly realm in Luke 1:35 "the power of the most high will cover you with its shadow." Thus, the reality of who Jesus is as a being is defined by the *shekinah* glory of God.[70] The baptism of Jesus points towards the descent of the mysterious reality of God, alluding to his unfathomable glory by means of the sentence construction in Luke 3:21–32, "Now when all the people were baptized, and when Jesus also had been baptized and was praying, the heavens were opened, and the Holy Spirit descended upon him in bodily form like a dove. And a voice came from heaven, "You are my Son, the beloved; with you I am well pleased." The purpose of this construction is to "lay stress on the supernatural phenomena and to play down the importance of the attendant earthly circumstances."[71] Through the heavens being opened, there is "an indication that divine revelation is about to take place."[72] In addition, the Isaianic Servant's endowment of the Spirit in Isa 42:1 and 63:14 is recalled as the Spirit descends upon Jesus in Luke 3:22; this same Spirit "from above" which will lead Jesus into the wilderness (Luke 4:1), strongly echoing the Exodus where God's theophanic presence led his people in the desert. Further, the voice from above recalls Isa 42:1 thereby linking this story to Luke 1:32 and Luke

---

69. See Appendix A for a biblical theology of the significance that the human nature plays in the reception and comprehension of the revelation of God.

70. O'Loughlin, "Losing Mystery," 17.

71. Marshall, *Luke*, 152.

72. Ibid.

23:35 via Isa 42:6, 49:6, and to the transfiguration voice via the use of Ps 2 and the LXX semantics underlying "chosen" and "delight."[73] Therefore, the three ideas present in Luke 3:21 are that the supernatural nature of this event has to do with God's majestic presence, God's unapproachable presence and a revelatory voice from the inaccessible heavenly realm. These ideas all contribute to the unfathomable core of a trinitarian revelatory event associated with God's presence or his *shekinah*.[74]

Luke makes both glory and splendor key themes in his account of the transfiguration (9:29, 31, 32), with details such as the inclusion of both Moses and Elijah who had unique experiences of God's glory (Exod 25–31; 1 Kgs 19:8–18).[75] In particular, the majestic Exodus-like presence of God is accentuated via repetition of the fact that God appears in a cloud (Luke 9:34b–35a, "a *cloud* appeared and enveloped them, and they were afraid as they entered the *cloud*. And a voice came from the *cloud* . . ."). The cloud is highly significant in this pericope. Nolland states, "The awesome and fearful presence of God is both hidden and revealed by the presence of the cloud."[76] It is "the sign of God's (hidden) presence (Ps 18:11; Exod 1 9:16, etc.) and the mode of his transportation (Isa 19:1; Pss 18:10–11; 104:3)."[77] This presence of God is unquestionably the glory of a God who is at the same time incomprehensible and transcendent. The cloud symbolizes the eschatological presence of God.[78] Though God is clearly present, from the disciples' point of view the scene is one of confusion in terms of their knowledge of God and his works: the cloud "evokes fear in the presence of the awesome mystery of God."[79] Peter "did not know what he was saying" (Luke 9:33b), and needed God's voice to interpret what his presence meant (Luke 9:35). This sense of confusion and the inability to recognize God is strengthened by two preceding sto-

---

73. Nolland, *Luke*, 1:161–63.

74. This is further heightened by the use of the dove in the story. However, Carson and Beale like many others "readily admit that the meaning behind the symbolism of the dove cannot be determined with any degree of certainty." Beale and Carson, *New Testament Use*, 280.

75. Ibid., 312.

76. Nolland, *Luke*: 2:504. Nolland notes that as far as the disciples are concerned, "They have seen the glory that by rightly belongs to Jesus, but it belongs to him on the other side of death and resurrection."

77. Nolland, *Luke*: 2:501.

78. Beale and Carson, *New Testament Use*, 311.

79. Nolland, *Luke*, 2:497.

ries of perplexity and of revelation. These are Herod's confusion about Jesus (Luke 9:7–9), and the disciples' confusion (at the feeding of the five thousand, Luke 9:12–13), which is followed by a revelation of Jesus' purpose (Luke 9:21–27). The parallel is that revelation takes place in the midst of human inability to understand the full extent of God's identity and work: who Jesus is as God (they cannot understand God's identity) and what God is doing in Jesus (they misunderstand what God is doing around them). The final transfiguration scene emphasizes the sleepiness of the disciples. This drives home the point that the disciples "manage to see the scene of glory, but only just: they are heavy with sleep."[80] Their silence about the event (Luke 9:36) means that for them "the whole experience has been as much puzzling as illuminating."[81]

The transfiguration account begins with a simple reference to Jesus, which does not indicate an identity other than his human form as a servant of God (Luke 9:28). In direct contrast, the actual transfiguration event emphasizes Jesus' glory (Luke 9:31) and his changed, dazzling appearance (Luke 9:29). A key point is that God's inner life is qualitatively (and quantitatively!) different to human life (Luke 9:28–36). Jesus' "transcendence," equivalently stated as his "heavenly glory," is the key attribute revealed so that "Jesus' glory reveals who he really is and how he will ultimately manifest himself."[82] Therefore, we must bear in mind that only in events such as the transfiguration (Luke 9:28–36) do we have a partial insight into the fullness of God's own answer to Herod's question about Jesus' identity (Luke 9:9: "but who is this about whom I hear such things?").[83] Therefore, there is a contrast in both accounts *within the same person of Jesus* as a human servant of God, and his glorious identity.

Though the majesty of God is never far from sight in Jesus' ministry (Luke 9:43), Jesus' essential glory is mostly veiled in flesh.[84] For example, "the majesty of God" is used as a phrase to conclude the pericope that immediately follows the transfiguration account. In this story, Jesus delivers a boy from a demon, and the response of the crowd was "they were astonished at the majesty of God" (Luke 9:43). The weight of this account

80. Ibid., 2:504.
81. Ibid., 2:502.
82. Bock, *Luke*, 1:862, 76.
83. Fitzmyer, *Luke*, 793; Bock, *Luke*, 1:862.
84. Lee, *Transfiguration*, 71.

means that an accent lies on the glory and majesty of Jesus, rather than on his humanity or humiliation alone. However, his divine Sonship is never stated without his role as Servant in mind. For example, the voice at the transfiguration alludes to both Ps 2:7 and Isa 42:1. In fact, the voice from heaven provides a double emphasis, "stressing that Jesus is both Son and Suffering Servant." This confirmation of Jesus as both Son and Servant is "the high point of the narrative."[85] Therefore, even in revelatory moments, the messianic nature of Jesus in the economy of salvation is a key feature of the biblical witness. Jesus' sonship is never revealed aside from his humanity and its roles. The exegetical conclusion is that in Luke's narrative of the transfiguration, the revelation of Jesus' essential glory means that this divine glory is mostly veiled by his flesh and his economic role.[86] It is only at special events, such as the transfiguration that we see that, though Jesus retains his physical embodiment, at the same time "another identity illuminates it, the source of which is God's own self."[87] Dorothy Lee expresses the point well. At the transfiguration: "an astonishingly brilliant light flaming forth from Jesus—the radiance of his body shining through garments in flashes of fire, like light pouring through a window . . . More generally this language belongs to the heavenly realm where white and light are intimately associated with celestial beings, manifestations of divine presence, holiness and beauty."[88]

The revelation of the "celestial light of Christ,"[89] displaying Jesus' divine identity as God's Son,[90] is re-affirmed in Luke 24. This narratival unit includes Jesus within the Jewish Monotheistic view of God.[91] This,

85. D. A. Carson, comments made in Biblical Theology Lectures, Trinity Evangelical Divinity School, 2009.

86. A point that is often overlooked in this debate is this issue is the degree of consensus on the position that the transfiguration reveals something otherwise hidden. It is not just Protestant Christians who understand that the transfiguration shows of more of Jesus' divinity than is revealed during the common course of his ministry. Cole, *Holy Spirit*, 164.

87. Lee, *Transfiguration*, 133.

88. Ibid., 71.

89. Ibid., 132.

90. "The transfiguration symbolizes the salvific and eschatological purpose of the incarnation, revealing the human Jesus in his identity as the divine son." Lee, *Transfiguration*, 133.

91. At the outset of his article, Johnson states his agreement with Yeago's comment that "the Nicene *homoousion* . . . describes a pattern of judgments present *in* the texts, in the texture of scriptural discourse concerning Jesus and the God of Israel." Yeago,

inclusion into the divine identity via his inclusion within the divine life in 24:49 draws upon the resurrection account in which again one sees that, alike the transfiguration account, notions of physicality, identity, presence and worship are changed in view of who Jesus really is.

Luke Timothy Johnson puts together the aspects that unite Jesus' resurrection and his inclusion within the divine life:

> Jesus' appearances are not only appearances of one who has been eschatologically transformed, *but of one who has already been exalted to the right hand of God as Lord and begun his reign, one who sings the eschatological presence of Yahweh himself.* This is highlighted by the way Luke concludes his Gospel . . . Jesus leads his followers out to Bethany where he ascends into heaven . . . It functions to confirm that the narrative's redefinition of both messiah and of Yahweh's δόξα has been divinely given. As the embodied risen Son gradually fades from the narrative spotlight and becomes unfollowable once again, our last images is one of a transformed, yet fleshly embodied, human being ascending into the abode of God using his crucifixion-marked hands to pronounce divine favor on his followers. Such a portrait continues Luke's process of forging in the imagination of his audience a cosmology that breaks the bounds of the popular understanding of the place of human flesh in the cosmos. It uncompromisingly sews together the light, airy, eternal world above with the "crass, heavy, physical/material stuff" of the temporal world below. And in the process, Luke is presenting . . . new and illuminating combinations of forms that are meant to become the new meaningful forms through which the audience understands the identity/deity of the one God of Israel. In fact after the one who now embodies Yahweh's eschatological glory/presence can no longer be followed . . . the disciples quite appropriately "worship" him. This is something that in Luke-Acts, and in first century Judaism as a whole, is typically reserved for God alone.[92]

The starkest contrast between Jesus' divinity and his veiling flesh, however, occurs on the cross. A flayed Jesus hangs on a cross. Paradoxically, though he is exhausted and dying, he can simultaneously promise the thief "Paradise" (Luke 23:43)! The One who can promise and grant entry into Paradise concurrently has his glory veiled by his

---

"The New Testament and the Nicene Dogma," 88; Johnson, "Ripples," 88–89. Italics are Johnson's.

92. Johnson, "Ripples," 103–4.

disfigured humanity.[93] Together with the transfiguration (Luke 9:28–36) and the resurrection (Luke 24), the promise of Paradise to the thief on the cross (Luke 23:43) provides an insight into the complex issue of Jesus' veiled divine identity in key revelatory moments in salvation history. Thus, the claim to isomorphism between God's taxis in the economy of salvation and the immanent taxis (as claimed by the SRR of RR) is challenged by the very veiling nature and role of Jesus' humanity during his earthbound mission.

JESUS' FUTURE REVELATION OF HIS GLORY

In Luke-Acts there are a series of contrasts between Jesus' lowly state and work in the context of his humiliation, and the final revelation of his *eschatological* glory.[94] That there will be a final revelation of God the Son's *eschatological* glory at the time of judgment reinforces the need for hermeneutical caution regarding claims about any knowledge of God's inner life based upon Jesus' earthly life. The temporary state of humiliation in the life of Christ is re-affirmed at the end of Luke's Gospel and in Acts when Jesus is said to enter and return to his glory. For example, in the passage immediately preceding the transfiguration account (Luke 9:18–27), Peter's confession of Jesus' identity (Luke 9:20: Jesus asked "But who do you say that I am?" Peter answered, "The Messiah of God."), is matched by Jesus' own definition of his identity in terms of suffering, rejection, death and resurrection (Luke 9:22: "The Son of Man must undergo great suffering, and be rejected by the elders, chief priests, and scribes, and be killed, and on the third day rise again"). This is immediately contrasted with the eschatological revelation of the glory of the Son of Man and the glory of the Father (Luke 9:26). Further, this kind of glory (also attributed to Jesus in Luke 24:26) is the eschatological presence and glory of Yahweh. This glory of Jesus Christ, into which he has already entered, is a glory which will be more fully realized, and will finally be seen at the time of his return to earth from his position

---

93. Also Luke 24, which includes Jesus within Jewish Monotheism as God. Johnson, "Ripples," 88ff.

94. Smith, "Beloved Son," 79.

of power at the right hand of God (Acts 2:33–34) at the eschaton (Luke 9:26; 21:27).[95]

The book of Acts presents the ascension account in a way that stresses that the identity Jesus has with God is one of shared glory which will be more fully revealed when he returns to restore all things (Acts 1:22; 3:21).[96] This suggests that one cannot search for a theology of God's inner life from the economy of salvation as the SRR of RR does, because the economy of salvation itself is not yet complete. In our view therefore, the SRR of RR is working with an inherently incomplete set of data because it cannot account for the consummation of salvation history.

Jesus' Limited Knowledge of the Actions of God the Father

Prima facie Jesus had limited knowledge, and was not continually omniscient during his earthly ministry. Jesus' development, including the intellectual growth he underwent, is recorded in Luke 2:52: "As Jesus grew up, he increased in wisdom and in favor with God and people." This verse has prevented the imposition of non-scriptural norms about God's being onto the text. Noting this, Nolland observes that: "Traditional theology has stumbled here at what might be taken to undermine the conviction that Jesus was at all times and in all respects utterly without flaw. Luke speaks, rather, out of the conviction that the human maturing process even in perfect form involves not only growth in size but also in development in wisdom and in the capacity to execute that which is pleasing both to God and one's fellows."[97]

Surely we cannot read Jesus' development with reference to God as an activity that has an isomorphic trinitarian corollary within the development of the second person of the Trinity within God's own being. If the SRR of RR were taken with respect to this text, what would the theological result be? What would a development of God the Son with reference to God the Father mean in the immanent taxis as far as the being of God is concerned? What would this suggest for the full divinity of the second person of the Trinity? How could Jesus be really Lord other than in an adoptionist or gradational sense?[98] Nolland's use of the word

---

95. Johnson, "Ripples," 98–99.
96. Cifrak, *Beziehung zwischen*, 73–74.
97. Nolland, *Luke*, 1:132.
98. This question also needs to be raised with respect to many theologies of the procession of the Son from the Father such as Karl Rahner's own gradationist Christology,

"flaw" is unhelpful here, as the focus of the narrative is on limitation and ignorance rather than imperfection or error.

The point is that extra-scriptural norms and theologies, including views of the attributes of God, and the SRR of RR, are resisted by this text.[99] This resistance is consolidated in Luke 8:45–47 which reads as follows: "'Who touched me?' Jesus asked. When they all denied it, Peter said, 'Master, the people are crowding and pressing against you.' But Jesus said, 'Someone touched me; I know that power has gone out from me.' Then the woman, seeing that she could not go unnoticed, came trembling and fell at his feet. In the presence of all the people she told why she had touched him and how she had been instantly healed." This text clearly presents Jesus as limited in knowledge when he is touched by the bleeding woman.[100]

With reference to the incident of Luke 8:45–47, Fitzmyer states that "what is startling is that not even Luke has suppressed the question."[101] The question itself and the material that follows (8:45b–46) point to Jesus' ignorance regarding who had touched him.[102] Erickson rightly comments that "It is difficult to account for the fact that Jesus' knowledge was extraordinary in some matters, but definitely limited in others . . . Perhaps we can say that he had such knowledge as was necessary for him to accomplish his mission; in other matters he was as ignorant as we are."[103]

It is true that Luke's Gospel does not emphasize the limitation of Jesus in terms of his knowledge. One reason is that "[s]eemingly in response to this Christological problem, Luke leaves out all of Mark 13:32."[104] The idea that Luke would leave out details of the narrative due to personal conviction is not surprising, as, for example, he leaves out

---

and adoptionist christologies such as Mcquarrie's. For example, see Helfing, "Reviving Adamic."

99. Erickson, *Theology*, 727. See also Morris, *Lord*, 45–48.

100. There has been great debate on this issue throughout Christian history. For example, the Arians joined the limitation of Jesus' knowledge to other issues such as texts which may be interpreted as teaching that Jesus is a creature (Prov 8:22; Acts 2:36; Heb 3:2), who was changeable (Luke 2:52), and inferior to the Father (John 14:28) who is the only "true God." Walker, "Arianism," 29–30. Erickson, *Theology*, 713.

101. Fitzmyer, *Luke*, 1:746.

102. Stein, *Luke*, 261.

103. Erickson, *Theology*, 726.

104. Marcus, *Mark*, 913.

the Markan note that the woman with the bleeding had suffered much at the hands of doctors. However, despite Luke omitting Jesus' words found in Mark 13:32, what Luke says in Luke 8:45 is in concert with that pericope as it points to Jesus' noetic limitation as a human person. What is said in Mark 13:32 is an unavoidable aspect of the incarnation if it truly is an assumption, a "taking on," of human flesh:

> [t]here has been some preparation for this statement in Jesus' admission to the sons of Zebedee that it is not within his power to decide who will sit at his right or left hand in the kingdom of God (10:40). These sayings are not the kind of material that early Christians would have created on their own, and so they may well represent the authentic voice of Jesus and provide an important perspective on the meaning of the incarnation (see Phil 2:6–11). However, they have also provided ammunition throughout the centuries for those who question Jesus' divinity and equality with God in the Trinity.[105]

That Jesus' limitation is an unavoidable entailment of his real humanity is revealed by His response to the question about the ushering in of God's end-time kingdom. Jesus states that "it is not for you to know the times or periods the Father has set by his own authority" (Acts 1:7). This means that we should include Jesus as a member of humanity in this statement. The theological significance is that "Jesus' ignorance of the day and hour as a necessary part of his participation in the limitations of human existence."[106] Jesus does not explicitly admit his own ignorance of these "times or periods." The point is not that the disciples do not know anything of the times and seasons, rather, it is not their business. However, the implication is that the Father is the one who knows the full extent of these times—not people. There is a contrast is between God and people,[107] and here Jesus, according to the main text from Acts, clearly belongs to the category of "people." Barth captures the significance of the incarnation for Jesus' knowledge: "If the Word became flesh, if God became man, he necessarily existed as a man in a human history, and trod a human way, and on this way had human wants, was subject to human temptations and influences, shared only a

---

105. Donahue, *The Gospel of Mark*, 376.
106. Marcus, *Mark*.
107. Larkin, Briscoe, and Robinson, *Acts*, 40.

relative knowledge and capacity, and learned and suffered and died as a man."[108]

There can be no doubt then that for Luke the humanity of Jesus is a limiting factor on his knowledge of the things of God, as it is for all people.[109] In terms of a contrast between the Father and the Son, the end times are set solely by the Father's authority. The authority of Jesus is not included in this. The limitation experienced by Jesus is proper to one who is bound by space and time because he belongs to the class "humanity," as is clear from Acts 1:7. From this verse, it is clear that "[a]s far as the Son is concerned, only during the days of his humiliation did he restrict himself in the use of this as of the other divine attributes to what was needed in his mediatorial work."[110] Therefore, his knowledge of, and relationship to God the Father in the economy of salvation cannot be taken to be a clear reflection of the relationship of knowledge he shared with God the Father before the incarnation. If this were so, then both Mark 13:32 and Acts 1:7 would be problematic for Christians on a SRR of RR as "the Second Person of Trinity did not know something the First Person was unwilling to share cf. 10:40; Acts 1:7)."[111]

Conclusion

The burden of this chapter has been firstly to uphold the richness of the messianic purpose of Jesus' incarnation and secondly to explain its significance for resisting the SRR of RR. We have demonstrated that Luke clearly presents Jesus' life and work in the salvation-historical context of his messianic "humiliation," and as such Jesus' relationships with the other persons of the Trinity in this setting cannot be read as isomorphic reflections of the eternal relationships (and the nature of these relationships) between the persons of the Trinity. The particular points which have built this argument are that according to Luke-Acts, Jesus' work in the economy of salvation takes place within Jesus' state of humiliation,

---

108. Barth, *CD* 4/2, 95.

109. Peterson, *Acts of the Apostles*, 110.

110. Lenski, *Interpretation*, 30–31.

111. Boring, *Mark,* 376–77. Boring helpfully notes that whereas Mark 13:32 accents the "truly human" side of the Chalcedonian formula, whereas in the previous verse (13:31), Jesus speaks the words of God from Isa 40:7–8, and equates his own with God's emphasize the other aspect of his person, thereby Mark accents "truly God" nature of Jesus.

which is one aspect of the two states of Christ; further, Luke-Acts presents Jesus' work in the economy of salvation as taking a particular messianic shape which determines Jesus' actions, evident particularly in his obedience to God the Father. In addition, Luke-Acts presents Jesus' work in the economy of salvation as taking place under the veiling effect that his humanity has upon his essential glory. Also, given his anticipated eschatological work and revelation, Luke-Acts presents Jesus' work in the economy of salvation as an incomplete revelation of who he is. Lastly, Luke-Acts presents Jesus as limited in regards to his knowledge of the actions of God. This cannot be taken as a representation of an essential aspect of the relationship between the second person of the Trinity and God the Father.

The next two chapters will explore the interpersonal relations between God the Father and God the Son, and God the Son and God the Holy Spirit. These chapters will demonstrate Luke-Acts' resistance to the SRR of RR with respect to the economic relationship between God the Father, and God the Son (chapter 4), and the economic relationship between the Holy Spirit and God the Son (chapter 5).

4

God the Father and God the Son

THE PREVIOUS CHAPTER PROVIDED arguments against the SRR of RR from the Messianic and salvation historical concerns of Luke-Acts. This chapter explores the significant problems for the doctrine of God that stem from the application of the SRR of RR to Luke-Acts. We shall outline cautions from Luke-Acts against a SRR of RR that arise from the nature of the Father-Son relationship in Luke-Acts.

For the sake of this book, the Father-Son relationship in Luke-Acts will take its point of departure from the fact that Jesus is presented as Lord throughout this two-volume account. As C. Kavin Rowe argues: "there is a kind of 'inner rhythm' to Luke's use of *kurios*—a regular occurrence of similar features variously put to use in the service of a coherent meaning . . . *kurios* in Luke's Gospel (and really, Luke-Acts) constitutes something of a *Leitwort* for the Lukan narrative." Rowe then gives an example from chapter one of Luke's Gospel:

> The manner of Jesus' introduction into the story as *kurios* in 1:43 ("the mother of the *kurios*") effects the duality in the referent of the word *kurios*, which then allows the ambiguity of 1:17 ("to prepare for the *kurios*"), 1:76 ("you will go before the *kurios* to prepare his ways"), and 3:4 ("prepare the way of the *kurios*") to emerge narratively with theological force . . . to ask after the identity of the *kurios* is to answer *theos* and *Iesous* . . . within the ambiguity the structure and movement of the story shift the focus from *Christos ho theos*. The narrative itself is the theology:

the coming of the *kurios Christos* is the coming of the *kurios ho theos*.¹

This claim entails that God the Son is as much Lord as the Father is, and that any differentiation between the Father and the Son only ever occurs within the complex, one-ness of the Lord who is strongly internally related.² In referring to Luke-Acts' continuity with the OT assumption that there is one God, Rowe states this internal unity in Lukan categories:

> [T]his assumption [the assumption that only God the Father is YHWH], however, will not stand under exegetical scrutiny. The New Testament texts never identify the Father as the Son or vice-versa, but they do give the divine name *kyrios* (= YHWH) to both the Father and the Son. The word *kyrios* (and less frequently *theos*) and the way in which it is used in the New Testament in Old Testament citations, hymns of worship, prayers, soteriological statements, etc. exerts a unitive pressure in two directions with respect to its referent, toward the Father and toward Jesus. This pressure moves us to the conclusion that YHWH is not the Father alone. There is a differentiation into Father and Son within the unity of the one Lord (*kyrios heis* in Deut 6:4).³

The complexity of the God's inner life as it relates to the SRR of RR will continue to be examined in the next chapter. This present chapter will examine the relationship between God the Father and God the Son, and the following chapter will examine the relationship between God the Son and God the Spirit. These relationships will be outlined in a manner which pinpoints the narratival logic and theology within

---

1. Rowe, *Narrative Christology*, 199–200. (Italics are Rowe's, transliteration is mine).

2. Yandell states this complexity as follows: "Each part of a necessarily internally connected being is such that its existence is a necessary condition of the existence of each other part of that being. Given these definitions we can see how to define the notion that I have been building toward, namely that of an *ultimate individual composed only of essential parts which are necessarily internally connected*. Here is the definition: '. . . X is an *ultimate composite necessarily internally connected individual composed only of essential parts* if and only if X exists. X is an individual, X is ultimate and composite, X has no part that is not essential, each part of X is necessarily internally connected to every other part of X, and neither X nor any part of X depends for its existence on anything other than X to the parts of X.' A trinitarian deity is an ultimate composite necessarily internally connected individual composed only of essential parts." Yandell, "Most Brutal," 204–5. (Italics are Yandell's).

3. Rowe, "Biblical Pressure," 303.

Luke-Acts which resists the logic of a SRR of RR, and furthermore, the problematic conclusions for the doctrine of God that flow from a SRR of RR based on the narrative of Luke-Acts.

In this chapter we shall attempt to show that the narrative of Luke-Acts implicitly resists the logic of the SRR of RR when this norm is applied to the text for the following reasons. *In our view, it may be possible to conclude from the application of the SRR of RR Luke's work that God the Father is subordinate to God the Son's will in at least one instance.* Though this is not a universally held view, *it* may mean there is evidence of a reversed subordination between the Father and the Son's wills in Luke's Gospel. Also, the ascension of Jesus resists any theology whereby the sending of Jesus the Son into the economy of salvation is taken to be a reflection of the begetting of the Son in the trinitarian taxis. Another issue is that the loose appropriation of God's *ad extra* revelation of the Father in the Son reflects a fluidity or interchangeability of actor and action (which indicates profound unity) in the narrative which resists the SRR of RR. In addition, the loose appropriation of soteriological works in Luke-Acts between God the Father and God the Son also reflects a fluidity of actor and action that resists the SRR of RR. Furthermore, the book of Acts presents a profound continuity between the persons of God the Father and God the Son that resists the SRR of RR. A broader point is that the fluidity of actor and action between God the Father and the Son, which disallows the strict appropriation of divine actions and relations as the norm for immanent trinitarian relationships, is not unique to Luke-Acts.

The Subordination of God the Father to God the Son's Will

In Luke 10:22, Jesus is emphatically presented as the sole person who reveals the Father. In the role of revealer, Darrell L. Bock contends: "the persons of the Son and the Father literally 'switch' roles, to the extent that 'the Son functions like the Father.' He grounds this in the text as follows: 'Knowledge of the Father is left in the hands of the Son and is given to whomever the Son wished to give it. The Father and the Son have switched roles from the description of 10:21.'"[4] Significantly, there is no corresponding declaration that runs the other way: "and the one to

---

4. Bock, *Luke*, 2:1012. Cf. Luke 22:29–34; 23:42–43.

whom the Father chooses to reveal him."[5] This has important implications for trinitarian theology in terms of the Father-Son relationship in the economy of salvation.[6] If the SRR of RR is applied to this situation, and this relational pattern is read as isomorphic with respect to God's inner life, then the conclusion follows that there is a succession of subordinations between God the Father and God the Son within God's own life: the Son's will is first subordinate to the Father, then the Father's will is subordinate to the Son.

The application of the SRR of RR would also detract from the focus of this passage. This passage is not about the nature of the subordinations or power-relationships within God. Instead, the revelation of the relationship between Jesus and his Father means firstly, that: "the revelation itself is bound up with a particular human life, that of Jesus. It implies, second, that the revelation is therefore fundamentally historical and narratable, because human life . . . is 'entangled' in (hi)stories. The revelation of the Father through the Son in this way comes together at the point of the narrative, in which the narration of the life of Jesus is an apocalyptic . . . [narrative] of the life of God."[7] If this yields a contradictory theology, then both the norm that lead to it and its entailments are logically problematical.

Luke's point in 10:22 is distinctive to his gospel within the Synoptics, and therefore cannot be glossed over. According to Smith, it is a stark contrast to the Markan Jesus who is not presented as claiming to be God himself, but is only ever presented as the One who serves, and defers to, God's authority:

> The Markan Jesus does not [in my view directly] claim to be God, but only the authoritative representative of God . . . Explicitly related to this idea of the eschatological authority [Mark 10:28–31;

---

5. Rowe, *Narrative Christology*, 141.

6. A proponent of the SRR of RR, or another strict realist view, might counter that the accent falls on the Father handing over the authority to the Son (Luke 10:22a). This is certainly arguable but less convincing when placed in the overall argument of Luke-Acts. We shall shortly consider one such proponent of the opposing view, that of Légasse. Ware also provides an opposing view. He deals with the analogous passage from Matthew 11:25–27. Ware employs this passage to argue that Jesus acknowledges that the Father is supreme over all other persons of the Trinity. This is arguable but it is less persuasive given the considerations brought forward in chs 4–6. See Ware, *Father, Son and Holy Spirit*, 46–48.

7. Rowe, *Narrative Christology*, 141.

13:9–13], are the words Jesus speaks to James and John in response for seats on his right and left when Jesus comes in glory (10:35–45). Jesus makes no claim to having authority to grant them what they want . . . he again points to God as the sole authority who has prepared . . . these seats, and as the one who has authority to give these seats.[8]

However, this is not the case in Luke, as in fact the author of Luke 10:22 has made an even stronger point about who Jesus is. This is striking given how the author of Luke-Acts is at pains to demonstrate that people are never to be confused for God.[9] An example is in Acts 14:8–15, especially verse 15. As the priest of Zeus and the crowd come forward to offer sacrifices to Barnabas and Paul as Zeus and Hermes respectively (vv. 12–14), Barnabas and Paul shout "Friends, why are you doing this? We are mortals just like you, and we bring good news, that you should turn from these worthless things to the living God, who made heaven and the earth and the sea and all that is in them."

In John's gospel we find a theology which is in line with the theology of Luke 10:22. Based upon John 5:23; 14:8–11; 17:2, 6, and Matt 11:27 par; Mark 1:22 par; 11:27 par; and Luke 10:22, Jenson draws together the theological coherence of the Johnanine and synoptic tradition in terms of the Father's role being handed over to the Son. He writes:

> Of the Father it is said that the Father has turned over the role of God to the Son. To be related to God we are therefore directed *not* to the Father but to the Son. . . . John but provides formulas for what the Synoptics too depict. The saying, 'All things have been handed over to me by my Father,' states the ground of the single greatest impact of Jesus' teaching and action as told by the Synoptic Gospels: that he had unique and underived—indeed underivable—authority, the kind of authority that could only belong to the one God.[10]

Luke 10:22 directs us to the exegetical conclusion that in the economy of salvation God the Father is served by God the Son to the extent that God the Father is dependent upon (and thus subordinate in terms of action) to God the Son *in the economy of salvation*, in at least this one instance. In this passage, the authority in decision-making as to who

---

8. Smith, "Beloved Son," 79.
9. Kezbere, *Umstrittener Monotheismus*.
10. Jenson, *Systematic Theology*, 1:109.

relates to God the Father lies in the hands of God the Son. Thus, we may say that in this instance, God the Father is dependent upon the will of God the Son. God the Son is the gatekeeper of the knowledge of God the Father. Within the sweep of Luke-Acts, this dependence of God the Father to God the Son should not be taken as a mark of inferiority of God the Father as it occurs in the economy of salvation.[11] However, if the SRR of RR is taken, then the conclusion is that in this instance there is an executive superiority of God the Son over God the Father.

Due to the implications of applying the SRR of RR to Luke 10:22, scholars such as Légasse have tried to argue a counter-case so that the Father could not be subordinate to God the Son: "the quality of the reciprocity they share is perfect" and "the greatness which the Father and the Son share is a greatness of the same order. They are fully equal."[12] However, the response to the passage itself is quite telling. He has to make Arian-like arguments in order to substantiate his position. For example, in order to mount his ultimate argument that the Father and Son do not have the same greatness and reciprocity due to the superiority of the Father over the Son, he appeals to the nature of Jesus' humanity and to the fact that there is a subordination of Jesus to God the Father throughout the NT which follows the OT pattern of sons being subordinate to their fathers.[13] This rebuttal does not provide a sufficient theological account of Christ nor is it exegetically strong. For the author of Luke, the unity of the life of the Father and the Son extends to allowing the Father to be the recipient of the Son's will at least once in the economy of salvation. Légasse's case is further weakened by the fact that Jesus and God the Father are later shown to have distinct yet aligned wills (Luke 24:46–49), and that the presentation of Jesus as Lord in Acts

11. When the relations between persons of the Trinity in Luke-Acts are read with a LRR of RR, the result is more satisfactory. In the light of this trinitarian norm, the result is that the persons of the Trinity are simultaneously distinct in their service of one another in the economy of salvation whilst also all sharing to different degrees in all the works and revelation they accomplish in the one mission of the one God. This is captured in the use of the unifying names used for God in Luke-Acts (*kyrios*), and in Matt 28:19 "the name of the Father, and of the Son and of the Holy Spirit," which are clarified by Jesus' language in John ("one . . . us" John 17:21).

12. My own translation from the French, which reads: "la connaissance réciproque que ce texte exprime entraînerait une déduction capitale: «réciprocité absolute et parfaite», donc «Pére et Fils sont des grandeurs du même ordre, Ils sont mis sur pied d'égalité» cited in Légasse, "Logion," 261.

13. Légasse, "Logion," 261–62.

1:21 demonstrates, according to Cifrak, that Jesus continually "works as God the Father does."[14]

In sum, the exegetical conclusion is that God the Father is subordinate to the will of God the Son in Luke 10:22. This is a challenge for the SRR of RR. If the SRR of RR is applied to Luke's Gospel, the theological conclusion would be that there is a reversed subordination in the inner-divine taxis between the Father and the Son. Whereas in much of the Gospel of Luke the Father is portrayed as the person of the Trinity whose will determines the mission and actions of the Son as his Messiah, in this instance these roles are reversed. Rowe notes that the Son as the sole revealer of the Father in Luke 10:21–22 is an instance of the non-reciprocal relationship between the Father and the Son, which is also witnessed in the "distinction between the *kyrios* Messiah and the κύριος God, where the former is sent by the latter, prays to the latter, and, ultimately, is dependent upon the latter for the continuity of his identify as *kyrios* through crucifixion and death . . . (Acts 2:36)."[15]

The role reversal entailed in applying the SRR of RR to Luke 10:21–22 simply cannot be taken to be an isomorphic reflection of the inner taxis of God. If the SRR of RR is right then what is the eternal analogue of the Son's role? Is this Son the gatekeeper of the Spirit's knowledge of the Father? If so, what do we make of 1 Cor 2:10–16? In this passage, the Spirit's role within God and with reference to knowledge is spoken of as follows: "These things God has revealed to us through the Spirit; for the Spirit searches everything, even the depths of God. For what human being knows what is truly human except the human spirit that is within? So also no one comprehends what is truly God's except the Spirit of God. Now we have received not the spirit of the world, but the Spirit that is from God, so that we may understand the gifts bestowed on us."

The proposition that the Father is subordinate to the will of the Son poses multiple problems for the SRR of RR. These include the following: How to hold this result in coherent tension with the other exegetical conclusions stemming from the application of the SRR of RR in terms of the Father-Son relation. The issue is that its exegetical conclusion requires that it be taken complementarily with the other results of the SRR of RR in terms of the Father and Son: that the Father is the "Lord"

14. "Jesus im Himmel ist kúpios (Apg. 1,21) und wirkt so wie Gott, sein Vater, wirkt." Cifrak, *Beziehung zwischen*, 74. (My own translation).

15. Rowe, *Narrative Christology*, 142.

over Jesus as Messiah. Thus, we have a situation that may be described as 'subsequent subordinations' of the Father and the Son. Further, this subsequent subordination clashes with the static and unidirectional nature and order of relations within God. This is both the assumption and conclusion at play in both Rahner's own use of his *Grundaxiom*, and of those who employ the SRR of RR or the SRRT[16] (who are doing something like Rahner). Furthermore, there is a focus on the immanent life of God that is foreign to the text.

In view of these issues, we can say that given the apparent relational and epistemic dependence of God the Father to God the Son in the economy of salvation and what this means for God's immanent taxis according to the SRR of RR, the coherence and theology stemming from the SRR of RR faces a large obstacle. In essence the problem with Rahner's norm and its strict realist reading is that it seeks a simplistic (not to be confused with "simple") level of clarity that the Scriptural narrative does not allow. A more robustly biblical solution, which Evangelicals in particular should pursue, is one whereby theological construction is attentive to the narrative of Scripture: "This is sometimes the way of theology: to take a plain phenomenon of the gospel's narrative that causes difficulty in certain conceptual connections and remove the difficulties by adjusting not the narrative *but the connections*."[17] If the theological connections made by the SRR of RR cannot do justice to the narrative of Luke-Acts, a reading such as the LRR of RR may be a better approach to, and reflection of, the narrative of Scripture in general and Luke-Acts in particular. However, to explore this idea further would require a separate work.

THE ASCENSION AND ITS ETERNAL ANALOGUE

The ascension of Jesus has many narratival and theological functions within Luke-Acts. These include (but are not limited to) Jesus giving a blessing to his disciples following the OT pattern of blessing (Luke 24:50), his share in God's glory as the completion of the resurrection

---

16. In a nutshell, the SRRT literalistic literary hermeneutic which can be described as closely approximating the SRR of RR, but is better described as a SRRT even though Ware appears to deploy the SRRT selectively. This aspect of Bruce Ware's theology will be dealt with in a follow up work.

17. Jenson, *Systematic theology*: 124.

event,[18] and the fulfillment of the covenantal, Davidic and Messianic and world-blessing hopes of Israel. Other aspects of the ascension in Luke-Acts include Jesus entering into fuller power and authority (Acts 2:33), and the possibility of Jesus' worldwide presence and mission empowerment through the donation of his Spirit (Acts 1:9–10; 2:33). In tandem with this gift of the Spirit, perhaps the most significant aspect of the ascension is that it is the grounds for the confession that Jesus is Lord and Christ (Acts 2:36), the one who can now convey forgiveness of sin (Acts 2:38).[19] Ostensibly none of these has anything to do with the inner-trinitarian taxis. So, why apply the SRR of RR to such a passage?

It would be a grave mistake to employ the return of Jesus to his Father in heaven as a basis for speaking about the nature of the immanent relations within God. However, if the SRR of RR is to be applied evenly across the biblical text whenever there are references to relationships between persons of the Trinity, the ascension of Jesus would be included in this group. Yet, applying such a reading of Rahner's norm would prove to be problematic for the doctrine of God. It would entail a theology whereby in the immanent Trinity there is a return of Jesus to God the Father. This would raise questions beyond scriptural and Chalcedonian boundaries.

If the SRR of RR is not applied to the ascension of Jesus to his Father in heaven, then why is the sending of the second person of the Trinity into the economy of salvation, as read through the lens of the SRR of RR, employed as the ground for theologies which attempt to establish the relation of origin within the Trinity? Weinandy proposes that the conception of the Son in Mary's womb has an eternal analogue of the begetting of the Son by the Spirit in the immanent Trinity. For Weinandy, Luke 1:35 is the clearest insight into the trinitarian inner life with reference to the Son and the Spirit. His exegesis and conclusion follow his comment on Matthew's infancy narrative: "from Matthew's Infancy Narrative . . . at least we can discern a nascent trinitarian pattern. Jesus was conceived of the Holy Spirit, and Yahweh (the Father) was instrumental in his conception to the extent that he sanctioned it in his confirmation to Joseph . . . Luke's account of the conception of Jesus illustrates this trinitarian paradigm more clearly."[20] For Weinandy, Luke's

18. Scobie, *Ways*, 455.
19. Beale and Carson, *New Testament Use*, 527–44.
20. Weinandy, *Father's spirit*, 40–1.

presentation of the virginal conception draws upon a biblical theology of the temple and the presence of the Spirit such that a very particular pneumatological "descriptive picture" is drawn:

> the power of the Most High . . . the Holy Spirit of Yahweh (the Father) will overshadow Mary . . . an allusion to Exodus 40:34–35 where the glory of the Lord . . . filled the tabernacle in the form of a cloud. The descriptive picture discloses why Jesus will be called the Son of God. Firstly, because he is conceived by the Holy Spirit, he possesses the very holiness of God and therefore is God. Secondly, Mary, as the new ark or tabernacle, bears within her the very presence and glory of God . . . The depiction of the Father begetting his Son in the womb of Mary by the Holy Spirit becomes, I believe, a temporal icon of his eternally begetting the Son by the Spirit.[21]

For Weinandy, the immanent begetting of the Son in the Spirit has three economic parallels:

> Firstly, as the Son is sent forth from the Father into the world by the power of the Holy Spirit, so the Son is eternally begotten of the Father in the Holy Spirit. Secondly, as the Son is conceived in the womb of Mary by the power of the Holy Spirit, and so conforms the Son to be Son now as man, so the Holy Spirit conforms the Son to be the eternal Son of the Father within the immanent Trinity. Thirdly, as the economic "sending" of the Son, effected by the power of the Spirit, a mission for the forgiveness of sins, makes the Father *our* Father, so similarly, within the immanent Trinity, the Spirit by which the Father begets the Son is the same Spirit by which he himself becomes the Father of the Son.[22]

Weinandy also wrote that "The Father spirates the Spirit in the same act by which he begets the Son, for the Spirit proceeds from the Father as the fatherly Love in whom or by whom the Son is begotten."[23] For Weinandy, this proposal allows for the Spirit's role in constituting the relationships and identities of who the divine persons are:

> Because each of the persons now actively plays a role in determining the subjectivity of the others, they complement one another. The Father is Father not only in opposition to the Son and the

---

21. Ibid., 41–42.
22. Ibid., 42. (Italics are Wienandy's).
23. Ibid., 69.

> Son is Son not only in opposition to the Father, but they also, in their relatedness, complement one another as being, respectively, Father for the Son and Son for the Father. This complementarity of the persons as subsistent relations is due again to the Holy Spirit . . . The Trinity of persons then subsists in opposition to one another only as complimentary relations.[24]

Be this as it may, the point is that if one is to take the economy of salvation as the basis for trinitarian relations, then a number of questions arise. These include: Why is an act of God's will (the sending of the Spirit into the economy of salvation) taken to be a strict reflection of inner-trinitarian relationships? For the sake of theological consistency, if one is going to employ the SRR of RR in that instance then one must apply the SRR of RR to all trinitarian relations in the economy of salvation. The problem is that this consistency comes at the price of theological coherence. The ascension of Jesus suggests that the SRR of RR cannot be applied to Luke-Acts without being resisted by the surface message of the narrative, and also yielding very problematic results for the doctrine of God.

The problem created by attempting to apply the SRR of RR to the ascension raises the issue of the economy of salvation as a basis for establishing a theology of inner-trinitarian origins aside from direct biblical teaching on this matter.[25]

THE "LOOSE" APPROPRIATION OF GOD'S AD EXTRA REVELATION

The author of Luke-Acts is greatly concerned with the identification of who God truly is. That Jesus is true God is identified in Luke 3:21ff; 9:28–36; 24:50–53 and Acts 1:9–11. He is identified in the face of multiple pretenders who engage in various forms of "false apotheosis"— Luke 4:5–8; Acts 10:25 ff; Acts 12:21–23; Acts 14:8–20; Acts 16:25–34; Acts 28:1–6.[26] In each passage listed above, there is a false pretender,

---

24. Ibid., 97–98.

25. The history of the *Filioque* debate should also cause us to pause before attempting to construct theologies about relations of origin within the Trinity from the text of the Bible without making the distinctions between "'dogmas,' 'theologoumena,' and 'theological opinion.'" Baker cites Bolotov's work on this point. Baker, "Eternal 'Spirit of the Son,'" 395.

26. Kezbere, *Umstrittener Monotheismus*.

or one who is mistakenly understood to stand in the place and receive the honour that is due to God alone. These varied figures are the Devil, Peter, Herod, Barnabas, and Paul, and then Paul alone respectively. None of these figures deserves to be worshipped as God, only Jesus does. Yet, even though the identification of God in Jesus is a concern from a formal point of view, the material identification of the structure of relations within God is not as clear as proponents of the SRR of RR would assert.

This lack of a focus on the taxis within God is especially true in the book of Acts. Bibb writes: "There is a clearer distinction between God, portrayed as Father, and Jesus in Luke than in Acts . . . it is easier to determine the meaning of *theo*-logical titles, such as κύριος in the gospel [of Luke] than in Acts. This may be attributed to sources for the gospel tradition as well as less clearly defined roles and actions related to the narrative after Pentecost."[27] There is a looseness and a lack of determined patterns of relations amongst the persons within God in Acts. Schweizer contends that Luke the author of Acts: "is very reluctant to give us any clear christological statements or titles. Neither are there definite patterns of God's nature or of his role in history. Luke certainly says that God can use and does use history to manifest himself, but there are no rules that we could handle to detect his acts or even predict them. Nor is there a definitive pneumatology in Luke. How confusing are the reports in Acts!"[28] He is not alone is his assessment. Rowe, who builds upon Conzelmann's work, agrees with Schweizer's conclusion, and provides a clear explanation for this phenomenon. He writes: "in Acts the fully ambiguous uses of κύριος increase significantly, as Jesus has now been exalted to the right hand of the Father. From the perspective of the Christian community . . . Jesus' 'location' in heaven tightens, as it were, the *Verbindung* between God and Christ in their acting as κύριος, for the work of the Father and the Son from earth appears undifferentiated."[29] This in-differentiation may be applied to both God's work of revelation and salvific action.

---

27. Bibb, "Characterization," 300–301.

28. Cited in ibid.

29. Rowe, *Narrative Christology*: 201. (Italics are Rowe's). Rowe translates Conzelmann as: "From the point of view of the community . . . the work of Jesus seems completely identical with that of the Father, therefore both can be designated as 'lord' and can be represented as the instigator of the saving events which the community experiences." Conzelmann, *Mitte der Zeit*, 184.

This argument does not entail modalism, rather, narratival sensitivity. The shared identity between Jesus and the God of Israel "in no way approaches a *Vermischung*, as Luke 2:11 and the use of Ps 110:1 in Luke 20:41–44 make particularly clear: *theos* and *Iesous* are never *vermischt*. Luke is not . . . an early modalist."[30] Instead, "the sense is that if a narrative *Verbindung*, a coherent pattern of characterization that binds God and Jesus together through the word κύριος such that they finally cannot be separated or abstracted from one another in the story."[31]

Returning to Schweizer's conclusion we note that according to Luke-Acts, there are "no rules that we could handle to detect his acts or even predict" God's self manifestation in terms of both nature and role. Thus, for Schweizer, and we agree with him on this point, the Lukan understanding of the self-presentation of God is one that resists the SRR of RR as the nature of inner trinitarian relations is somewhat opaque in Luke-Acts.

An example of the fluidity found in trinitarian relationships in Luke-Acts is that the persons of the Father and the Son loosely appropriate the revelation of themselves. That is, the Father does not clearly reveal himself aside from revealing the Son, nor does the Son clearly reveal himself aside from revealing the Father and likewise with the Holy Spirit. Therefore, it is difficult to answer the question: what does the Son's revelation in the economy of salvation reveal about the Son as a trinitarian person both *per se* and *in se*? In what follows we take the example of the Son revealing the Father as a demonstration of the fact that persons of the Trinity are not self-revealing in the strict sense. God the Son's own self is not revealed in his revelation, rather the Father's is. Therefore, theological conclusions about how the Son relates to the Father and the Spirit from his *ad extra* works of revelation seem difficult to substantiate.

Some trinitarian theologians who employ theologies with very close affinities to the SRR of RR argue that the revelation of the Son includes revealing the nature of his eternal relation to God the Father. For example, evangelical theologian Bruce Ware claims that "One must come to terms with the fact that God specifically revealed himself to us with the names 'Father' and 'Son' for the first and second persons of the Trinity. Certainly these names carry the connotations of authority and

---

30. Rowe, *Narrative Christology*, 201. (Italics are Rowe's).
31. Ibid., 201. (Italics are Rowe's, transliteration is mine).

submission, as is confirmed by the Son's uniform declaration that he, the Son, sought only to do the will of the Father . . . God's self-revelation . . . indicates[s] an identity of the Persons of Father and Son which also marks their respective roles."[32]

However, once again, Luke 10:22 provides a challenging case in point. In this pericope "Knowledge of the Father is left in the hands of the Son and is given to whomever the Son wished to give it. *The Father and the Son have switched roles from the description of 10:21* . . . This indeed is a strong description of the Son's central, mediatorial work in salvation. *He functions like the Father.*"[33] The Son may indeed reveal the Father, but this does not tell us much about the Son himself, other than that he reveals the Father.

Torrance, drawing upon Athanasius, recognized the same phenomena with regards to the Spirit's revelation of the Son. The Spirit does not reveal himself, he reveals the Son instead. Therefore, the Spirit's revelation cannot be taken to be a strict revelation of himself, including his relationships to the Father and the Son. Torrance states:

> Athanasius says, "It is natural that I should have spoken and written first about the Son of God that from our knowledge of the Son we may be able to have proper knowledge of the Spirit" (*Ad. Ser.* 3.1) . . . this is the only proper procedure because of the propriety of the Spirit to the Son, and because it is only in and through the Son or Word that God has revealed himself. The Spirit does not utter himself but the Word and is known only as he enlightens us to understand the Word . . . it is only *in the Spirit* that we may know the Son . . . It is from the Son that the Spirit *shines forth* (*eklampei, Ad. Ser.* 1:18), and *in the Spirit* (*en Pneumati*) that God is known.[34]

---

32. Ware, *Father*, 83.

33. Italics added. D. L. Bock, *Luke*, 2:1012. Note the parallel between Luke 10:21–22 and Matt 28:18–9: the authority of Jesus is highlighted in tandem with the identity of God being revealed in terms of mutually constituting relations.

34. Torrance, *Theology in Reconstruction*: 214–15.

THE "LOOSE" APPROPRIATION OF GOD'S SOTERIOLOGICAL WORKS

A related issue to those discussed above is the "over-individuation" of the persons of the Trinity which may result from the use of the SRR of RR. An example of this is Ware's treatment of God the Father.[35] If the divine relations are compartmentalized as a result of the SRR of RR then an "over-individuation" of the relations and works of any person of the Trinity occurs. This comes at too great a cost to Christian theology as it ultimately ignores the immanent oneness of God within which the person-constituting relations of the Father, Son, and Spirit occur.[36]

The narrative of Luke-Acts presents a fluidity of actor and action (and hence their unity) that is reflected in a looseness of the appropriation of some of God's soteriological work, such as the divine role and authority to receive a person into heaven. In Acts 7:59–60, shortly before dying, Stephen calls out: "Lord Jesus, receive my spirit." This parallels Luke 23:46, when on the cross, Jesus cries out "Father, into your hands I commit my spirit." Stephen could do this because he believed that it was equally fitting for Jesus to receive his spirit as it was for God the Father. This is an example of a looseness of appropriation of this particular role that the Son and the Father played in the economy of salvation. This looseness of appropriation is established by the fact that Jesus is presented as Lord in this same passage.[37] Further, this role equality between Jesus and his Father is extended to the forgiveness of sins. Stephen calls out to Jesus: "Lord, do not hold this sin against them" (Acts 7:60), which directly parallels Jesus' own call to God the Father (Luke 23:34). This is noteworthy because according to Jesus himself, forgiveness of sin is a work of God alone (Luke 5:21).

The cooperative work of God the Father and God the Son also poses problems for the SRR of RR. There is a dependent mutuality between

---

35. Ware, *Father*.

36. For example, we note how little material attention is given to the unity of God in Bruce Ware's works on the Trinity. Each person of the Trinity is treated discretely and the extent of their particular characteristics (as Ware understands them) is taken to the most extreme degree of differentiation. The accent lies on the individuation of the person of the Trinity, not the unity of God. In *Father*, each person of the Trinity receives a separate chapter whereas the unity of God, his will and his works can only be gleaned via occasional references throughout the work.

37. This is also reflected in John 10:30, and is reflected in the Nicene *homoousion*. See also Pelikan, *Acts*, 107.

the persons of the Trinity in the economy of salvation with reference to the sending of the Holy Spirit. Luke 24:49 records Jesus' words that: "I myself am going to send the promise of my Father upon you. Stay in the city until you are clothed with power from on high." In this situation, the Son is more than the instrument of the Father. The Son himself will send the Spirit. Thus, the Father's promise is given over to the Son, and the Spirit is dependent upon being sent by the Son and being promised by the Father.[38] This demonstrates a mutuality of trinitarian relations and shared work in the economy of salvation, which if read with a SRR of RR would mean that within the Godhead, the Spirit would be transferred from the Father to the Son in some sense before being given to believers. Luke's terminology also presents a fluidity of actor and action, as reflected in a looseness of the appropriation of God's soteriological works shared between God the Father and God the Son. For example, the term "Father" is not used in the narrative after Acts 2:33, whereas the term "God" is used for the agent of salvation.[39] Furthermore, the Father-Son language is not appealed to in any significant way by the witnesses to God's work in Jesus.

The above two points are brought together in Stephen's speech in Acts 7, which is a "witness to Jesus by retelling the scriptural story from the point of view of Jesus at God's right hand. Telling the story from this point of view leaves God as the central character. The first agent and prime subject of this story is not Israel, but 'the glory of God (7:2).'"[40] That is, the focus of the story is God, and though Jesus is integral to this story, neither the inner life of God nor the Father-Son relation is significant. This is made clear by the fact that "In the first six verse of the speech, 'God is the subject of every main verb' except one, and 'without these verbs the story has no movement,'[41] and yet there is no mention of his taxis at all. This is reinforced by the fact that it is at the point when Stephen "includes Jesus in God's glory (and thus, in God's very identity)" that his speech becomes unbearably blasphemous and offensive to (Acts 7:55).[42] Thus, we have the employment of God, and Jesus as Lord, as the markers of the divine *identity* in this

---

38. Johnson, "Ripples," 107.
39. Mowery, " Disappearance."
40. Laytham, "Stephen's," 3.
41. Kilgallen, *Stephen Speech* cited in Laytham, "Stephen's," 3.
42. Laytham, "Stephen's," 12.

key speech in Luke-Acts, without reference to Father-Son language in order to explicate God's *inner nature*. Therefore, we can say that Luke-Acts upholds God's identity yet does not highlight God's inner nature in terms of inter-personal relations.

A PROFOUND CONTINUITY BETWEEN GOD THE FATHER AND GOD THE SON

The identity of God is radicalized in Luke-Acts, in terms of the way we see into the root of the divine identity—albeit opaquely. Rowe states this in Lucan terms:

> Luke does not think that the Father and the Son are the same person or character, but he sees in the very relation that constitutes who they are—their identity—a profound continuity that extends through the word *kurios* to the Father and the Son. In the Lukan Gospel, the God of Israel and Jesus are so joined in the narrative that to speak of *ho kurios* is to speak of *ho theos* and *Christos*, of *patēr* and *huios*.[43]

In the book of Acts the mission of the new people of God is tied to a new understanding of the economy of salvation in view of the inclusion of Jesus and the Spirit within the identity of God. If God the Son were viewed as subordinate to God the Father in any way which called into question his identity within God, then the gospel and the mission *about him* as "Lord and Messiah/Savoir" (Luke 2:11; Acts 2:36) are in conflict with OT faith. A subordinate Jesus would also be in conflict with Jesus' own claims and those about his divinity in the broader New Testament. In chapters 1 and 2 of Acts we noted an emphasis on the unity of the work of the Trinity, yet there is an appropriation of divine works to each person of the Godhead. In these chapters we noted the way in which the identity of Jesus is placed at the centre of God's trinitarian being as he is clarified as the "Lord" (Acts 1:24; 2:25), raised by God (2:24, 32), prophesied by the Spirit (1:16), who in turn dispenses the Father's gift of the Spirit (2:33), and is therefore God's "Lord and Messiah" (2:36). The deepened understanding of who God is does not compromise God's unity at all. Pervo draws together the facts of the triune identity, and the

---

43. Rowe, *Narrative Christology*, 201.

narrative and missional focus of Luke-Acts as reflected in 2:32–36 as follows:

> Verses 32–36 show the development of the Christian creed. Resurrection, exaltation/ascension, session at God's right hand, and the gift of the Spirit are distinct theologoumena, sequential events in Luke's thought . . . but not without some integration. The fundamental assumption is that Jesus had to be exalted . . . as the ground for bestowal of the Spirit. For Acts, Jesus is the source of the Spirit received by believers. The Father had promised the Spirit to him. The result of this is the phenomenon seen and heard by the audience, thus cementing the claim of vv. 16–21 [the fulfillment of Joel's prophesy].[44]

That this identification occurs in the context of describing God's missional phenomena and its implications for the whole world is no surprise as the purpose of Acts is not trinitarian but missiological (Acts 1:8). Thus, to read these missiological statements about trinitarian relationships in order to glean references to God's inner life oversteps the bounds of the text. In fact, Acts 1–2 is an example of a narratival section that could be misread as subordinationist or adoptionist if a norm akin to the SRR of RR were employed to make ontological statements from Jesus' ascension movement from below to above. This mistaken theology would undermine the central proclamation that Jesus is Lord.

An issue raised by this section, which has great relevance to the doctrine of the Trinity, is how to derive doctrine from narrative. On this, Pervo writes: "One of the important contributions of literary analyses of Luke-Acts has been to indicate that the author communicates theological views by showing rather than telling, through story rather than through exposition."[45] It would appear that the SRR of RR inadequately addresses the narratival nature of much of Scripture. Hence it seems that the SRR of RR must follow a simplistic trajectory—from the economy of salvation univocally into the being of God. Scripture arguably follows a different logic.

---

44. Pervo and Attridge, *Acts*, 83.
45. Ibid., 43.

CONCLUSION

This chapter has brought the witness of Luke-Acts to bear on the viability of a "strict realist" reading of Rahner's Rule with respect to the relations of God the Father and God the Son. As a result, we found that the SRR of RR fails because of the theological issues that would ensue from its use. These issues include the following: *if the SRR of RR is applied to Luke's Gospel, God the Father is subordinate to the Son's will in at least one instance. What eternal analogue answers to this? We also saw that attempting to find an eternal analogue for the nativity account is unconvincing. Such attempts raise the question as to why the ascension story should not be treated similarly given a SRR of RR.* In addition, the SRR of RR is resisted by Luke-Acts' presentaion of a "loose," rather than the "strict," appropriation of God's *ad extra* revelation of the Father in the Son. The "loose," rather than the "strict" appropriation of soteriological works between God the Father and God the Son also resists the SRR of RR. Finally, the book of Acts presents a profound interchangeability of some actions between the persons of God the Father and God the Son, which also resists the SRR of RR.

5

God the Son and God the Spirit

IN THIS CHAPTER WE will explore the economic relations between God the Holy Spirit and God the Son in Luke-Acts. We will do so with a view to the significance of these relations for a SRR of RR. This chapter will seek to outline exegetical conclusions about this relationship, and the theologies that would follow if the SRR of RR was employed to project salvation-historical conclusions onto God's inner life. That is, we will raise the question of whether or not the witness of Scripture challenges the theological viability of the SRR of RR. The exegetical work undertaken in this chapter will raise issues, some of which other writers have recognized, and some which are new. The work of a recent Evangelical writer, who recognizes the challenge to the SRR of RR based on the successive reversed subordinations of the Son and the Spirit to one another in the economy of salvation, will also be considered before overall conclusions are drawn.

THE SPIRIT AS THE ETERNAL GENERATOR OF THE SON?

The Holy Spirit Plays a Significant Role in the Conception of the Person of Jesus Christ

For Second Temple Jews, the Temple was the specific location of, and expression of, God's desire to be Immanuel—God with his people. The language of God's specific presence amongst his people in the Temple, which anticipates an incarnation, is on the lips of Gabriel at the annunciation to Mary: God will "overshadow you" (Luke 1:35). This language of overshadowing "is used of God's presence resting on the Tabernacle in the cloud (Exod 40:35)."[1] The special presence of God's Spirit in generating the person of Jesus is captured in Luke 1:35a ("The Holy Spirit will come upon you . . ."). This instrumental language makes it clear that Jesus is conceived by the Holy Spirit.[2] In the incarnation, the Jewish understanding of God dwelling in the midst of his people via his Spirit-presence, takes the form of God dwelling in the midst of his people via the Spirit conceived Son. The link here between Christology and pneumatology is such that in the incarnation, a descent of the Spirit takes place alongside the descent of the second person of the Trinity.[3] The joyful outcome is that Jesus comes "promising future decisive personal action to save Israel and the world."[4] Drawing upon a Temple view of God's presence within Mary, we can say that she will become pregnant because of God, *and with*, the special presence in the world in human form.

Jesus is conceived by the Spirit, and as such owes his entry into the world of humankind to the Holy Spirit as well as to Mary.[5] Because of the overshadowing of the Spirit, the child to be born to Mary is "holy." The nature of this holiness is made clear by the parallelism between Spirit and "power" in Luke 1:17a ("With the Spirit and power of Elijah he will go before him . . ."). This parallelism entails that the power that achieves the conception of the child without a human father is none other than the power of God, which is God's Spirit. Therefore it is clear that Jesus is conceived without human instrumentality, and therefore is holy in the sense of divinity, not merely by designation or dedication as in a

---

1. Marshall, *Luke*, 70.
2. Johnson, *Luke*: 38–39, 75. Morris, *Luke*, 81.
3. Bobrinskoy, *El Misterio*, 102.
4. The Synoptic Gospels attest to Jesus' self-understanding as the true Temple-image, which in turn explains his antipathy towards the misuse of the Temple in Jerusalem because he understood himself as God's true presence. Wright, "Jesus' Self-Understanding," 56–58.
5. G. Schneider goes too far in asserting: "Not only is he filled with the Spirit as John is, rather he has the Spirit to owe for his very existence." The original text reads: "nicht nur vom Geist *erfüllt* wie Johannes (1:15), sondern er verdank seine *Existenz* diesem Gottesgeist." G. Schneider, *Evangelium nach Lukas*, 53 cited in Turner, "Jesus," 35. (Translation is my own).

first-born child.⁶ The contrast between Jesus' conception and the conception of the greatest of God's prophets anticipating the kingdom (Luke 7:28 "among those born of women, no one is greater than John") drives this point home. Like Mary, Elizabeth is also miraculously pregnant (Luke 1:36), with a special son (Luke 1:66, 76–77). However, the "juxtaposition of the two conception stories shows—given the highlighted role of the Holy Spirit—that in Mary's case something very special indeed and qualitatively different was taking place, as the account is *sui generis* in the pages of Scripture."⁷ The full Lukan sense of Jesus' unique origination from God is understood when Jesus' pre-conception actions *as* God are spoken of in Acts 3:14a–15, "But you rejected the Holy and Righteous One . . . and you killed the Author of life, whom God raised from the dead."⁸ Therefore, when the phrase "he shall be called the Son of God" is employed, the reader will ultimately understand that in Mary's case, God really was personally present within her.

The significance of Jesus' Spirit-conception is continually developed by the author's narrative. His identity is borne out in Luke 2:41–51, where Jesus states that his familial origin lies beyond Mary and Joseph, which is confirmed by the misunderstanding of those around him after his boyhood temple visitation (Luke 2:49–50). In this event Jesus "said to them, 'Why are you searching for me? Did you not know that I must be in my Father's house?' But they did not understand what he said to them." Jesus' true origin and familial intimacy is more broadly developed via the Father-Son theme throughout the gospel (Luke 10:22; 22:29; 24:49).⁹

That Luke has a theology of Jesus' conception by the Spirit is clear. What is not clear, however, is the significance of this event in history as a mirror of eternal events or relationships within God. If the SRR of RR is taken, then the origination of the Son by the Spirit is either a reflection of the origination of the Son in God's eternal taxis, or the reflection of an event in the life of God where the Spirit gives of himself so that the Son receives his personhood.

Weinandy is one theologian who has applied the SRR of RR to the implications of this Lukan theology. He insists that the Son is begotten by the Father in the Spirit, and that the conception of Jesus in Mary's

6. Marshall, *Luke*, 70–71.
7. Cole, *Holy Spirit*, 155.
8. See also the rhetorical and theological use of Jesus as a holy being in Acts 4:27, 30.
9. Turner, "Jesus," 35–36.

womb is an analogue of an eternal reality.[10] He outlines his view of the "Spirit of sonship" and its trinitarian consequences below. Firstly, the Spirit of sonship:

> The begetting of the Son and the proceeding of the Spirit are simultaneous, and while distinct, mutually inhere one another. The Father is the Father because in the one act by which he is eternally constituted as father, the Spirit proceeds as the Love (Life and truth) in whom the Son is begotten of the Father. The Son is Son because, having been begotten by the Father in the Spirit of sonship, he loves the Father as Son. This act of filial love, enacted in the Spirit of sonship, is what makes him the Son.[11]

Secondly, Weinandy then outlines what the Spirit's role means for the particularization of the Father and the Son, which we shall treat with respect to the Spirit and the Son later in this chapter. Weinandy writes:

> The one action by which the Spirit is the Spirit is then twofold in effect—pertaining to the Father and to the Son. The Spirit, springing forth within the Father as his love in or by which the Son is begotten, conforms the Father to be the Father for the Son and concurrently conforms the Son to be the Son for the Father. Putting it more strongly . . . it is by the Spirit that the Father substantiates or "persons" himself as Father because it is by the Spirit that he begets the Son. In so doing the Father substantiates, or "persons," by the same Spirit, the Son and the Son personally re-acts, and so is "personed" in the Spirit of sonship, as Son of the Father.[12]

The Oversight of Jesus' Development by the Holy Spirit: If the SRR of RR Is Taken Then Is the Spirit the Eternal Generator and Particularizer of the Second Person of the Trinity?

The agent responsible for the unity of the divine and human natures in Jesus is the Holy Spirit. Not only is Jesus conceived by the Spirit at a foundational level, but the human nature and personal unity within that human nature is also the work of the Spirit. These are all aspects of the particularization of the person of Jesus in his messianic mission (which has been treated previously in chapter 3). Exegesis of Jesus' origins as

---

10. Weinandy, *Father's spirit*, 73, 75.
11. Ibid., 72–73.
12. Ibid., 73.

reported in Luke 1–3 demonstrates the significance of the Spirit's work for the person of Jesus of Nazareth. The Spirit's work bathes Jesus' entire birth narrative and connects this with the Spirit's work in Acts. In Luke 1:49,

> Mary is exhorted to rejoice . . . and offers praise because God has done great things . . . while Elizabeth rejoices because the Lord has magnified mercy to her . . . (1:58). As pious and upright children of Zion, the two women experience divine renewal within themselves and respond very much in keeping with the expectations of the prophet Joel. In Joel, this passage about joy [2:21-26] leads directly into Joel 2:28-32 . . . quoted by Peter in Acts 2, where it provides the foundation for a number of themes developed in the ensuing narrative . . . the arrival of the Spirit, the salvation of all who call on the name of the Lord, the gathering (salvation) of the Gentiles.[13]

Therefore, in Luke-Acts a pneumatological undercurrent must be assumed for those spheres of divine action where a full explanation of divine instrumentality with reference to Jesus is not provided. This includes the specific actions by the Spirit that bring about the addition of a human nature to the Son's divine nature.[14] The annunciation to Mary (Luke 1:35) is a fulfillment of Isa 7:14 "Therefore the Lord himself will give you a sign. Look, the virgin is with child and shall give birth to a son, and shall name him Immanuel." The canonical interpretation of this Isaianic verse highlights two unique aspects of the virgin's son—he is human and yet also "God with us" in this same humanity. The pneumatological fulfillment and clustering of these two natures within Mary, who is a virgin, (Luke 1:27, 34), is made clear in "the child to be born . . . will be called the Son of God" (Luke 1:35). This strand of thought goes beyond the kingship of Jesus which is highlighted in Luke 1:32: "He will be great, and will be called the Son of the Most High, and the Lord will give him the throne of his ancestor David." Importantly, in Luke 1:35, "we have a different understanding of what it means to be the Son of God, tracing it to divine intervention at conception and a resulting special

---

13. De Long, *Surprised*, 174.

14. N. T. Wright claims that the Temple approach to the person and thus the natures of Christ is a superior route to Jesus' identity as it avoids unnecessary nuances which distract the Christian from the salvation which God has already brought about via Jesus, and which he will further once Jesus returns. Wright, "Jesus' Self-Understanding," 56–58.

nature."[15] This understanding is confirmed by the sentence structure of 1:35. The *"therefore"* in Luke 1:35 which links "The Holy Spirit will come upon you, and the power of the Most High will overshadow you" and "he will be called the Son of God," means that "he will be called the Son of God," is not merely a title of grandeur. Rather the precise construction of the sentence is used by Luke to "entitle one to the following supposition: The Evangelist evaluates . . . what they already knew about him . . . that the manner of speaking about the Spirit's work of the life-origination of Jesus is more than a mere possibility, rather it is the vivid grounds for the truth of the church's Son-of-God-proclamation."[16] Thus this "Son of God" is not merely called the "Son of the Most High" in functional terms alone (Luke 1:32). This union of humanity and divinity in Jesus is not merely the creation of a static union, but rather the creation of a union which will be driven by the Spirit through history in such a manner that it takes a particular shape for the sake of others: "through the activity of the Holy Spirit in the historical events of Jesus Christ's life, death, and resurrection, Christ was *constituted* the messianic Son *for us.*"[17]

Given the exegesis above, the witness of Scripture confronts us with multiple questions if one takes a SRR of RR. If this relationship between the Son and the Spirit were read according to the SRR of RR, then it would appear that within the divine taxis, God the Spirit generates God the Son. Also, the Spirit would be understood to particularize the Son's person. Thus, the Holy Spirit-Son relationship would entail that the Son is entirely dependent on the Holy Spirit for his being. Further, both conclusions would be made without reference to the relationship with God the Father—the eternal analogue would thus be that the Son proceeds from the Spirit alone.

---

15. Tannehill, *Luke*: 50.

16. The original reads: "Dies bereichtigt zu der Vermutung: Der Evangelist wertet die ihm . . . schon bekante . . . Redeweise von der geistwirkten Lebensentstehung Jesu bloß als eine Möglichkeit, die Wahrheit der kirchlichen Sohn-Gottes-Verkündigung anschaulich zu begründen." Kremer, "Dieser ist," 144, see also 43. (Translation is my own).

17. Groppe draws together the elements of a Spirit Christology which includes the dynamic connection between the personhood and works of the Spirit and the Son: "The Spirit who wrought the *kenōsis* of Incarnation, baptism, and death is also the Spirit of Christ's glorification–a glorification not of dominion but of communion. Jesus Christ exercises his divine Sonship precisely by giving the Spirit to others such that they, too, may become sons and daughters of God." Groppe, *Yves Congar's*, 57.

The theological issues at hand include whether or not an *autotheos*[18] can be maintained for God the Son if the economy of salvation is taken as the basis for speaking about God's taxis. A second issue would be whether the Son's procession from the Spirit as an *essentialiter* view is possible or not. Thirdly, an eternal subordination of the Son to the Spirit would be in view, because the Son would be dependent upon the Spirit for his being.

An historical resource for considering how to uphold the christological and pneumatological unity of Luke-Acts via sound exegesis simultaneously with strongly maintaining God the Son's *autotheos*, is John Calvin. He held his view in distinction to other views of the time, including the belief that the Son was *deuterotheos or heterotheos*.[19] Commenting on Luke 1:35, Calvin not only noted that the human nature of Jesus is "generated" by the Holy Spirit, but also that the Holy Spirit secures the unity of the natures into the person of the Christ. Calvin notes that the use of the future tense in the verb he "shall be called" the Son of God, refers to God the Son's clothing with flesh alone.[20] The significance is that Calvin notes that at his birth the eternal Son of God was clothed with flesh, and that the agent responsible for this is the Holy Spirit. Such

---

18. By *autotheos*, we mean "*of himself God; i.e., God by nature*; a term applied to each of the persons of the Trinity, in particular to the Son and the Spirit, in order to identify them as divine by nature rather than by grace. The term is specifically applied to the Son to distinguish him from 'sons' by creation and 'sons' by adoption." Italics are Muller's. Muller, *Latin and Greek*, 54. It must be noted here that we are not arguing for *autoprosopon*. Muller draws out the nature of the Son's aseity as he makes the distinction between aseitas, which he understands to be used "synonymously with *autotheos*," and *autoprosopon*. He writes: "The Reformed orthodox . . . define the consubstantiality of the Son and the Spirit with the Father as essential *aseitas* of each of the three persons. In this definition, they distinguish between *aseitas personalis* and *aseitas essentialis*, the former term, personal aseity involving trinitarian error and the latter term, essential aseity interpreting *homoousios* correctly. Thus, insofar as the *deitas* or divinity, of the Son and the Spirit is communicated . . . insofar as they are persons in relation to the Father, they are not a se, but *a Patre*, from the Father. *Aseitas* therefore, does not indicate *autoprosopon*, a person of itself. Nevertheless, the *deitas* that the Son and the Spirit have fully and completely is not derived deity or divinity. In order to be truly God, the Son and the Spirit, considered according to their divinity or according to the divine essence that is theirs, must be *autotheos* and have the attribute of *aseitas* . . . The doctrinal alternative . . . is the essential subordination of the Son and Spirit on grounds of generation and procession." Muller, *Latin and Greek*, 47.

19. Muller, *Triunity*, 77, 81.

20. Therefore, for Calvin, Jesus did not become the Son of God at birth as Servetus claimed. Calvin, *Harmony*, 1:43, 37.

is the executive and creative role of the Holy Spirit with reference to the person of Jesus that the Spirit also ensures the sinless nature of Christ (1:35).[21] Further, the narrative of the birth of Jesus demonstrates that the Holy Spirit was the instrument of Jesus' birth itself (Luke 2:1–7).[22] On Jesus' development in Luke 2:40–52, Calvin stated that with reference to his human nature, Christ "received . . . according to his age and capacity, an increase of the free gifts of the Spirit," and that it was necessary for Christ to grow in knowledge under the direction of the Holy Spirit.[23] In terms of Jesus' ministry, he is led into the wilderness by the Spirit, where the presiding role of the Spirit over the Son is heightened to emphasize the fact that Jesus was "more abundantly imbued with the grace and the power of the Spirit, in order that he might be more fortified for the battles which he had to fight."[24]

The breadth of the Spirit's work with reference to the Son's entry into the world shows how seriously Calvin took this particular work of the Spirit. However, Calvin did not face the problems faced by those who argue for the SRR of RR because he did not expect the economy of salvation to be a mirror of the eternal taxis within God. For him this would not be possible because of the dogmatic weight he accorded to the *autotheos* of God the Son. Calvin therefore avoided any kind of subordinationism or gradationism involving God the Son's relationship to other persons of the Trinity. Though Calvin unambiguously affirmed that God the Son derived his personhood from the person of the Father, yet his divinity is essential to himself because he has divinity intrinsic to himself. His personhood is dependent on the Father, but his divinity is not.[25] This is achieved by Calvin's use of Christ's *autotheos* as an interpretive norm. The essential and full deity of the Son of God is maintained, yet without detracting from his inter-personal relationship to God the Father. This encapsulation was unique to Calvin when he was writing. The genius of his thought is that in the *autotheos* of God the Son, he captures the intent

---

21. Calvin, *Harmony*, 1:43.

22. "[C]ertainly Luke's whole narrative may well lead believers to acknowledge that Christ was led by the hand of God "from his mother's belly," (Ps. 22:10)." Calvin, *Harmony*, 1:109.

23. Calvin, *Harmony*, 1: 165-68.

24. Ibid., 1:211.

25. Calvin, *Institutes*, I.13.23-5; Warfield, *Calvin and Augustine*, 275.

of Nicea, yet simultaneously protects Christianity from the dangerous ambiguity of the Nicene expression.[26]

The significance of this work is not lost on Warfield. Warfield states the following on Calvin's conception of the *autotheotys* of God the Son: "By this assertion the *homoousiotys* of the Nicene Fathers at last came to its full right, and became in its fullest sense the hinge of the [Trinitarian] doctrine."[27] Therefore, in Calvin we have an example of a theologian whose christology was not diminished by a strong pneumatology because he held both in a mutually enriching manner.

Jesus' Double Reception of the Spirit: A Puzzle for Eternal Analogues?

In Luke's record of salvation history, Jesus received "the Spirit at least twice: once at the Jordan River (Luke 3:21f) and once at Pentecost (Acts 2:33)."[28]

Jesus' first reception of the Spirit occurred during his prayer after his baptism by John (Luke 3:22). The coming of the Spirit upon him was his "consecration and empowerment for ministry. Although Jesus was conceived by the Holy Spirit and therefore already a holy person consecrated to God's service, as a baby (Luke 1:35), this special empowerment with the Holy Spirit is necessary for Jesus to begin his work."[29] This was not a passing enablement, rather, Luke the author "makes it clear that that this is a permanent endowment that leads to ministry, for Jesus is 'full of the Spirit' in 4:1, returns to Galilee 'filled with the power of the Spirit' in 4:14, and announces in 4:18 that 'the Spirit of the Lord is upon me.'"[30]

Jesus' second reception of the Spirit occurred at his enthronement as Lord (Acts 2:21, 33–36). Peter's use of Joel 3:1–5 (LXX), demonstrates that Jesus' Lordship assumes his rule via the Holy Spirit. Peter's use of Joel 3:1–2 (LXX) established the pneumatological basis of the glossolalia, and the immediately preceding call for salvation in the Lord alone is based upon the very next section in Joel, Joel 3:3–5 (LXX). Eckhard Schnabel has persuasively argued that this theology was established by Jesus himself in Luke 24:49 when he promised that he would send the

---

26. Warfield, *Calvin and Augustine*, 284.
27. Ibid.
28. Turner, "Jesus and The Spirit in Lucan Perspective," 10–11, 28.
29. Tannehill, *Luke*, 84.
30. Ibid., 84.

Spirit. This enabled Peter to employ the same hermeneutical lens in order to overcome the issue that "according to Jewish conviction, only God can pour out the Spirit, since the Spirit of God is the active presence of the one true God revealing himself personally to creation." Therefore, he was able to give "the explanation that the Spirit of God is the Spirit of Jesus, that Jesus is 'Lord' of the Spirit, that Jesus 'poured out' the Spirit" even though it "must have been surprising and provocative for Peter's Jewish listeners."[31] In Acts, Jesus is understood to have "received" the Spirit, which is a "gift" (Acts 2:38; 8:20; 10:45; 11:17). Whether or not this reception is based on an allusion to Ps 67(LXX), it is consistent with the theology of Eph 4:8. More importantly, it is an aspect of the rule that is proper to the Messiah of the new people of God. The notable point is that this is a different reception of the Spirit by Jesus from that recorded in Luke 3:22 and Acts 10:38.[32]

If a SRR of RR is applied to Jesus' double reception of the Spirit in Luke-Acts, then what would these exegetical conclusions from Scripture mean for our understanding of God's taxis? One possible conclusion (a theologoumenon to be sure) is that within God's taxis the nature of the relations mean the Son's first reception of the Spirit is not sufficient. This taxis thus requires two separate acts whereby the Spirit is given over to the Son. On the other hand, the conclusion for God's inner life may be that the structure of this relational life is open to continuous change. That is, with respect to the Son and the Spirit there are various directional "occasions," and these occasions may repeat or produce change in God. Either of these "fluid" versions of God's inner life could result from applying the SRR of RR to Luke-Acts. Ironically, the choice amongst these speculative theologies stemming from the SRR of RR could lead to much confusion. Many would ultimately conclude that we cannot say much that is certain or coherent about the inner life of God with respect to the Son-Spirit taxis. This potential for confusion or agnosticism about the inner life of God arguably undermines the aims of those who hold the SRR of RR.

---

31. Schnabel, *Early*, 401.
32. Beale and Carson, *New Testament Use*, 541–42.

SON AND SPIRIT: REVERSE SUCCESSIVE SUBORDINATIONS

The reversed subordinations of God the Son to God the Spirit in Luke-Acts has been noted by many scholars.[33] The first aspect of this point is taken from Luke's Gospel where Jesus is presented as being subordinate to the Spirit in numerous ways. The Spirit oversees the development of the person of Christ, the nature of his ministry, the actual events of his ministry, and is the final promise of his ministry. Surprisingly, these roles are reversed in the book of Acts where Jesus is described as having a presiding authority over the Holy Spirit.

The Comprehensive Subordination of God the Son to the God Spirit in the Gospel of Luke

The Particularization of Jesus by the Holy Spirit

As already described, the Holy Spirit had a developmental role regarding God the Son. After Jesus' conception, the Spirit was active in placing and leading Jesus into relationships and roles which ultimately constitute the form Jesus takes as an individual person.[34] This activity of the Spirit is described as follows by Höhne, who draws heavily upon the work of Colin Gunton:

> "The Son's particularity will be perfected as the Spirit enables him to progressively contextualize his actions on the basis of his relation to the Father as Son and to Israel as Savior. In the final analysis, the quality and nature of the relations between characters will be an essential referent for determining their identity . . . The Spirit will act with and for the Son to perfect his identity in relation to God and his people as the events of the Scriptural drama reach their climax."[35]

This particularity into which the Son is constituted by the Spirit as Israel's savior is illuminated by comparing Luke 1:15, 80 and 2:52. John the baptizer's growth is attributed to the Spirit filling him from birth (Luke 1:15): "the child grew and became strong in spirit, and he was in the wilderness until the day he appeared publicly to Israel." John's

---

33. For example, Turner, "Jesus," 28–29. Plantinga, Jr., C., in Giles, *Jesus and the Father*, 7.

34. Gunton, *Act and Being*, 143.

35. Höhne, *Spirit and Sonship*, 41.

development is paralleled in Jesus throughout Luke 2:40–52. In particular, Luke 2:52 reads: "And Jesus increased in wisdom and in years, and in divine and human favor."[36] Thus, there is a development in Jesus' life (Luke 2:52; drawing upon 1:80), under the direction of the Spirit. This is established by the fact that there is a strong circularity and parallelism in Luke 1:5—2:52,[37] especially as it relates to the Holy Spirit as the agent who ensures Jesus' development as a prophet,[38] and the Lukan equating of the Spirit's work with transformative wisdom.[39] This shows that God the Son adjusted to new economic conditions, which were foreign to his essential relations within the Godhead. Also, this adjustment occurred under the guidance of the Spirit, who not only had authority over the God the Son incarnate, but also had developmental oversight over his total person.

The Davidic Nature of Jesus' Ministry as the Messiah Is Overseen by the Holy Spirit

Not only does the Spirit enable the entry of the Son enfleshed into the world, unite the natures and foster the development of Jesus, he also oversees the Davidic-Messianic nature of Jesus' ministry. The announcement of Jesus' birth (Luke 1:26–38) confirms that Jesus is in line with

---

36. Calvin, *Harmony*, 1: 1:79.

37. "As it stands there are at least three beginnings in Luke. Luke 1:1–4, as is commonly acknowledged, is a conventional introduction in which the implied author speaks directly to the implied reader about the work. Luke 3:1–2 is a scenic introduction. In between, we have Luke 1:5—2:52, a series of birth and infancy accounts that functions in a similar way to that of the dramatic prologue. These accounts provide a particularly effective frame for the gospel, containing phenomena of circularity and parallelism." Tyson, "Birth Narratives," 113.

38. In the infancy narratives in Luke's Gospel, "On the discursive level, the Spirit functions to insure the narrative reliability of the prophetic figures found in these chapters. In effect, the Spirit stands in the background, content to tell us more about God and Jesus than itself . . . the characterization [of the Spirit] is coherent, as the Spirit would seem to have one primary function: to inspire the speech and action of other characters, to make prophets of them. A secondary function of the Spirit is to announce and assist in the births of new prophets, John and Jesus . . . Indeed, the Spirit is highly active in these two chapters [Luke 1–2], hard at work among the prophetic figures. Luke shows the reader in these first few pages that this is a book about action—God's action, working through the Spirit . . . the Spirit fills, abides with, leads and inspires the prophetic figures . . . the focus in the infancy narrative has been on the birth of the prophetic figures John and Jesus, Jesus being the chief of the two. The Spirit functions to show that both these children are prophets . . ." Shepherd, *Narrative*, 125–26.

39. Turner, "Work," 150–51.

a Davidic understanding of the Messiah.[40] In fact, the christological continuity between the Lukan nativity scenes and the book of Acts is achieved through emphasizing the Davidic nature of Jesus' Messiahship (Luke 1:32–33, 69; Acts 2:29–31; 13:23–37) and the titles of Χριστός and κύριος (Luke1:43; 2:11; Acts 2:36; 10:36).[41] Thus, the Spirit's role is to ensure this typological fulfillment. Jesus' anointing by the Holy Spirit at his baptism (Luke 3:21–23) and his pneumatically-empowered declaration in the Nazareth manifesto (Luke 4:16–30), highlights the significant role the Spirit played in David's life. This typology means that though there is a "*conforme*" which this particular human "Son of God" must carry out as God the Son,[42] it is Davidic. His vocation is as a Davidic Messiah at a precise point in salvation history. Therefore, we can say that Jesus' divine sonship and his human mission as the Son of God are overlapping yet not mirroring concepts. The Davidic nature of his messianic call is a "buffer" between the immanent and economic relations of God the Son.

By way of anticipation, at this point one notes that the Davidic Messiah is necessarily a ruling Messiah, and as such the means or instrument of his rule is of great significance (Luke1:33 cf. Ps. 110:3).[43] This points toward the fact that the messianic rule will be a rule whereby the ruler will reign with power, anticipating Jesus' reign via the Holy Spirit himself who is the personal power of God.[44] In the book of Acts, the messianic rule of Jesus will be carried out via the Holy Spirit.

The Holy Spirit Directs the Actual Events of the Ministry of Jesus in Luke's Gospel

Luke's baptism and anointing narrative (3:21–22) is a pivotal moment in this Gospel, as it makes the point that Jesus' ministry is carried out

---

40. This view is widely held, for example, Scobie, *Ways*, 301 ff. Johnson and Harrington, *Luke*, 51–53; Hendricksen, *Gospel*, 86–87. This view has also been held in the past, for example, see Calvin, *Harmony*, 1:37–38.

41. Strauss, *Davidic Messiah*, 80.

42. Bosc, "Dieu," 58.

43. Calvin, *Harmony*, 1:39.

44. Significantly, this is due mainly due to the nature of historic Messianic *rule* rather than merely the ontology of the ruler. The narrative of Luke-Acts makes it clear that Jesus rules via the Spirit because he is the Messiah, not due to his sharing his "Substance" with the Spirit as Cyril of Alexandria believed. See Cyril's "Homily 10," in his "Commentary on Luke," cited in *Ancient: Luke*, 63. Ferguson, *Holy Spirit*, 35–36.

"in the sphere of the Holy Spirit,"[45] under the "reign,"[46] or lordship of the Spirit.[47] This economic relationship is compounded in the temptation narrative (Luke 4:1–13), where Jesus is "full of the Spirit" (Luke 4:1) because he received the Spirit as the Messiah.[48] Luke 4:14 ensures that the reader continues to observe the presence of the power of the Spirit in Christ's ministry. Luke 4:14–44 is a single narrative unit that emphasizes (via references to the Spirit in Luke 4:14 and 4:18) the outworking of the Holy Spirit's empowerment of Jesus at his baptism and temptation (Luke 3:21—4:13).[49] The significance of the words "The Spirit of the Lord is upon me," in the 'Nazareth Manifesto' (Luke 4:16–30) reveals the extent of the dependence of Jesus the Messiah upon the Holy Spirit.[50] The Spirit is the source of authority and power for Christ's ministry, as Jesus is the one uniquely anointed by the Holy Spirit.[51] This is demonstrated by the Holy Spirit provoking the "gracious words" which came from Jesus mouth (Luke 4:22).[52] The Spirit's guidance of Jesus' ministry and person is reinforced at the critical juncture of Luke 10:21,[53] where Jesus is begin-

45. Green, *Luke*: 853. Nolland, *Luke*: 1:158–82.

46. Fitzmyer, *Luke*: 1:229, 479–83.

47. "Jesus was baptized with the Spirit and lived under his lordship." Ferguson, *Holy Spirit*, 46. Commenting on 3:23, which reads: *Jesus was about thirty years old when he began his work,* Calvin states that with reference to his human nature, "When Christ was preparing to preach the Gospel, he was introduced by Baptism into his office; and at the same time he was endued with the Holy Spirit . . . that he comes as a godlike man . . . in whom the power of the Holy Spirit reigns." Calvin, *Harmony*, 1:204.

48. Johnson, *Luke*, 81.

49. Evans and Gasque, *Luke*, 70. Green, *Luke*, 230.

50. "Luke 4:18 being of programmatic significance: Jesus quotes Isa 61:1 to show that the Spirit of God rests upon Him as anointing his work. This verse to some extent counterbalances Matt 12:28 which attributes Jesus' exorcisms to the Spirit of God; the parallel in Luke 11:20 has instead 'the finger of God.'" Marshall, *Luke*, 177–80. Significantly, the "finger of God" in Luke's Gospel has a different divine referent. Woods attributes this, and the work of the "finger of God," to God the Father rather than God the Holy Spirit. See Woods, *Finger of God*, 223–25. Woods writes: "With the 'finger of God' expression, God the Father is acting with power and mercy through Jesus his spirit-anointed Son (Acts 2:22; cf. Lk. 8:39) . . . the phrase 'finger of God' at Luke 11:20 refer[s] to God the Father himself in a non-instrumental sense, because the Holy Spirit is already involved in miracles through the authoritative word of command and release."

51. Calvin is right to state that these words indicate that "He [Christ] does nothing by the suggestion or advice of men, but everything by the guidance of the Spirit of God." Calvin, *Harmony*, 1:228.

52. Ibid., 1:230.

53. Ibid., 1:115; Morris, *Gospel according to St. Luke,* 203. Contra Turner, *Power,*

ning his final journey to Jerusalem, towards the cross.[54] This reinforces the fact that Jesus' ministry and journey towards the cross is carried out as the One anointed by the Holy Spirit.[55]

Jesus' saving work on the cross is dependent upon his virginal conception by the Holy Spirit. It is only in this power of the Holy Spirit that the promises about God's saving action recorded in the infancy narratives can be brought about. The Holy Spirit conceives someone who can miraculously be so radically different to other people that only he can accomplish that which is "necessary" in salvation history. The infancy narratives in Luke 1 and 2 "leave no doubt that God's 'remembering his mercy which he promised to our fathers, and to his posterity forever' (1:54, 72–73), is to be found in the son born of Mary, named Jesus." Finally, "Simeon punctuates this Lukan overture about the linkage between Jesus and salvation with his own song after he had seen the Lord Christ: 'Now . . . my eyes have seen thy salvation' (2:26, 29–30)."[56] This salvation can only ever be accomplished by the enablement of the Spirit because only a miraculous conception forms someone who can carry this out. By the Spirit, Jesus is a person outside the paradigm for all mere human persons and can therefore accomplish the "musts" of Luke 24:46–47—the Messiah *must* suffer, be rejected, and be the basis for the preaching of repentance and forgiveness for God's people. Luke brings out the miraculous enablement of God by the means of emphasizing that his salvation has indeed arrived. Luke achieves this by employing a group of "songs of thanksgiving" around the events of Jesus' birth, his death on the cross, and Stephen's faith at his stoning (Luke 2:29–32; Luke 23:46; Acts 7:59). Luke weaves a pattern whereby the person who is the *pray-er* in each situation asks God for salvation given their status as part of a *Todesgeweihten* (a doomed people). This prayer is answered when Jesus becomes the ruling Messiah of both the Jews and Gentiles whose relationships with God and each other are radically and savingly altered

---

263–64. Calvin attributes Jesus' joy at this point, and Christian joy, as a function of the Holy Spirit. Calvin, *Harmony*, 1:115. Therefore, the joy Christ experiences more generally after the mission of his disciples is due to the Holy Spirit. The extension of this in terms of the relation between the Spirit and God the Son is that the Holy Spirit had in some sense direct control over the affections of God the Son. This is consistent with Luke's theology.

54. Green, *Luke*, 422.

55. Ibid., 422.

56. Schroeder, "Luke's Gospel," 337.

via his Spirit (more shortly).[57] Jesus is, by his provenance from the Spirit, enabled to live and minister in a way which is not possible for other humans including the Israelites. González writes:

> We have seen that human beings cannot liberate themselves from the scheme of the law. Only God can set us free from the scheme of the law. If Jesus of Nazareth lived at the margins of the law, this is an achievement that is not merely a human achievement. Nor is it something he was able to do due to his noble heritage—a prostitute (Rahab) is included in his genealogy. If Jesus lived at the margins of the scheme of the law, it is because he did not proceed only from flesh and blood, but rather from God too.[58]

In sum, this third point demonstrates the breadth of the Spirit's presiding authority over Jesus' ministry in Luke. This provides a strong contrast to the relational reversal that is evident in the book of Acts.

The Holy Spirit Is the Final Promise of Jesus' Ministry, Anticipating a Reversal of the Executive Function in the Relationship Between the Son and the Spirit

John the Baptizer's preaching about Jesus and the Holy Spirit in Luke 3:7–18 anticipates a change in the economic relationship between God the Son and God the Holy Spirit. Christ will be the bestower of the Holy Spirit and will have an executive role over the Spirit. The trial of Jesus before the Sanhedrin crystallizes a central issue within Luke's Gospel regarding who God's chosen leader for his people is. The messianic role of Jesus is in view, and this includes his reign at the right hand of God. The use of the phrase "from now on" (Luke 22:69: "From now on the Son of Man will be seated at the right hand of the power of God"), indicates that the death-resurrection and ascension together make up a complex unit that culminates in the enthronement of Jesus.[59]

---

57. Berger, "Canticum Simeonis," 27, 37.

58. The original reads: "Hemos visto que el ser human no puede liberarse por sí mismo del esquema de la ley. Solamente Dios nos puede liberar del esquema de la ley. Si Jesús de Nazaret vivió al margen del esquema de la ley, esto no es un simple logro humano. Tampoco es algo explicable por los meritos de su noble cuna. En la genealogía de Jesús aparece incluso una prostituta, Rahab . . . Si Jesús vivió al mergen del esquema de la ley, es porque él no procedía solamente de carne y de sangre, sino también de Dios." González, *Teología de la Praxis,* 298. (My own translation).

59. Green, *Luke,* 181, 793–96. Talbert, *Patterns,* 115–16. Nolland, *Luke,* 1:52.

The relations between the Spirit and Christ in the passages which compose this complex need to be seen as part of the enthronement of Christ as the Messiah anointed by the Spirit.[60] Thus far this section's exegesis agrees with that of scholars such as Green[61] and Penney.[62] However, this section would like to take a step further and show that though the trial, death and resurrection of Jesus are all carried out by Jesus in the power of the Spirit, there is a change in the narrative when Jesus promises the gift of the Spirit. It is significant that Jesus' promise of the Spirit to the disciples occurs in the context of his enthronement. Even though Jesus speaks of the "Father's promise" (Luke 24:49), it is Jesus who can both promise the Spirit and will send him: "Amazingly . . . it is not the Father who will dispense the Spirit, but Jesus himself. This recalls the words of John in Luke 3:16, and his message finds parallels later in Acts 1:5; 11:16."[63]

Thus, by the close of the Gospel of Luke we have an anticipated reversal in the economic relations between the Spirit and the Son. This role reversal is very clearly driven by the messianic nature of Jesus' work and not by the self-expression of God in the economy of salvation. It is driven by salvation-historical concerns and not ontological ones pertaining to the immanent Trinity.

In sum, the weight of the biblical witness presents two theological conclusions that are exegetically based. Firstly, Jesus' entire life—conception, development, ministry, death, and resurrection—is carried out under the reign of the Holy Spirit. Secondly, a change in economic relations between God the Son and God the Holy Spirit for salvation-historical reasons is anticipated. If the SRR of RR were applied at this point, the conclusion would be that given the relationship between these two persons in Luke's Gospel, God the Son is subordinate to God the Spirit in the eternal taxis.

---

60. Nolland, *Luke*, 3:1220–22.

61. Green concludes that "the material related to Jesus and the Spirit in the birth narrative, the account of Jesus' anointing, and the description of his testing make clear the Spirit's activity with regard to Jesus is integral to his birth, identity, and mission as Son of God." Green, *Luke*, 205.

62. "[I]n Luke's Gospel . . . even Jesus is never 'Lord of the Spirit'; rather he is directed and empowered by the Spirit." Penney, *Missionary Emphasis*, 112.

63. Green, *Luke*, 853; Green, *Luke*, 859; Johnson, *Luke*, 403–6; Marshall, *Luke*, 907; Morris, *Luke*, 374.

THE COMPREHENSIVE SUBORDINATION OF THE SPIRIT TO THE SON IN THE BOOK OF ACTS

The Economy of Salvation in the Book of Acts Is Christologically Focused Not Pneumatologically Focused

The christological focus of the book of Acts is introduced in Acts 1:1. Whereas in the Gospel of Luke Jesus was led by the Spirit, in Acts Jesus directs the actions of God in the economy of salvation, including the activities of the Spirit. The interpretation of ἤρξατο in Acts 1:1 is crucial for understanding the economic relationships taught in this narrative. The theology of Acts, rather than the syntax, demands that Acts 1:1 be translated as "of all that Jesus did and taught as a beginning until the day."[64] This adverbial use of ἤρξατο means that Jesus continues the work he began with no end in sight (Luke 2:47; 9:34; 14:3; 16:14; 18:10).[65] Therefore, the relationship between God the Son and God the Holy Spirit in Acts is primarily christological in that the narratival focus is upon Jesus rather than the Holy Spirit. N. T. Wright captures this with reference to the end of Luke's Gospel: "The final four verses round off the Gospel as a whole, and simultaneously overlap with the beginning scene of Acts . . . Jesus himself [is] the exalted lord of the world, ready to begin the second phase of his work. (Acts opens by speaking of '*all that Jesus began to do and teach (1:1); it describes his continuing ministry of word and deed*')."[66]

God the Son has Executive Authority Over God the Holy Spirit in the Book of Acts

The content of the first *kerygma* in the book of Acts (Acts 2:14–22) clearly has a christological rather than pneumatological priority. In this regard the Spirit is seen as part of the ministry of the reigning Jesus.[67] Jesus is the "promised Messiah-Lord, who sits at God's right hand exercising authority from above." Therefore, the activity of God in Acts

---

64. Hull, *Holy Spirit*, 180.

65. "The implication of Luke's words is that his second volume will be an account of the things Jesus *continued* to do and teach after his ascension—by His Spirit and followers" (Emphasis is Bruce's). Bruce et al., *New International*, 32.

66. Italics are Wright's. Wright, *Resurrection* 647; Cf. Ladd and Hagner, *A Theology*, 239.

67. Williams, *Acts*, 48–50.

is consistent with that of Luke, yet it is directed by Jesus, not the Holy Spirit.⁶⁸ This is expressed functionally in the executive role which Jesus has over the Holy Spirit beginning in Acts 2:33,⁶⁹ where it is as "Lord" that Jesus gives the Holy Spirit to believers (Acts 2:33; 7:55–56).⁷⁰ This is significant because the Christology of Luke's Gospel is very restrictive in its application of κύριος to Jesus. However, after the resurrection (marked at Luke 24:34), κύριος is frequently applied to Jesus.⁷¹ At Pentecost "what takes place in Acts is not that the church has inherited Jesus' anointing, but that the risen Lord himself continues his redemptive activity, as Lord of the Spirit (Acts 2:33; 16:7)"⁷² The act of giving the Spirit demonstrates that Jesus "had become the divine executor,"⁷³ and the "Lord of the Spirit (Acts 2:33; 16:7)."⁷⁴ This is in accordance with the OT typology of a ruling Messiah (Luke 1:33 cf. Ps 110:3).⁷⁵ Marshall states that "[i]n Acts the place of the Spirit is of great importance, but it is vital to notice that He is the Spirit of Jesus and that He is subordinate to Jesus."⁷⁶ This is evidenced in Acts 10:44, "While Peter was still speaking, the Spirit fell upon all who heard the word." Here, Jesus' gift of the Spirit to Cornelius' household demonstrates that Jesus "oversees" the constituency and mission of his church through the Spirit.⁷⁷ The Spirit is dependent on Christ's direction,⁷⁸ and is characterized as the gift, rather than the instigator of the gift.⁷⁹ In addition, Acts 11:16 recalls Jesus' promise about sending the Holy Spirit: "John baptized with water, but you will be baptized with the Holy Spirit."⁸⁰ As such, any view that the Spirit is inde-

---

68. Bock, *Luke*: 280, 73.

69. This relationship is not negated by the fact that Jesus' gift of the Spirit is received from the Father.

70. Ladd and Hagner, *A Theology*, 239.

71. Moule, "The Christology of Acts," 160, 65.

72. Turner, "Jesus," 28–28.

73. Williams, *Acts*, 53. Mittlestadt, *Spirit and Suffering*, 27–28. Contra Turner, *Power*, 179–85, 289, 349ff, 428ff.

74. Turner, "Jesus and The Spirit in Lucan Perspective," 28–29.

75. Ferguson, *The Holy Spirit*, 35–36.

76. Cf. Acts 16:7, Marshall, *Luke*, 92.

77. Cf. Acts 11:16. Kistemaker, *Exposition*, 414.

78. Hurtado, "First-Century Jewish Monotheism."

79. Acts 1:4; 2:33; 10:45; 11:17. Shepherd, *Narrative Function*, 247.

80. Kistemaker, *Exposition*, 414.

pendent of Christ is implausible.[81] The Spirit is the gift of God the Father (Luke 24:49; Acts 1:4–5), and is received exclusively in Jesus' name (Acts 2:38), given *through and by God the Son* (Acts 2:33). Given that the book of Acts communicates that the Spirit is the primary instrument of the continuing work of Jesus in his divine executive capacity,[82] the Spirit is depicted as subordinate to Jesus' mission and authority. The Holy Spirit is presented as an agent or personal means, who is subordinate to Jesus as the Messiah seated at the right hand of God. This takes into consideration the larger biblical theology of Jesus' states of humiliation and glorification (cf. Phil 2: 5–11; 1 Tim 3:16).

The witness of Luke-Acts is that Jesus is the Lord of the Spirit in the book of Acts, and that this stands in relational contrast to the picture of the Spirit as the Lord of Jesus in Luke's Gospel. This conclusion confronts us with the following questions if one takes a SRR of RR: firstly, how can these complementary pictures of the successive reversed subordinations between the Spirit and the Son cohere if they are true of their eternal referents? And, secondly, what is the correspondence between these relationships within temporal history and those within the divine taxis? Is it isomorphic?

Theologians from Augustine to Von Balthasar have wrestled with this issue. Von Balthasar wrote that "No analogy from creation or the economy of salvation suffices to permit an unbroken statement about the trinitarian life. And most confusing of all is the *economic reversal of the relation between the Son and the Spirit.*"[83]

Though Augustine clearly did not deal with the SRR of RR per se, he dealt with the methodological and theological issues at hand. He noted that Acts 10:38 proposed a reversal in economic relations. He believed that whereas Jesus received the Holy Spirit when he became incarnate in the womb of Mary, he then dispenses the Holy Spirit for the church. Augustine attempted (unsuccessfully) to reconcile this by the hermeneutical move of speaking separately of the distinct natures of Christ.[84]

81. Hurtado, "First-Century Jewish Monotheism," 3–26.

82. González, *Acts: Gospel,* 16–17. Calvin, *Acts,* 2: 1:78.

83. Italics are von Balthasar's. von Balthasar, *Explorations: Spirit and Institution,* 4: 231.

84. Augustine, *The Trinity*: Book XV, 46, 174. Though Augustine is confusing when he states that Christ received the Spirit as a man, yet dispenses it as God, the unity of both His natures is reflected in his use of "the Lord Jesus" in that same discussion. Thus, though Augustine would like to compartmentalize the natures of Christ within

Augustine's struggle demonstrates the careful theological thought required to simultaneously uphold the unity of the economic work of God the Son and God the Holy Spirit, and the reversed subordinations of the Son and the Spirit to each other, whilst preserving the stability of Jesus' and God's identities.

Contemporary theologian François Bovon attempted a different solution, based on the entirety of the narrative of Luke-Acts. He believed that where the reversed subordinations of the Spirit and the Son are present, these mediations are carried out at the initiative of, and are the work of, the one God and are not related to his taxis.[85] What is most helpful about Bovon's appeal to the whole narrative of Luke-Acts is that he demonstrates the need for, and possibilities offered by, maximizing the criterion "the sense of Scripture" for determining our theology. The "sense of Scripture" ensures that our theological exegesis has both a robust biblical basis and *parameters*. That is, there is no inconsistency in holding both the reversed subordination of the Son in the economy of salvation for the simple reason that this is the theatre of God's action *ad extra*. However, there is a clear incoherence in a theology that holds that the economic reversed subordinations between the Son and the Spirit are isomorphic reflections of relations *ad intra*. This raises *the* central problem with the SRR of RR: it cannot deal with the exegetical conclusion that there is a reversed subordination of God the Son to God the Spirit *and vice versa* in Luke-Acts. That the SRR of RR cannot handle such significant evidence from Luke-Acts severely weakens the validity of this theory for trinitarian interpretation.

The Economic Work of God the Holy Spirit Is So Closely Aligned with God the Son That the Spirit Is Not Only Understood as Economically Subordinate to Jesus, but Is Identified as the "Spirit of Jesus"

Acts 16:6 speaks of the action of the Holy Spirit in directing the expansion of Christianity by restricting the apostles' travels. It reads, "They went through the region of Phrigia and Galatia, having been forbidden by the Holy Spirit to speak the word in Asia." In the very next verse, the

---

the unity of his person, he ultimately unites them, as should any scriptural and creedal theology of the Messiah. Augustine, *The Trinity*, 174–75. Calvin resolves this matter differently to Augustine with reference to the natures of Christ and the Mediator. Calvin, *Commentary Upon the Acts of the Apostles*, 2: 1:68–69. A better approach may be T. F. Torrance's appeal to perichoresis. Torrance, *Perspectives*, 92–93.

85. Bovon, "Médiations," 35.

same agent who carries out the same action is called "the Spirit of Jesus". We read: "When they had come opposite Mysia, they attempted to go into Bithynia, but the Spirit of Jesus did not allow them" (Acts 16:7). The view that the "Spirit of Jesus" is a reference to the Holy Spirit is consistent with Jesus' continuing active role in the narrative of Acts (7:56; 9:5, etc.). In this role, he is the exalted Lord who "continued to direct the progress of the gospel through the Spirit which he 'received from the Father' and 'poured out' on his disciples at Pentecost."[86] This "transverse actor and action" definition of the Holy Spirit as the Spirit of Jesus also occurs in Rom 8:9–10 ("the Spirit of Christ") and in Phil 1:19 ("the Spirit of Jesus Christ").[87] The nature of the identification between the Holy Spirit and the Spirit of Jesus is strong. In this case a mere predicative identity is not in view, but an identity that approaches a numerical identity—hence something akin to an identity thesis.[88] If this is the case, equating the Holy Spirit with the Spirit of Jesus forbids a strict compartmentalization of the works of the Son and the Spirit in the economy of salvation, which resists the SRR of RR at the outset. Here is another instance of the fluidity between actors and actions that we saw with regard to the Father and the Son in the previous chapter. Again, this fluidity indicates a deep unity between these actors. If statements equating the "Spirit of Jesus" with the "Holy Spirit" are read through the lens of the SRR of RR, then what is the eternal analogue to this? One possible conclusion may be that there must be some kind of ontological "blurring" between the Spirit and the Son within the Godhead.

---

86. Peterson, *Acts*, 455.

87. Ibid. This verse was a significant factor in instituting the *filioque* clause in the Nicene Creed. Lenski, *Interpretation*, 646.

88. Again, we draw upon McCall's work for this distinction. He writes: "According to the Identification Thesis, the 'is' used in such statements as 'God is the one who rescued Israel and raised Jesus from the dead' is the 'is' of predication. The point made here is simply that there is no God other than the deity revealed in Jesus Christ . . . is the traditional way to do theology . . . The Identity Thesis, on the other hand, arguably is opposed to traditional understandings of the nature of God and of the God-world relation. Here 'is' is not the 'is' of predication but the 'is' of identity. Here the reference is not what is sometimes called 'qualitative identity'; it is clearly not what is meant by phrases such as 'the twins are identical.' What is on view here is numerical identity, according to which identity is normally understood to be *reflexive, transitive,* and *symmetric*." McCall, *Which Trinity?*, 129–30.

REFUTATION OF A PROPOSED ALTERNATIVE: THE PROBLEM REMAINS

In his work *Father, Son and Holy Spirit*, Ware does acknowledge the succession of reverse subordinations between the Son and the Spirit but is able to dismiss their significance via his argument in John 16:12–14[89] and Jesus' ascension.[90] With regard to John 16:12–14, Ware writes that the fact that the Spirit "will speak what Jesus *tells* him to speak" demonstrates the hierarchy within the Trinity. He concludes:

> Jesus does not say, "Just as I spoke only what the Father taught me, and just as I glorified the Father, so the Spirit, when he comes, likewise will only speak what the Father teaches him, for he will glorify the Father." No, the direct lines of authority and submission here run between the Spirit and the Son, not the Spirit and the Father. Although Jesus submitted fully to the Spirit in his incarnate life, still, the Spirit's eternal role is to uphold the will and the word of the Son; in his coming, the Spirit seeks in all he does to glorify Jesus.[91]

For Ware the ascension of Jesus is very significant for revealing a hierarchical order of relationships within the essential Trinity. Jesus' return to the Father demonstrates the true structure of inner-trinitarian relationships as follows: "Although the Son is in submission to the Spirit in the incarnation, in his exaltation the Son 'returns' to his place under the Father yet over the Spirit. So the Spirit is the 'Spirit of Jesus,' ... and the Spirit comes to 'glorify' Jesus."[92]

These twin pieces of text form an unsatisfactory exegetical argument. It appears selective in terms of its textual basis. As a result of his handling of the changed relationship between the Son and the Spirit in the economy of salvation, Ware does not appear to recognize the extent of the challenge that this phenomenon poses to his use of a theology that very much approximates the SRR of RR (the SRRT).[93]

---

89. Ware, *Father*, 94–95.

90. Ibid., 97.

91. Ibid., 94–95.

92. Ibid., 97.

93. In a nutshell, the SRRT literalistic literary hermeneutic which can be described as closely approximating the SRR of RR, but is better described as a SRRT even though Ware appears to deploy the SRRT selectively. This aspect of Bruce Ware's theology will be dealt with in a follow up work.

Whilst Ware adjusts his theology—in my view in a question begging way—in order to deal with these successive subordinations, in a recent successful doctoral thesis Andrew Moody has recognized that the challenge this poses for the SRR of RR is foundational.[94] Moody is a true employer of the SRR of RR. Moody recognizes that if the SRR of RR fails, then his own approach to responsive intra-trinitarian willing will be a casualty.[95] By extension, all other similarly founded projects such as Ware's will also face a significant obstacle. Given Moody's appreciation of the stakes, he proposes his own solution. We will explore his solution before concluding on its legitimacy.

Moody recognizes the challenge as follows: "One of the most acute challenges to the RITW ["responsive intra-trinitarian willing"] case—indeed to the whole Rahnerian theory—is the argument that the immanent Trinity cannot align with the economic because the earthly Jesus is subordinate to the Spirit."[96] He cites Cole who has also highlighted this issue. Cole has raised the following questions concerning the reversed successive subordinations between the Son and the Spirit: "[I]f we too quickly move from the narrative of the economy to the inner life of the Trinity, what are we to make of the 'lordship' of the Spirit over the Son prior to glorification? What is the counterpart to this subordination in the eternal internal life of the Trinity? . . . Do we have to posit an executive role to the Spirit within the essential Trinity?"[97]

Given this challenge, Moody attempts to meet it by making two points. Firstly, he cites what he believes is a hermeneutical principle taken from Gregory of Nazianzen. This is a principle on the relative clarity of the identity of divine persons. Moody writes:

> we should not allow that which is unclear to cloud that which is abundantly clear. If Jesus' relationship to the Spirit in his earthly ministry seems to overturn the traditional understanding of his relationship to the Spirit in the life of God *ad intra*, then we

---

94. Moody provides an example of an Evangelical who is consciously indebted to RR and to the SRR of RR, in contrast to other Evangelicals who employ something analogous to the SRR of RR.

95. Moody's project is Moody, "Will of Him Who Sent Me: An Exploration of Responsive Intra-Trinitarian Willing."

96. Moody, "Will," 243.

97. Cole, *Holy Spirit*: 172. In the footnotes, Moody also cites von Balthasar on this difficulty; however, he does not deal with Balthasar's solution. von Balthasar, *Explorations: Spirit and Institution*, 4: 231–32.

might do well to remember Gregory of Nazianzen's comments on the relative clarity with which the persons are revealed:

> The Old Testament proclaimed the Father openly, and the Son more obscurely. The New manifested the Son, and suggested the deity of the Spirit. Now the Spirit himself dwells amongst us, and supplies us with a clearer demonstration of himself.[98]

Moody uses this argument in tandem with what he claims is binitarian evidence from the New Testament supported by the opinions of Doyle and Karl Rahner. Moody's argument appears to be arguing for something less than an equal divine and personal existence for the Spirit as for the Father and the Son. Moody cites Doyle approvingly; Doyle writes: "clearly the N.T. states that the Holy Spirit is God, and Person in God, but that he is God and Person in a different way from Father and Son." [99]

Not only does this appear to stray from orthodox trinitarianism, but the use of Gregory's point misses the mark as it does not seem to be relevant to the issue of the clear record of the successive reverse subordinations of the Son and the Spirit in the economy of salvation.

A further point to be made at this point is to ask why do the Father and the Son require mediation between them—*why would they need a mediator*? Indeed, does such a mediation view allow for the perichoresis between the Father and the Son? How does this mediatorial view accommodate the "oneness" and "in-ness" language about the Father and the Son (John 10:30, 38)?

The second argument Moody employs to overcome the problem facing the SRR of RR, is an argument for the inner-divine and historical mediatorship of the Holy Spirit. Moody states:

> It would seem that the Holy Spirit fulfils the same mediatorial or interstitial role between the Father and Jesus that he later fulfills in relation to us as the Spirit of God and the Spirit of Christ . . . In the light of the Spirit's economic role in the relations between the Father and the Son, an alternative conclusion might be that the Spirit's relationship vis á vis Jesus does correspond to his *opera*

---

98. Moody, "Will," 244.

99. Doyle, Robert, "The Spirit of the Father and the Spirit of the Son," 25–27 cited in Moody, "Will," 245. Moody's approach is interesting because the other Evangelical theologian who we studied as a proponent of SRR of RR (Bruce Ware) believes that the Spirit is "all the time third." Ware, *Father*, 129. Thus, both Moody and Ware lean towards a low pneumatology which perhaps is indicative of the fact that that the use of the SRR of RR produces a weak pneumatology.

ad intra after all; not an "eternal executive role" but an eternal *mediatorial* role. There are certainly affinities with this suggestion in the Augustinian depiction of him as the bond of love (*vinculum amoris*) between the Father and Son, or with the view Graham Cole himself sets forth—that the Spirit is the way God knows himself . . . Cole thus provides a very plausible answer to the problem he and others raise. If the Spirit is the "epistemic bond" *within* the Godhead, then it is entirely appropriate that he also mediate between the Father and the Son *ad extra*.[100]

What is significant for our project is that Moody's "mediation of the Spirit" view does not cohere with Luke-Acts' presentation of the Son-Spirit relationship. According to Luke-Acts, there is only one true mediator role in the economy of salvation. The sweep of salvation history and the canonical shape of progressive revelation clearly locate the Spirit's work between the Father and the Son in a once-off temporary role. The only one who is accorded the role of mediator, is Jesus, the reigning king. Therefore, there is no salvation-historical analogue for any eternal the permanent Spirit-mediation between God the Father and God the Son.

In order to counter Moody's argument, three prominent New Testament scholars may be taken as representative of the fact that across the breadth of the theological spectrum there is a consensus view on this issue: namely that in Luke-Acts and in the New Testament more broadly there is only one mediator- Jesus Christ, not the Holy Spirit. Firstly, we turn to the work of N. T. Wright, a proponent of a "maximizer's" view of Jesus' historical mediating reign. For Wright, Jesus is the one whose exalted status means that he has "World Lordship."[101] Wright states that at the end of Luke's Gospel: "The readers are left for the moment where they began, worshipping in the Temple; but Jesus himself ends as the exalted lord of the world, ready now to begin the second phase of his work. (Acts opens by speaking of 'all that Jesus began to do and teach' (1.1); it describes his continuing ministry of deed and word.)"

Secondly, the more "moderate"[102] historical view of James D. G. Dunn. He presents us with the fact that regardless of how people viewed the relationship between God and Jesus, they approached God via

---

100. Italics are Moody's. Moody, "Will," 246–47.

101. Wright, *Resurrection*, 728 ff.

102. It is deemed "moderate" because his use of the historical-critical method mutes the fuller capacity of some of the claims of the New Testament.

Jesus.[103] That is, in Dunn's thinking, Jesus alone is the mediator between people and God. In his most recent work Dunn writes:

> [T]here is a consistent thought through the New Testament of Jesus sharing in the glory of God. The thought is not only of Jesus as the agent or embodiment of God's glory, but of glory being given to Jesus, as glory is given to God. And in the benedictions that begin and conclude Paul's letters, "the Lord Jesus Christ" is presented equally with "God our Father" as the source of grace and peace, and as the one through whom pre-eminently the grace of God has come and still comes to expression.
>
> In reflecting further on how this relationship of the Lord Jesus Christ with God is conceived, we should recall also the repeated conviction that thanks to God are given "through Jesus Christ" or "in the name of our Lord Jesus" ... Christ, in other words, seems to have been thought of as on both sides of the worship relationship—as in at least some degree the object of worship. But also as the enabler or medium of effective worship.[104]

Thirdly, we have the scholarship of an historical "minimalist"— Dale Allison. Despite his caution with regards to the "historicity of Jesus," there is no doubt in his mind that Jesus envisioned a kingdom of God. Moreover, Jesus understood himself as the eschatological king of that kingdom. Despite Allison's stripped back, bare-bones approach to the historical Jesus, he contends that the New Testament claim is that Jesus is the ruler over the kingdom of God as anticipated by Ps 110 and by Jesus' followers:

> Jesus himself is, in the canonical gospels, the eschatological king, or destined to be such. The mainspring of Matthew's infancy narrative is that the Davidic Messiah ... has been born, and he will rule "my people Israel" (2:6). As "king of the Jews" (2:2), he is Herod's rival, which is why the tyrant decrees death for Bethlehem's children. Luke's infancy narrative is similar, for it too records the birth of royalty. The angel Gabriel announces to Mary, regarding her child, that "the Lord God will give him the throne of his ancestry David," and that he "will reign over the house of Jacob forever, and of his kingdom there will be no end" (1:32–33) ... Soon after Easter, some of his followers envisaged him as enthroned because, already before Eater, they had expected his enthronement ... they had hoped God would install

---

103. Dunn, *Did the First Christians?* 28.
104. Ibid.

him as king, so when they became persuaded of his divine vindication, they naturally came to believe that God had seated him upon a heavenly throne—a conviction that . . . could find support in Scripture, above all in Ps 110.[105]

This survey of recent New Testament scholarship, which I find convincing, reveals that Moody's proposal for a mediating view of the Holy Spirit simply does not sit well within current scholarly agreement. Moody has not captured the biblical witness to Jesus' unique and fundamental identity as the reigning Lord and mediator between God and humankind.

The proposal by Moody therefore suffers from a lack of clarity, especially when the NT only identifies one person as the mediator. Paul states that there is "one mediator between God and humankind, the man Christ Jesus" in 1 Tim 2:5, and so does the writer to the Hebrews (Heb 8:6 "Christ has obtained a ministry that is as more excellent than the old as the covenant he mediates is better"; 9:15 "Therefore he is the mediator of a new covenant, so that those who are called may receive the promised eternal inheritance"; see also 6:17 and 12:24). Given the New Testament presentation, we conclude that Moody's language confuses the relationship between christology and pneumatology. This confusion is unfortunate and akin to deploying the term "the Word" to refer to the Spirit if it suited our theological purposes.

In our view, Moody's attempt to handle the biblical witness regarding the successive reversed subordinations between the Spirit and the Son requires greater warrant. Given that Moody's attempt is the most serious attempt of which we are aware, these successive reversed subordinations remain a roadblock to the application of the SRR of RR to Scripture. The challenge to the SRR of RR by the witness of Scripture is currently insurmountable by proponents of the SRR of RR.

CONCLUSION

Given the exegesis above, Scripture presents us with grounds for doubts and questions about the value of employing SRR of RR. Firstly, exegesis from Luke-Acts shows that according to the narrative the Spirit is (together with Mary) responsible for the origination and personal unity of

---

105. Allison Jr., *Constructing Jesus*, 245, 50.

Jesus. The Spirit also shapes and leads Jesus' ministry as God's chosen Messiah for distinct purposes within the economy of salvation. Further, Jesus' mission under the influence of the Spirit is not intended to be interpreted as an expression, or strict reflection, of the intra-trinitarian life. *If* the Spirit's generating role were read according to the SRR of RR, then a view which counters both the Western and Eastern views of generation would apply: the Son is generated by the Holy Spirit with no direct relation to God the Father or to the life of God the Son. Further, the ensuing theology of relations within the Godhead would have great affinity with pantheism as God the Son is absolutely tied to history for his development. Secondly, we noted that in the narrative of Luke-Acts Jesus receives the Spirit twice. These receptions have salvation history concerns in mind and do not relate to events within the trinitarian taxis. *If* these events did relate to an eternal correlate within the Godhead *ad intra*, several speculative theologoumena ensue as it is would be difficult to conceive why it is necessary that this event be repeated, and how this dual reception presents a coherent theology of God's inner relationships. The level of speculation required at this juncture surely presses against the epistemological security sought by those who employ the SRR of RR. Thirdly, we also noted that there is a reversal of the economic executive relations between God the Son and God the Holy Spirit in the Gospel of Luke and the book of Acts. *If* these reversed economic relations are read into the eternal trinitarian taxis, then a theology arises whereby God is a being who may morph at the ontological level. In addition, little could be said about God's eternal being due to these changes, unless one took a two-tiered view of God in which the Father is relationally stable but the Son and the Spirit are not. Even in this case, not much could be said of the relations between the Spirit and the Son: we would be somewhat agnostic about the current state of God's being because a further change may have occurred within him, or perhaps a relational change may occur in the future.

After our exegetical work was completed we raised various questions regarding the eternal analogues of the phenomena we see in Luke-Acts. We addressed Andrew Moody's work in which he acknowledges that in order for his own SRR of RR-based project to stand, he needed to provide a counter to our third observation regarding the successive reversed subordinations between the Son and the Spirit in Luke-Acts. His answer was duly considered, found wanting from an exegetical point of view and thus rejected.

6

Conclusion

Our book has engaged with Rahner's Rule and its "Strict Realist Reading." McCosker was right to say that "One can safely say . . . that this 'rule' generated more theological reflection in the second half of the twentieth century than any other single sentence."[1] After exploring its foundations and implications within Rahner's thought, we outlined the *Grundaxiom's* importance. Following this, we engaged in an exegetical study of Luke-Acts with special reference to Jesus' messianic vocation, the relationships and works between the persons of God the Father and God the Son, and also between God the Son and God the Spirit in the economy of salvation.

The cumulative result of this study has been to suggest that the SRR of RR may be questionable given some aspects of the witness of Luke-Acts. Firstly, there is indirect resistance to the SRR of RR by select sections of the text of Luke-Acts. Secondly, there is also the specter of the problematical theological conclusions that could stem from the application of this norm to various texts in Luke-Acts. These two issues raise questions about the usefulness of the "strict realist reading" of Rahner's Rule as a conceptual tool from an Evangelical standpoint. Thus, the SRR of RR appears to be problematic for constructing a doctrine of the essential Trinity. This conclusion is reinforced when we return to some of Erickson's criteria for assessing the relative strength of competing theories, which we outlined in chapter 1.

We begin with the "consistency criterion." This criterion requires that a theory be consistent within itself and not be inconsistent. In view

---

1. Cited in O'Byrne, *Spirit Christology*, 168n.

of our results from chapters four and five, we can see that the SRR of RR cannot be applied to Luke-Acts in a manner which yields consistent results. The SRR produces inconsistent results in terms of the changing patterns of relationships between the Father and the Son, and also the Son and the Spirit because of the dynamic and somewhat fluid nature of the trinitarian actors and actions in Luke-Acts.

In chapter four of our work, we argued that Luke 10:22 may provide a case in point for our "economic trinitarian person fluidity thesis." The inconsistency in a relational order between the persons of the Trinity was more clearly evident in the results outlined in chapter five. In that chapter, the successive reversed subordinations between God the Son and God the Spirit to each other were noted. Based on the SRR of RR, one might expect that this pattern of relationships to be an analogue of an eternal relationship. However, it is hard to see how the conclusions about this aspect of the Son-Spirit relationship in Luke-Acts can be made to comport with this view.

The "applicability criterion" deals with the issue of whether or not what is stated is an accurate representation of biblical reality. Evangelicals will surely stand behind Erickson's statement that whether or not a proposition emerges from the Bible should be taken to be the grounds for its validity or invalidity respectively. Given this, the SRR of RR has been tested against the Bible and found wanting. This is because theological conclusions that arise from the use of the SRR of RR meet resistance from the Scriptures themselves. In particular, the conclusion that God the Son is eternally obedient to God the Father in the divine taxis was resisted by the fact that Scripture is very clear that Jesus' messianic role determined his actions and relationships in the economy of salvation, including his obedience to God the Father (as we saw in chapter three).

The "adequacy criterion" asks whether all or most of the data from Luke-Acts can been taken into account by those who hold to a SRR of RR. An adequate theory should be able to take up all or the majority of the data within itself.[2] However, our study of trinitarian relations in

---

2. "One sees often in theological discussions where certain biblical texts are appealed to while others that also bear on the subject are bypassed. The difficulty comes when because there are often numerous relevant texts, at least some of which tend to support opposing conclusions... Picking and choosing in such a way as to support the conclusion to which one is already committed betrays a weak theory. Good theories are built upon taking account of all the data, not that which is favorable." Erickson, *Tampering*, 99.

Luke-Acts has provided evidence that the SRR of RR cannot include the following within its set of data: Jesus' messianic vocation, Jesus' limited knowledge with reference to God the Father, the fuller revelation of Jesus to come at the eschaton, the transfigurational cue that Jesus' revelation of himself in salvation history is limited, and the veiling effect that Jesus' humanity and messianic vocation have upon what is revealed of trinitarian relationships in the economy of salvation. Further, the SRR of RR cannot include within it the eternal analogues it would create in terms of Jesus' double reception of the Spirit, Jesus' ascension, nor the successive reversed subordinations of the Son and the Spirit to each other. These significant aspects of the testimony of Luke-Acts simply cannot be left aside by a theory. Therefore, the SRR of RR does not comport well with Luke-Acts and so fails the "adequacy" criterion. As a result we may say that a SRR of RR is, at best, a weak theory because it cannot include much of the witness of Luke-Acts (nearly 1/3 of the New Testament record) within the boundaries of its data.

The "personal criterion" maintains that a key criterion for assessing any view is to take into account the motivation behind it. As we saw in chapter two, in Rahner's case, the motivation behind his *Axiom* and its SRR interpretation, was pastoral, and anthropological, rather than rooted in a significant exegetical engagement with the Bible. Thus at the outset, a SRR of RR *was not posited with a view to reflecting an exegetically warranted biblical truth*. Our cumulative case against the SRR of RR argues that given the exegetical results of our study, these motivations for the SRR of RR may be commendable but cannot function as the basis for our theology of God.

Finally, the "status of the conclusion criterion" is a highly significant criterion for strong theories. A strong theory will emerge over competing theories because it can account for more evidence than another, however, at the same time it will not claim to take all the data into account. The finding of this study is that the SRR of RR is a weak theory because it cannot accommodate much of the data from Luke-Acts. Further, our study of Luke-Acts implicitly calls for a theory, other than the SRR of RR, to provide a norm for a doctrine of the triune God. This new norm will hopefully be much more closely based upon the biblical witness.

Given the biblical case outlined in this work, and the issues faced by the SRR of RR, one may wonder what may be helpful avenues for future research into the relationship between the economic work of the

Trinity and God's eternal taxis. One possible avenue for future research, in line with this work, might be to show that the trinitarian conclusions found in Luke-Acts are in line with various soundings taken from across the NT. Passages for such a study might be John 17:5, 2 Cor 8:9, Phil 2:5–11, Heb 5:8, 1 John 3:1–2 among others.

The fact of the presence of a fluidity of actor and action (and hence a deep unity) between trinitarian persons disallows a strict appropriation of actions to be employed as the norm for trinitarian relations. This fluidity between the Father, the Son and the Spirit is not unique to Luke-Acts. It is borne out in the lack of a consistent order of relations between the persons of the Trinity throughout the New Testament. For example, the lack of a consistent order of relations shows that the trinitarian taxis is not fixed hierarchically, nor is it a priority for biblical writers. Erickson observes:

> we should note that, especially in Paul, the persons are not invariably named in the order, Father-Son-Spirit. Those who hold to the priority of the Father would contend that the order Father-Son-Spirit is normative, indicating a superiority or priority of the Father to the Son and of both the Father and the Son to the Holy Spirit. There is however, a lack of uniformity of this pattern in the New Testament. Indeed, occasionally the reverse order occurs, as in 1 Corinthians 12:4–6 . . . Another example is Ephesians 4:4–6.[3]

Moreover, there are passages in which even the reverse order of a so called pattern of relations is not proposed, such as in 2 Cor 13:14.[4]

This suggestion for future research is made in the hope that Evangelical theologians will be challenged to find a better tool than the SRR of RR for exploring Scriptural trinitarian theology. This suggestion is offered with a view to deriving a doctrine of the Trinity that may be a true fount of living worship, union, love, and mission.

---

3. Erickson, *Making sense of the Trinity: 3 Crucial Questions*, 88.

4. Ibid. Observation of this lead B. B. Warfield to the following conclusion: "The question naturally suggests itself whether the order Father, Son, Spirit was especially significant to Paul and his fellow-writers of the New Testament. If in their conviction the very essence of the doctrine of the Trinity was embodied in this order, should we not anticipate that there appear in their numerous allusions to the Trinity some suggestion of this conviction." Cited in ibid.

Bibliography

Adam, Peter. *Written for Us: Receiving God's Word in the Bible*. Nottingham, UK: InterVarsity, 2008.

Allison Jr., Dale C. *Constructing Jesus: Memory, Imagination, and History*. Grand Rapids: Baker Academic, 2010.

Anderson, Kevin L. *"But God Raised Him From the Dead": The Theology of Jesus' Resurrection in Luke-Acts*. Paternoster Biblical Monographs. Milton Keyes, UK: Paternoster, 2006.

Augustine. *The Trinity*. Edited and abridged by Charles Dollen. Boston: St. Paul, 1965.

Baker, Matthew. "The Eternal 'Spirit of the Son': Barth, Florovsky and Torrance on the Filioque." *International Journal of Systematic Theology* 12.4 (2010) 382–403.

Balserak, J. "The God of Love and Weakness: Calvin's Understanding of God's Accommodating Relationship with His People." *Westminster Theological Journal* 62.2 (2000) 177–95.

Barnes, Michael H. "Demythologization in the Theology of Karl Rahner." *Theological Studies* 55.1 (1994) 24–45.

Barth, Karl. *Church Dogmatics 4/2: The Doctrine of Reconciliation*. Translated by G. W. Bromiley et al. Edinburgh: T. & T. Clark, 1978.

Battaglia, Vincent. "An Examination of Karl Rahner's Trinitarian Theology." *Australian EJournal of Theology* March (2007). No pages.

Bauckham, Richard. *God Crucified: Monotheism and Christology in the New Testament*, Didsbury Lectures. Carlisle, UK: Paternoster, 1998.

Beale, G. K., and D. A. Carson. *Commentary on the New Testament Use of the Old Testament*. Grand Rapids: Baker Academic, 2007.

Bénétreau, Samuel. "Appellation et Transcendence: Le Nom mystériux de Phillipiens 2,9." *Revue D'Historie et de Philosophie Religieuses* 89.3 (2009) 313–31.

Benner, Drayton C. „Augustine and Karl Rahner on the Relationship between the Immanent Trinity and the Economic Trinity." *International Journal of Systematic Theology* 9.1 (2007) 24–38.

Berger, Klaus. "Das Canticum Simeonis (Lk. 2:29–32)." *Novum Testamentum* 27.1 (1985) 27–39.

Bibb, Wade. "The Characterization of God in Luke-Acts." PhD diss., The Southern Baptist Theological Seminary, 1996.

Bird, Michael F. "Jesus Is the 'Messiah of God': Messianic Proclamation in Luke-Acts." *Reformed Theological Review* 66.2 (2007) 69–82.

———. "Jesus Is the Christ: Messianic Apologetics in The Gospel of Mark." *Reformed Theological Review* 64.1 (2005) 1–14.
Blackburn, Simon. "Isomorphic " In *The Oxford Dictionary of Philosophy*, edited by Simon Blackburn. Oxford: Oxford University Press, 1996.
Bobrinskoy, Boris. *El Misterio de La Trinidad*. Translated by David Gasa i Castell. Salamanca, Spain: Secretariado Trinitario, 2008.
Bock, Darrell L. *Luke*. 2 vols, Baker Exegetical Commentary on the New Testament. Grand Rapids: Baker, 1994.
Bøe, Sverre *Cross-Bearing in Luke*, Wissenschaftliche Untersuchungen zum Neuen Testament. Tübingen: Mohr Siebeck, 2010.
Bonaventure. *The Breviloquium*, IV.2.2. No pages. http://www.catholic.uz/tl_files/library.
Boring, M. Eugene. *Mark: A Commentary*. New Testament Library. Louisville: Westminster John Knox, 2006.
Bosc, Jean. "Le Dieu de la bible est un Dieu Trinitaire." *Revue Reformee* 181.3 (1994) 53–67.
Bovon, Francois. *Das Evangelium Nach Lukas (Lk 19,28—24,53)*. 4 vols. Vol. III/4, Evangelisch-Katholischer Kommentar zum Neuen Testament. 1989. Reprint. Düsseldorf: Neukirchen-Vluyn: Neukirchener, 2009.
———. "Les Médiations dans l'oevre de Luc." *New Testament Studies* 21 (1975) 23–39.
Bracken, Joseph A. *What Are They Saying About the Trinity?* New York: Paulist, 1979.
Brueggemann, Walter. *Old Testament Theology: An Introduction*, The Library of Biblical Theology. Nashville: Abingdon, 2008.
———. *Theology of the Old Testament: Testimony, Dispute, Advocacy*. Minneapolis: Fortress, 1997.
Buckwalter, H. Douglas. *The Character and Purpose of Luke's Christology*. Cambridge: Cambridge University Press, 1996.
Calvin, John. *Commentary on A Harmony of the Evangelists*. Vol. 1. Translated by W. Pringle. Edinburgh: Calvin Translation Society, 1845.
———. *Commentary Upon the Acts of the Apostles*. Vol. 2. Translated by Henry Beveridge. Edinburgh: T. & T. Clark, 1859.
———. *Institutes of the Christian Religion*, The Library of Christian Classics; v. 20–21. Edited by J.T. McNeill. Philadelphia: Westminster, 1960.
Cifrak, Mario. *Die Beziehung zwischen Jesus und Gott nach den Petrusreden der Apostelgeschichte: Ein exegetischer Beitrag zur Christologie der Apostelgeschichte.* Würzburg, Germany: Echter, 2003.
Coffey, David. *Deus Trinitas*. Oxford: Oxford University Press, 1999.
———. "The 'Incarnation' of the Holy Spirit in Christ." *Theological Studies* 45.3 (1984) 466–80.
———. "Trinity." In *The Cambridge Companion to Karl Rahner*, edited by Declan Marmion, and Mary E. Hines, 98–111. Cambridge: Cambridge University Press, 2005.
Cole, Graham A. *God the Peacemaker*. Downers Grove, IL: InterVarsity, 2009.
———. "God, Doctrine of." In *Dictionary for Theological Interpretation of the Bible*, edited by K. J. Vanhoozer, et al., 259–63. Grand Rapids: Baker Academic, 2005.
———. *He Who Gives Life: The Doctrine of the Holy Spirit*. Wheaton, IL: Crossway, 2007.
Conzelmann, Hans. *Die Mitte der Zeit: Studien zur Theologie des Lukas*. 5. Aufl. ed. Beiträge zur historischen Theologie. Tübingen: Mohr, 1964.

Cooper, John W. *Panentheism: The Other God of the Philosophers: From Plato to the Present*. Grand Rapids: Baker Academic, 2006.
Coppedge, Allan. *The God Who Is Triune: Revisioning the Christian Doctrine of God*. Downers Grove, IL: InterVarsity, 2007.
Corkery, James. "Rahner and Ratzinger: A Complex Relationship." In *Karl Rahner: Theologian for the Twenty First Century*, edited by Padriac Conway and Fainche Ryan, 77–100. Bern: Lang, 2010.
Dallavalle, Nancy Ann. "Revisiting Rahner: On the Theological Status of Trinitarian Theology." *Irish Theological Quarterly* 63.2 (1988) 133–50.
———. "Saving History and the Salvation of History in Karl Rahner's Trinitarian Theology." PhD diss., Notre Dame, 1993.
Davis, John Jefferson. "Incarnation, Trinity, and the Ordination of Women to the Priesthood." In *The Deception of Eve and the Ontology of Women*, edited by William David Spencer, 10–20. Minneapolis: Christians for Biblical Equality, 2010.
Dempster, Stephen. "Exodus and Biblical Theology: On Moving into the Neighbourhood with a New Name." *The Southern Baptist Journal of Theology* 12.3 (2008) 4–24.
Di Noia, Joseph A. "Karl Rahner." In *The Modern Theologians: An Introduction to Christian Theology in the Twentieth Century*, edited by David F. Ford, 118–33. Oxford: Blackwell, 1997.
———. "Nature and Grace, and Experience: Karl Rahner's Theology of Human Transformation." *Philosophy and Theology* 7.2 (1992) 115–26.
Donahue, J. R. Harington. *The Gospel of Mark*. Edited by Daniel Harington. Sacra Pagina. Minnesota: Liturgical, 2002.
Doud, Robert E. "Rahner's Christology: A Whiteheadian Critique." *Journal of Religion* 57 (1977) 144–55.
Duffy, Stephen J. "Experience of Grace." In *The Cambridge Companion to Karl Rahner*, edited by Declan Marmion, and Mary E. Hines, 43–62. Cambridge: Cambridge University Press, 2005.
Dumbrell, William J. "Worship and Isaiah 6." *The Reformed Theological Review* 63.1 (1984) 1–8.
Dunard, Emmanuel. "L'identité rahnérienne entre la Trinité économique et la Trinité immanente à l'epreuve de ses applications." *Revue Thomiste* 103 (2003) 75–92.
———. "«Trinité immanente» et «Trinité économique» selon Karl Barth. Les declinaisons et la distinction et son dépassement (Aufhebung)." *Revue des Sciences Philosophiques et Theologiques* 90.3 (2006) 453–78.
Dunn, James D. G. "The Book of Acts as Salvation History." In *Heil und Geschichte: Die Geschichtsbezogenheit des Heils und das Problem der Heilsgeschichte in der biblischen Tradition und in der theologischen Deutung*, edited by Jorg Frey, 385–99. Tübingen: Mohr Siebeck, 2009.
———. *Did the First Christians Worship Jesus? New Testament Evidence*. Louisville: Westminster John Knox, 2010.
———. *Jesus Remembered*. Christianity in the Making, vol. 1. Grand Rapids: Eerdmans, 2003.
Dych, William V. *Karl Rahner*. Outstanding Christian Thinkers. Collegeville, MN: Liturgical, 1992.
Egan, Harvey. "Rahner, Karl." In *The Dictionary of Historical Theology*, edited by Trevor A. Hart, 449–51. Carlisle, UK: Paternoster, 2000.

———. "A Rahnerian Response to *Dominus Jesus.*" In *Australian EJournal of Theology*, 2004. No pages. http://dlibrary.acu.edu.au/research/theology/ejournal/aejt_2/HarveyEgan.htm

———. "Theology and Spirituality." In *The Cambridge Companion to Karl Rahner*, edited by Declan Marmion, and Mary E. Hines, 13–28. Oxford: Oxford University Press, 2005.

Egbulefu, John. "Theologie und Ausdrucksmittel: Bemerkungen zum Denken Karl Rahners." *Zeitschrift für Katholische Theologie* 126.1 (2004) 23–31.

Eicher, Peter. *Die anthropologische Wende: Karl Rahners philosophischer Weg vom Wesen des Menschen zur personalen Existenz*. Schweitz: Universitätsverlag Freiburg, 1970.

Ellingworth, Paul. *The Epistle to the Hebrews: A Commentary on the Greek Text*. New International Greek Testament Commentary. Carlisle, UK: Paternoster, 1993.

Endean, Phillip. "Has Rahnerian Theology a Future?" In *The Cambridge Companion to Karl Rahner*, edited by Declan Marmion, and Mary E. Hines, 281–96. Cambridge: Cambridge University Press, 2005.

Erickson, Millard J. *Christian Theology*. 2nd ed. Grand Rapids: Baker, 1998.

———. *God in Three Persons: A Contemporary Interpretation of the Trinity*. Grand Rapids: Baker, 1995.

———. *God the Father Almighty: A Contemporary Exploration of the Divine Attributes*. Grand Rapids: Baker, 1998.

———. *Making Sense of the Trinity: 3 Crucial Questions*. Grand Rapids: Baker, 2000.

———. *Who Is Tampering with the Trinity? An Assessment of the Subordination Debate*. Grand Rapids: Kregel, 2009.

Eslinger, Lyle M. "The Enigmatic Plurals Like 'One of Us' (Genesis i 26, iii 22, xi 7) in Hyperchronic Perspective." *Vetus Testamentum* 56.2 (2006) 171–84.

Evans, Craig A., and W. Ward Gasque. *Luke*. New International Biblical Commentary. Peabody, MA: Hendrickson, 1990.

Fee, Gordon D. *Pauline Christology: An Exegetical-Theological Study*. Peabody, MA: Hendrickson, 2007.

Ferguson, Sinclair B. *The Holy Spirit*. Downers Grove, IL: InterVarsity, 1996.

Fitzmyer, Joseph A. *The Gospel according to Luke: Introduction, Translation, and Notes*. 2 vols. The Anchor Bible. Garden City, NY: Doubleday, 1981.

Flender, Helmut. *St Luke: Theologian of Redemptive History*. Translated by Reginald H. and Ilse Fuller. Philadelphia: Fortress, 1967.

Gander, Georges. *L'Evangile pour les étrangers du monde*. Lausanne: Lausanne, 1986.

Gathercole, Simon J. *The Preexistent Son: Recovering the Christologies of Matthew, Mark, and Luke*. Grand Rapids: Eerdmans, 2006.

Gelpi, Donald L. *Life and Light: A Guide to the Theology of Karl Rahner*. New York: Sheed and Ward, 1966.

Giles, Kevin. *Jesus and the Father: Modern Evangelicals Reinvent the Doctrine of the Trinity*. Grand Rapids: Zondervan, 2006.

———. "Salvation in Lukan Theology (I)." *The Reformed Theological Review* 42.1 (1983) 10–16.

———. "The Son of God Is Not Eternally Inferior, Subordinate, or Submissive." *Christian Research Journal* 31.1 (2008) 15–19.

González, Antonio. *Teología de la Praxis Evangélica: Ensayo de una Teología Fundamental*. Santander, Spain: Editorial Sal Terrae, 1999.

González, Justo L. *Acts: The Gospel of the Spirit*. New York: Orbis, 2001.

Görres, Albert "Wer ist Karl Rahner für mich?—Antwortes eines Psychotherapeuten." In *Karl Rahner. Bilder eines Lebens*, edited by Paul Imhof, and Hubert Biallowons. Freiburg: Herder, 1985.

Graham, Pat. "Psalm 77: A Study in Faith and History." *Restoration Quarterly* 18.3 (1975) 151–58.

Green, Joel B. *The Gospel of Luke*. The New International Commentary on the New Testament. Grand Rapids: Eerdmans, 1997.

Groppe, Elizabeth T. *Yves Congar's Theology of the Holy Spirit*. Oxford: Oxford University Press, 2004.

Grudem, Wayne. *Systematic Theology: An Introduction to Biblical Doctrine*. Grand Rapids: Zondervan, 1994.

———, ed. *Biblical Foundations for Manhood and Womanhood*, Foundations for the Family Series. Wheaton, IL: Crossway, 2002.

Gryglewicz, F. "Die Herkunft der Hymnen Des Kindheitsevangelium des Lucas." *New Testament Studies* 21 (1975) 265–73.

Gunton, Colin E. *Act and Being: Towards a Theology of the Attributes of God*. Grand Rapids: Eerdmans, 2003.

———. *The One, the Three, and the Many: God, Creation, and the Culture of Modernity*. Cambridge: Cambridge University Press, 1993.

Hanson, R. P. C. *The Search for the Christian Doctrine of God: The Arian Controversy 318-381*. Grand Rapids: Baker Academic 1988.

Helfing, Charles C. Jr. "Reviving Adamic Adoptionism: The Example of John MacQuarrie." *Theological Studies* 52.3 (1991) 476–94.

Hendricksen, William. *The Gospel of Luke*. Grand Rapids: Baker, 1978.

Höhne, David A. *Spirit and Sonship*. Ashgate New Critical Thinking in Religion, Theology and Biblical Studies. Aldershot, UK: Ashgate, 2010.

Holmes, Stephen R. "Reformed Varieties of the Communicatio Idiomatum." In *The Person of Christ*, edited by Stephen R. Holmes, and Murray A. Rae, 70–86. London: T. & T. Clark, 2005.

Hübner, Siegfried. "Die Nichtchristlichre Menschheit im Licht Christlichens Glaubens: Karl Rahners Überlegungen zur thema „anonyme Christen⊠." *Zeitschrift für Katholische Theologie* 126.1 (2004) 47–64.

Huffman, Douglas S., and Eric L. Johnson. *God under Fire: Modern Scholarship Reinvents God*. Grand Rapids: Zondervan, 2002.

Hull, John H. E. *The Holy Spirit in the Acts of the Apostles*. London: Lutterworth, 1967.

Hurtado, Larry W. "First-Century Jewish Monotheism." *Journal for the Study of the New Testament* 71 (1998) 3–26.

Iredale, Matthew. "Indirect Reciprocity." *The Philosophers' Magazine* 50.3 (2010) 68–69.

Jenson, Robert W. *Systematic Theology*. New York: Oxford University Press, 1997.

Johnson, C. Andrew. "Ripples of the Resurrection in the Triune Life of God: Reading Luke 24 with Eschatological and Trinitarian Eyes." *Horizons in Biblical Theology* 24 (2002) 87–110.

Johnson, Luke Timothy. *The Gospel of Luke*. Collegeville: Liturgical, 1991.

Johnson, Luke Timothy, and Daniel J. Harrington. *The Gospel of Luke*. Sacra Pagina Series. Collegeville, MN: Liturgical, 1991.

Jorgenson, Allen G. *The Appeal to Experience in the Christologies of Friedrich Schleiermacher and Karl Rahner*. New York: Lang, 2007.

Jowers, Dennis W. "A Test of Karl Rahner's Axiom, 'The Economic Trinity Is The Immanent Trinity and Vice Versa.'" *The Thomist* 70 (2006) 421–55.
———. *The Trinitarian Axiom of Karl Rahner*. New York: Mellen, 2006.
Kärkkäinen, Veli-Matti. *Christology: A Global Introduction. An Ecumenical, International, Contextual Perspective*. Grand Rapids: Baker, 2003.
———. "The Trajectories of the Contemporary 'Trinitarian Renaissance' in Different Contexts." *Journal of Reformed Theology* 3.1 (2009) 72–81.
———. *The Trinity: Global Perspectives*. Louisville: Westminster John Knox, 2007.
Kasper, Walter. *Der Gott Jesu Christi*. Mainz: Grünewald, 1982.
———. *The God of Jesus Christ*. Translated by Matthew J. O'Connell. New York: Crossroad, 1984.
———. *Jesus the Christ*. New Jersey: Paulist, 1976.
Keppeler, Cornelius. "Begnadung als Berichtigte Froderung? Gedanken zur Bedeutung des übernatürlichen Existentials in der Gnadenlehre Karl Rahners." *Zeitschrift für Katholische Theologie* 126.1 (2004) 65–82.
Kezbere, Ilze. *Umstrittener Monotheismus: Wahre und falsche Apotheose im lukanischen Doppelwerk*. Novum Testamentum et orbis antiquus, Studien zur Umwelt des Neuen Testaments. Göttingen: Vandenhoeck & Ruprecht, 2007.
Kilby, Karen. „Karl Rahner." In *The Modern Theologians: An Introduction to Christian Theology since 1918*, edited by David F. Ford, and Rachel Muers, 92–105. Oxford: Blackwell, 2005.
———. "Philosophy, Theology and Foundationalism in the Thought of Karl Rahner." *Scottish Journal of Theology* 55.2 (2002) 127–50.
Kilgallen, John J. *The Stephen speech: A Literary and Redactional Study of Acts 7, 2–53*, Analecta Biblica. Rome: Biblical Institute Press, 1976.
Kingsbury, Jack Dean. *The Christology of Mark's Gospel*. Philadelphia: Fortress, 1983.
Kistemaker, Simon. *Exposition of the Acts of the Apostles*. New Testament Commentary. Grand Rapids: Baker, 1990.
Kraus, Hans-Joachim, and Hilton C. Oswald. *Psalms 60–150: A Commentary*. Minneapolis: Augsburg, 1989.
Kremer, Jacob. "Dieser ist der Sohn Gottes (Apg 9, 20)." In *Der Treue Gottes Trauen: Beiträge zum Werk des Lukas*, edited by Claus Bussman, and Walter Radl, 137–58. Freiburg: Herder, 1991.
Kress, Robert. *A Rahner Handbook*. Atlanta: John Knox, 1982.
Ladd, George Eldon, and Donald Alfred Hagner. *A Theology of the New Testament*. Rev. ed. Grand Rapids: Eerdmans, 1993.
Larkin, William J., D. Stuart Briscoe, and Haddon W. Robinson. *Acts*, The IVP New Testament Commentary Series. Downers Grove, IL: InterVarsity, 1995.
Laytham, D. Brent. "Stephen's Storied Witness to Jesus." In *Courage to Bear Witness*, edited by L. Edward Phillips, and Billy Vaughan, 1–13. Eugene, OR: Wipf and Stock, 2009.
Lee, Dorothy. *Transfiguration*. London: Continuum, 2004.
Lee, Seung Goo. "The Relationship between the Ontological Trinity and the Economic Trinity." *Journal of Reformed Theology* 3 (2009) 90–107.
Légasse, S. "Le Logion sur le Fils révélateur (Mt., XI, 27 par. Lc. X, 22) Essai d'analyse prérédactionelle." In *La Notion Biblique de Dieu*, edited by J. Coppens, 245–74. Leuven: Gembloux et Louven University Press, 1975.

Lenski, Richard Charles Henry. *The Interpretation of the Acts of the Apostles*. Columbus, OH: Lutheran, 1934.
Letham, Robert. "Does the Son Submit to the Father in the Indivisible Unity of the Trinity?" *Christian Research Journal* 31.1 (2008) 12–15.
———. *The Holy Trinity: In Scripture, History, Theology, and Worship*. Phillipsburg, NJ: P & R, 2004.
———. "Reply to Kevin Giles." *The Evangelical Quarterly* 80.4 (2008) 339–45.
Long, Stephen D. *Speaking of God: Theology, Language and Truth*. Grand Rapids: Eerdmans, 2009.
Longenecker, Richard N. "The Foundational Conviction of New Testament Christology: The Obedience/Faithfulness/Sonship of Christ." In *Jesus of Nazareth: Lord and Christ*, edited by Joel B. Green, and Max Turner, 473–88. Grand Rapids: Eerdmans, 1994.
Madigan, Kevin. *The Passions of Christ in High-Medieval Thought: An Essay on Christological Development*. Oxford: Oxford University Press, 2007.
Marcus, Joel. *Mark: A New Translation with Introduction and Commentary*, The Anchor Yale Bible Series. New Haven: Yale University Press, 2009.
Marmion, Declan. "Some Aspects of the Theological Legacy of Karl Rahner." In *Karl Rahner: Theologian for the Twenty First Century*, edited by Padriac Conway and Fainche Ryan, 3–22. Bern: Lang, 2010.
Marshall, Bruce D. "The Unity of the Triune God: Reviving an Ancient Question." *The Thomist* 74 (2010) 1–32.
Marshall, I. Howard. *The Gospel of Luke: A Commentary on the Greek Text*. New International Greek Testament Commentary. Exeter: Paternoster, 1978.
———. *Luke: Historian and Theologian*. 3rd ed. Exeter: Paternoster, 1988.
Matera, Frank J. *New Testament Christology*. Louisville: Westminster John Knox, 1999.
McCall, Thomas H. *Which Trinity? Whose Monotheism? Philosophical and Systematic Theologians on the Metaphysics of Trinitarian Theology*. Grand Rapids: Eerdmans, 2010.
McCall, Thomas, and Keith Yandell. "On Trinitarian Subordinationism." *Philosophia Christi* 11.2 (2009) 339–58.
McKnight, Scot. *Jesus and His Death: Historiography, the Historical Jesus, and Atonement Theory*. Waco, TX: Baylor University Press, 2005.
Meeks, Wayne A. "Assisting the Word by Making (Up) History: Luke's Project and Ours." *Interpretation* 57.2 (2003) 151–62.
Merrill, Eugene H. "Image of God." In *Dictionary of the Old Testament: Pentateuch*, edited by T. Desmond Alexander, David W. Baker, and John H. Walton, 441–45. Downers Grove, IL: InterVarsity, 2003.
Metz, Johann Baptist. *Den Glauben lehren und Denken. Dank an Karl Rahner*. Munich: Kösel, 1984.
Milne, Bruce. *Know The Truth: A Handbook of Christian Belief*. Downers Grove, IL: InterVarsity, 1982.
Mittlestadt, Martin W. *The Spirit and Suffering in Luke-Acts*. London: T. & T. Clark, 2004.
Molnar, Paul D. *Divine Freedom and the Doctrine of the Immanent Trinity: In Dialogue with Karl Barth and Contemporary Theology*. New York: T. & T. Clark, 2005.
———. *Incarnation and Resurrection: Toward a Contemporary Understanding*. Cambridge: Eerdmans, 2007.

Moody, Andrew. "The Will of Him Who Sent Me: An Exploration of Responsive Intra-Trinitarian Willing." ThD diss., Australian College of Theology, 2010.

Morgan, Robert. "Unity and Diversity in New Testament Talk of the Spirit." In *The Holy Spirit and Christian Origins*, edited by Graham N Stanton, Bruce W. Longenecker, and Stephen C. Barton, 1–14. Grand Rapids: Eerdmans, 2004.

Morris, Leon. *The Gospel according to St. Luke: An Introduction and Commentary*. The Tyndale New Testament Commentaries. Grand Rapids: Eerdmans, 1974.

———. *The Lord from Heaven: A Study of the New Testament Teaching on the Deity and Humanity of Jesus Christ*, Grand Rapids: Eerdmans, 1958.

Morris, Leon L. *Luke*. Rev. ed. Leicester, UK: InterVarsity, 2004.

Motyer, J. A. *The prophecy of Isaiah*. Leicester, UK: InterVarsity, 1993.

Moule, C. F. D. "The Christology of Acts." In *Studies in Luke-Acts*, edited by L. E. Keck, and J. L. Martyn, 159–68. New York: Abingdon, 1966.

Mowery, Robert L. "The Disappearance of the Father: The References to God the Father in Luke-Acts." *Encounter* 55.4 (1994) 353–58.

———. "God the Father in Luke-Acts." In *New Views on Luke and Acts*, edited by Earl Richard, 124–32. Collegeville, MN: Liturgical, 1990.

Muck, Otto. *The Transcendental Method*. Translated by William D. Seidensticker. New York: Herder and Herder, 1968.

Muller, Richard A. *Dictionary of Latin and Greek Theological Terms: Drawn Principally from Protestant Scholastic Theology*. Grand Rapids: Baker Book House, 1985.

———. *The Triunity of God*, Post Reformation Reformed Dogmatics: The Rise and Development of Reformed Orthodoxy, ca.1520–ca.1725. Grand Rapids: Baker Academic, 2003.

Nolland, J. *Luke 1—9:20*. Word Biblical Commentary 35a. Nashville, TN: Thomas Nelson, 1989.

———. *Luke 9:21—18:34*. Word Biblical Commentary 35b. Nashville, TN: Thomas Nelson, 1993.

———. *Luke 18:35—24:53*. Word Biblical Commentary 35c. Nashville, TN: Thomas Nelson, 1993.

O'Brien, Peter Thomas. *The Letter to the Hebrews*. Nottingham, UK: Apollos, 2010.

O'Byrne, Declan. *Spirit Christology and Trinity in the Theology of David Coffey*. Studies in Theology, Society and Culture. Berlin: Lang, 2010.

O'Leary, Joseph S. "Rahner and Metaphysics." In *Karl Rahner: Theologian for the Twenty-First Century*, edited by Padriac Conway, and Fainche Ryan, 23–38. Bern: Lang, 2010.

O'Loughlin, Thomas. "Losing Mystery in History." In *New Perspectives on the Nativity*, edited by Jeremy Corley, 180–99. London: T. & T. Clark, 2009.

Ollenburger, Ben C. "Creation and Peace: Creator and Creature in Genesis 1–11." In *The Old Testament in the Life of God's People: Essays in Honour of Elmer A. Martens*, edited by Jon Isaak, 143–58. Winona Lake, IN: Eisenbrauns, 2009.

Olson, Roger. "Wolfhart Pannenberg's Doctrine of the Trinity." *Scottish Journal of Theology* 43 (1990) 175–206.

Ormerod, Neil. *Introducing Contemporary Theologies*. New York: Orbis, 1997.

———. *The Trinity: Retrieving the Western Tradition*. Milwaukee: Marquette University Press, 2005.

Pannenberg, Wolfhart. *Systematic Theology*. Vol. 2. Grand Rapids: Eerdmans, 1994.

Parsons, Mikeal C. *Acts*, Paideia Commentaries on the New Testament. Grand Rapids: Baker Academic, 2008.
Pearl, Thomas. "Dialectical Panentheism: On the Hegelian Character of Karl Rahner's Key Christological Writings." *Irish Theological Quarterly* 42 (1975) 119–37.
Pelikan, Jaroslav. *Acts*, Brazos Theological Commentary on the Bible. Grand Rapids: Brazos, 2005.
Penney, J. M. *The Missionary Emphasis of Lukan Pneumatology*. Sheffield, UK: Sheffield Academic, 1997.
Pervo, Richard I., and Harold W. Attridge. *Acts: A Commentary*. Minneapolis: Fortress, 2009.
Peter, Lombard, Giulio Silano, and Pontifical Institute of Mediaeval Studies. *The Sentences: Book 3, On the Incarnation of the Word*. Toronto: Pontifical Institute of Medieval Studies, 2008.
Peters, Ted. *God as Trinity: Relationality and Temporality in the Divine Life*. Louisville: Westminster John Knox, 1993.
Peterson, David. *The Acts of the Apostles*. Grand Rapids: Eerdmans, 2009.
Pfremmer De Long, Kindalee. *Surprised by God: Praise Responses in the Narrative of Luke-Acts*. Berlin: de Grutyer, 2009.
Phan, Peter C. "Rahner on the Unoriginate Father: A Comment." *The Thomist* 58.1 (1994) 131–38.
Placher, William C. *Mark*, Belief: A Theological Commentary on the Bible. Louisville: Westminster John Knox, 2010.
Propp, William Henry. *Exodus 19–40: A New Translation with Introduction and Commentary*. The Anchor Bible. New York: Doubleday, 2006.
Rae, Murray A. "Anthropomorphism." In *Dictionary for Theological Interpretation of Scripture*, edited by Kevin J. Vanhoozer, 48–49. Grand Rapids: Baker Academic, 2005.
Rahner, Karl. "Christology within an Evolutionary View of the World." In *Theological Investigations. Vol. V*, 157–92. Baltimore: Helicon, 1966.
———. "Concerning the Relationship between Nature and Grace." In *Theological Investigations. Vol. I*, edited by Cornelius Ernst, 297–317. Baltimore: Helicon, 1963.
———. "'Current Problems in Christology.'" In *Theological Investigations. Vol. I*, 149–200. Baltimore: Helicon, 1965.
———. "Der dreifaltige Gott als transzendenter Urgrund der Heilsgeschichte." In *Mysterium Salutis: Grundriss Heilsgeschichtlicher Dogmatic*, edited by Johannes Feiner and Magnus Löhrer, 317–47. Einsiedeln, Germany: Benziger, 1967.
———. „'Dogmatic Considerations on Knowledge and Consciousness in Christ'." In *Dogmatic vs. Biblical Theology*, edited by H. Vorgrimler, 241–68. Baltimore: Helicon, 1964.
———. "Exegesis and Dogmatic Theology." In *Theological Investigations. Vol. V: Later Writings*, edited by Karl Rahner, 67–93. Baltimore: Helicon, 1966.
———. "'Exegesis and Dogmatic Theology.'" In *Dogmatic vs. Biblical Theology*, edited by H. Vorgrimler, 31–65. Baltimore: Helicon, 1964.
———. *Foundations of Christian Faith*. New York: Crossroad, 1978.
———. *Foundations of Christian Faith: An Introduction to the Idea of Christianity*. New York: Seabury, 1978.
———. "The Mystery of the Trinity." In *Theological Investigations. Vol. XVI*, translated by David Morland, 255–59. Baltimore: Helicon, 1979.

———. "On the Theology of Symbolic Reality." In *Theological Investigations*. Vol. IV, 235–44. Baltimore: Helicon, 1966.

———. "On the Theology of the Incarnation." In *Theological Investigations*. Vol. IV: *More Recent Writings*, 105–20. Baltimore: Helicon, 1966.

———. "On the Theology of the Symbol." In *Theological Investigations*. Vol. IV: *More Recent Writings*. Baltimore: Helicon, 1966.

———. "The Ontology of Symbolic Reality in General." In *Theological Investigations*. Vol. IV, 222–34. Baltimore Helicon, 1966.

———. "Reflections on Foundations of the Christian Faith." *Theology Digest* 28 (1980) 209–13.

———. "Some Implications of the Scholastic Concept of Uncreated Grace." In *Theological Investigations*. Vol. I, 319–46. Baltimore: Helicon, 1961.

———. *Spirit in the World*. Translated by W. Dych. New York: Herder and Herder, 1968.

———. *Theological Investigations*. 23 vols. Baltimore: Helicon, 1961.

———. *The Trinity*. New York: Crossroad, 1970.

Rauser, Randall. "Rahner's Rule: An Emperor Without Clothes?" *International Journal of Systematic Theology* 7.1 (2005) 81–94.

Rooker, Mark F. "Theophany." In *Dictionary of the Old Testament: Pentateuch*, edited by T. Desmond Alexander, David W. Baker, and John H. Walton, 859–64. Downers Grove, IL: InterVarsity, 2003.

Rowe, C. Kavin. "Biblical Pressure and Trinitarian Hermeneutics." *Pro Ecclesia* 11.3 (2002) 295–312.

———. *Early Narrative Christology: The Lord in the Gospel of Luke*. Berlin: de Gruyter, 2006.

———. "History Hermeneutics and the Unity of Luke-Acts." *Journal for the Study of the New Testament* 28.2 (2005) 131–57.

———. "Luke and the Trinity: An Essay in Ecclesial Biblical Theology." *Scottish Journal of Theology* 56.1 (2003) 1–26.

Sanders, Fred. "Chalcedonian Categories for the Gospel Narrative." In *Jesus in Trinitarian Perspective*, edited by Fred Sanders, and Klaus Issler, 1–43. Nashville: B & H, 2007.

———. "Dennis W. Jowers, Karl Rahner's Trinitarian Axiom: The Economic Trinity is the Immanenet Trinity and Vice Versa." *International Journal of Systematic Theology* 11.3 (2009) 370–72.

———. *The Image of the Immanent Trinity: Rahner's Rule and the Theological Interpretation of Scripture*. Issues in Systematic Theology 2. New York: Lang, 2005.

Sarot, Marcel. "Trinity and Church: Trinitarian Perspectives on the Identity of the Christian Community." *International Journal of Systematic Theology* 12.1 (2010) 20–32.

Schnabel, Eckhard J. *Early Christian Mission*. Downers Grove, IL: InterVarsity, 2004.

Schreiner, Thomas R., and Bruce A. Ware. *The Grace of God, the Bondage of the Will*. 2 vols. Grand Rapids: Baker, 1995.

———. *Still Sovereign: Contemporary Perspectives on Election, Foreknowledge, and Grace*. Grand Rapids: Baker, 2000.

Schroeder, Edward H. "Luke's Gospel through a Systematician's Lens." *Currents in Theology and Mission* 3.6 (1976) 337–46.

Scobie, Charles H. H. *The Ways of Our God*. Grand Rapids: Eerdmans, 2003.

Sheehan, Thomas "Rahner's Transcendental Project." In *The Cambridge Companion to Karl Rahner*, edited by Declan Marmion, and Mary E. Hines, 29–42. Cambridge: Cambridge University Press, 2005.

Shepherd, William H. *The Narrative Function of the Holy Spirit as a Character in Luke-Acts*. Atlanta: Scholars, 1994.

Siebenrock, Roman A. "„Tranzentale Offenbarung:☒ Bedeutungsanalyse eines Begriffs im Spätwerk Rahners als Beispiel methodisch geleiteter Rahnerforschung." *Zeitschrift für Katholische Theologie* 126.1 (2004) 33–46.

Siebenrock, Roman A. "Foreword." In *Karl Rahner: Theologian for the Twenty-First Century*, edited by Padriac Conway and Fainche Ryan, xi–xiv. Bern: Lang, 2010.

Smith, C. Drew. "This Is My Beloved Son; Listen to Him." *Horizons in Biblical Theology* 24.2 (2002) 53–86.

Sosa Silézar, Carlos Raúl "La teología de la gracia en el pensamiento de Karl Rahner." *Cuadernos de Teología* 28 (2008) 137–55.

Stein, Robert H. *Luke*. New American Commentary. Nashville: Broadman, 1992.

Stolina, Ralf. "»Ökonomische« und »immanente« Trinität? Zur Problematic einer trinitätstheologischen Denkfigur." *Zeitschrift für Theologie und Kirche* 105 (2008) 170–216.

Strauss, Mark L. *The Davidic Messiah in Luke-Acts*. Sheffield, UK: Sheffield Academic, 2001.

Talbert, Charles H. *Literary Patterns, Theological Themes, and the Genre of Luke-Acts*. Missoula: Society of Biblical Literature, 1975.

Talbot, Mark R. "Does God Reveal Who He Actually Is?" In *God Under Fire*, edited by Douglas S. Huffman and Eric L. Johnson, 44–70. Grand Rapids: Zondervan, 2002.

Tannehill, Robert C. *Luke*. Abingdon New Testament Commentaries. Nashville: Abingdon Press, 1996.

———. *The Narrative Unity of Luke-Acts: A Literary Interpretation*. 2 vols. Philadelphia: Fortress, 1991.

Terrien, Samuel L. *The Psalms: Strophic Structure and Theological Commentary*. Eerdmans Critical Commentary. Grand Rapids: Eerdmans, 2003.

Thomas. *Summa Theologica*. Translated by Fathers of the English Dominican Province. Westminster: Christian Classics, 1981.

Torrance, Thomas Forsyth. *Theology in Reconstruction*. Grand Rapids: Eerdmans, 1975.

———. *The Trinitarian Faith: The Evangelical Theology of the Ancient Catholic Church*. Edinburgh: T. & T. Clark, 1993.

———. *Trinitarian Perspectives: Toward Doctrinal Agreement*. Edinburgh: T. & T. Clark, 1994.

———. *When Christ Comes and Comes Again*. London: Hodder and Stoughton, 1957.

Turner, Max B. "Jesus and the Spirit in Lucan Perspective." *Tyndale Bulletin* 32 (1981) 3–42.

———. *Power From on High: The Spirit in Israel's Restoration and Witness in Luke-Acts*. Sheffield, UK: Sheffield Academic, 1996.

———. "The Work of the Holy Spirit in Luke-Acts." *World and Word* 23.2 (2003) 146–53.

Tyson, Joseph. "The Birth Narratives and the Beginning of Luke's Gospel." *Semeia* 52 (1990) 103–20.

Vaceck, E. "Developments with Karl Rahner's theology." *Irish Theological Quarterly* 42.1 (1975) 36–39.

Van Asselt, Willem J. "The Fundamental Meaning of Theology: Archetypal and Ektypal Theology in Seventeenth-Century Reformed Thought." *The Westminster Theological Journal* 64.2 (2002) 231–52.

Vanhoozer, Kevin. "Forward." In *Communion with the Triune God: John Owen*, edited by Kelly M. Kapic, and Justin Taylor, 11. Wheaton: Crossway, 2007.

Vass, G. "The Future of Theology: Homage to Karl Rahner." *The Heythrop Journal* 45.4 (2004) 477–85.

Volf, Miroslav. "Allah and the Trinity." *The Christian Century*, March 8, 2011, 20–24.

———. *Allah: A Christian Response*. New York: HarperOne, 2011.

von Balthasar, Hans Urs. *Explorations in Theology: Spirit and Institution*. Translated by Edward T. Oakes. Vol. 4. San Francisco: Ignatius, 1995.

Walker, James B. "Arianism." In *The Dictionary of Historical Theology*, edited by Trevor A. Hart, 28–31. Carlisle: Paternoster, 2000.

Ware, Bruce A. "Cur Deus Trinus? The Relations of the Trinity to Christ's Identity as Saviour and to the Efficacy of His Atoning Death." *The Southern Baptist Journal of Theology* 10.1 (2006) 48–56.

———. "An Evangelical Reformulation of the Doctrine of the Immutability of God." *Journal of the Evangelical Theological Society* 29.4 (1986) 431–46.

———. *Father, Son and Holy Spirit: Relationships, Roles, and Relevance*. Wheaton: Crossway, 2005.

———. *God's Greater Glory: The Exalted God of Scripture and the Christian Faith*. Wheaton: Crossway, 2004.

———. *God's Lesser Glory: The Diminished God of Open Theism*. Wheaton: Crossway, 2000.

———. "How Shall We Think About the Trinity?" In *God Under Fire*, edited by Douglas S. Huffman, and Eric L. Johnson, 254–77. Grand Rapids: Zondervan, 2002.

———. "Male and Female Complementarity and the Image of God." In *Biblical Foundations for Manhood and Womanhood*, edited by Wayne Grudem, 71–92. Wheaton: Crossway, 2002.

———. "The Man Christ Jesus." *Journal of the Evangelical Theological Society* 53.1 (2010) 5–18.

———. *Their God Is Too Small: Open Theism and the Undermining of Confidence in God*. Wheaton: Crossway, 2003.

Warfield, Benjamin Breckinridge. *Calvin and Augustine*. Philadelphia: Presbyterian and Reformed, 1956.

Webster, John. "Trinity and Creation." *International Journal of Systematic Theology* 12.1 (2010) 4–19.

Weinandy, Thomas G. *Athanasius: A Theological Introduction*. Great Theologians Series. Aldershot, UK: Ashgate, 2007.

———. *The Father's Spirit of Sonship: Reconceiving the Trinity*. 1995. Reprint. Eugene, OR: Wipf and Stock, 2011.

Williams, David J. *Acts*. Peabody, MA: Hendrickson, 1985.

Woods, Edward J. *The "Finger of God," and Pneumatology in Luke-Acts*. Sheffield, UK: Sheffield Academic, 2001.

Wright, N. T. *Jesus and the Victory of God*. Christian Origins and the Question of God, Vol. 2. Minneapolis: Fortress, 1996.

---. "Jesus' Self-Understanding." In *The Incarnation: An Interdisciplinary Symposium on the Incarnation of the Son of God*, edited by Stephen T. Davis, Daniel Kendall, and Gerald O'Collins, 47–61. Oxford: Oxford University Press, 2002.

---. *The Resurrection of the Son of God*. Christian Origins and the Question of God, Vol. 3. Minneapolis: Fortress, 2003.

Yandell, Keith E. "The Most Brutal and Inexcusable Error in Counting? The Trinity and Consistency." *Religious Studies* 30 (1994) 201–17.

Yeago, David S. "The New Testament and the Nicene Dogma: A Contribution to the Recovery of Theological Exegesis." In *The Theological Interpretation of Scripture: Classic and Contemporary Readings*, edited by Stephen E. Fowl, 87–102. Oxford: Blackwell, 1997.

Zaragoza, Gonzalo. "La Communión trinitaria: La contribución de Karl Rahner " *Estudios Eclesiásticos* 80.313 (2005) 263–90.

www.ingramcontent.com/pod-product-compliance
Lightning Source LLC
Chambersburg PA
CBHW062046220426
43662CB00010B/1677